Hypnosis
for the
seriously
curious

CONTEMPORARY PSYCHOLOGY SERIES

Edward L. Walker, Editor

The frontiers of psychology are advancing—advancing in response to persistent and fundamental social problems, advancing as a result of improved technology in both research and application, advancing through individual creative effort.

Brooks/Cole Publishing Company will make contemporary ideas, research, and applications widely available to students and scholars through the Contemporary Psychology Series.

GANG DELINQUENCY
Desmond S. Cartwright, University of Colorado
Barbara Tomson, Denver General Hospital
Hershey Schwartz, Seoul National University

FEMININE PERSONALITY AND CONFLICT
Judith M. Bardwick, The University of Michigan
Elizabeth Douvan, The University of Michigan
Matina Horner, Harvard University
David Gutmann, The University of Michigan

ROLES WOMEN PLAY: READINGS TOWARD WOMEN'S LIBERATION
Michele Hoffnung Garskof, Quinnipiac College

HOMOSEXUALITY AND PSYCHOLOGICAL FUNCTIONING
Mark Freedman

PSYCHOLOGY AND THE BLACK EXPERIENCE
Roderick W. Pugh, Loyola University of Chicago

HYPNOSIS FOR THE SERIOUSLY CURIOUS
Kenneth S. Bowers, University of Waterloo

Hypnosis
for the
seriously curious

Kenneth S. Bowers
University of Waterloo

Brooks/Cole Publishing Company
Monterey, California

A Division of Wadsworth Publishing Company, Inc.

ISBN: 0-8185-0181-2
L.C. Catalog Card No.: 75-31448
Printed in the United States of America

10 9 8 7 6 5 4 3 2 1

Production Editor: *Fiorella Ljunggren*
Interior & Cover Design: *John Edeen*
Typesetting: *Instant Type, Monterey, California*
Printing & Binding: *Malloy Lithographing, Inc., Ann Arbor, Michigan*

Preface

This book seeks to present a coherent account of the puzzling and elusive phenomenon known as hypnosis and reviews current research on the topic within the context of its history and clinical applications. One of the important goals of the book is to resolve some of the apparent paradoxes surrounding hypnotic phenomena. For example, part of the book argues that deeply hypnotized persons can honestly deny perceiving various features of their environment, which nevertheless have a profound and pervasive impact on their behavior, thinking, and/or affect. Once these apparent paradoxes are properly understood, perennial questions regarding the authenticity or reality of hypnotic phenomena simply evaporate.

I have organized other parts of the book around a variety of questions, such as: Is hypnosis an altered state of consciousness or is it simply heightened suggestibility? Can anyone be hypnotized to some extent? If certain individuals are more hypnotizable than others, are they different in other ways as well? How effective is hypnosis in helping people to overcome various psychological and physical disorders? I hope that answers to these and related questions will emerge in a natural and coherent fashion out of a critical examination of the relevant (although by no means exhaustive) experimental and clinical evidence presented in the pages that follow.

The main prerequisite for this book is a genuine curiosity about hypnosis. The reader new to the topic should find the book a useful introduction to hypnosis; but even the informed reader should find in it some new and, hopefully, valuable insights. Persons interested in perception and cognition will find that research on hypnosis reveals the workings of the mind in a way that more conventional laboratory investigations barely hint at. Professionals interested in hypnosis as a treatment modality will find chapters 2 and 9 of special relevance, with the rest of the book providing a helpful background to the broader implications of hypnosis.

The book has profited greatly from the comments of its reviewers, who were both critical of and sympathetic to my presentation. To Leslie M. Cooper of Brigham Young University, William E. Edmonston, Jr. of Colgate University, Kenneth Graham of Muhlenberg College, and Ronald E. Shor of the University of New Hampshire I would like to extend my heartfelt thanks. I would also like to thank Ernest and Josephine Hilgard, who have been a constant source of inspiration to me during the years I have been struggling to understand hypnosis. My visit to their Stanford Laboratory of Hypnosis in 1970-1971 has been of lasting importance to me in ways too numerous and complex to detail here. I am also in debt to Martin Orne, who, in addition to reviewing this book, has gently encouraged me over the years to look more closely and write more carefully. Close to home, I have been ably assisted by Sandra van der Meulen, Anne Coe, Susan Dotzenroth, Heather Brenneman, Peter Birch, Jane Knox, and Kenneth Keeling. Their help was made available through the generous support, at one time or another, of The Ontario Mental Health Foundation, The Medical Research Council, and Canada Council. Finally, I would like to dedicate this book to my parents, who got me started, and to my wife, Patricia, who kept me going.

Kenneth S. Bowers

Contents

Introduction

A deeply hypnotized person experiences himself in some rather unusual ways. Typically, he feels a profound sense of relaxation, frequently accompanied by sensations that his body is light or heavy, floating or sinking, enlarging or shrinking. His behavior and perception are exquisitely sensitive to the hypnotist's communications. For example, in response to pertinent suggestions, the person's arm can float up into the air of its own accord with no sensation on the part of the person that *he* is doing the lifting. It's as if his arm itself heard and responded to the command to become lighter and lighter, to float up into the air effortlessly—as if tied to balloons full of helium. Suggestions to a hypnotized individual that the room is full of roses may result in expressions of wonderment at the hallucinated beauty and fragrance that surround him; he may even prick a finger on a thorn when he tries to pick up a particularly lovely garland.

Such a deeply hypnotized person may be "regressed" back to an earlier age and laugh at a circus clown he is seeing on his eighth birthday, or he may become tearful and upset as his parents tell him that his dog has died. If age-regressed to an even earlier time, our hypnotic virtuoso may begin talking in a foreign language that he hasn't spoken since he was 3 or 4 years old—and that he could not remember when awake. Returned to the here and now, our subject can be told to smell the Chanel #5 under his nose, and he will sniff delightedly at the ammonia that has been placed there instead.

The entire arm of our deeply entranced subject can be plunged into ice-cold water, and, protected by suggestions for analgesia ("your arm is like a block of wood; it can't feel anything"), he will show no sign of pain or discomfort, even though he would be in agony under ordinary waking circumstances. Yet, our subject will grimace in pain if his "unprotected" arm is plunged into room-temperature water that has been transformed by suggestion into ice water.

This ability of hypnosis to alter perception and thinking has many practical implications—*for some people.* Long-time sufferers of migraine headaches have been cured permanently by incredibly short periods of treatment with hypnosis. People dying from terminal cancer have been spared the final indignities of ceaseless and senseless pain that seems impervious to medication. Major surgery has been conducted with nothing more than hypnotic analgesia to eliminate the pain. Memories have been hypnotically recovered and disarmed of their ability to cause unconscious torment. Asthma has been cured, and weight lost; smoking habits have been broken, and skin disorders successfully treated—all by hypnosis. (Some clinical applications of hypnosis will be covered in the last chapter of this book.)

Anything that has such a dramatic impact on a person's condition and functioning cannot help attracting the attention of the clinician and scientist on the one hand and the sick or simply curious layman on the other. But, historically, hypnosis has received much more than attention; it has frequently been at the center of vigorous and even venomous controversy. Advocates of hypnosis have been denounced as charlatans and ne'er-do-wells; its adversaries, as narrow-minded bigots.

But why? Why should something so dramatic and apparently effective be so contentious? A key word here is "apparently." Bitter opponents of hypnosis during the 19th century charged that reports of hypnotic cures were fraudulent and that witnessed demonstrations of hypnotic phenomena were purposefully contrived. This sort of extreme charge is seldom heard nowadays, but modern critics have seriously proposed that hypnotic analgesia, to cite but one example, is not really what it appears to be but is instead attributable to incredibly stoical subjects who are simply trying hard to please the hypnotist—even as they endure the most excruciating pain.

Another basis for skepticism is the claim that hypnosis is merely responsiveness to suggestions, a proposition that presumably demystifies hypnosis, rendering it more amenable to scientific investigation. What is exorcized by this account is hypnosis as an altered state of consciousness. And indeed, for a hard-core behavioristic psychology, such altered states have approximately the same status as demons or ghosts; indeed, for behaviorism even the existence of mind is in serious doubt.

There are other sources of controversy, but we need not detail all of them here; the reader by now has the idea that the study of hypnosis has not always had smooth scientific sledding. And the truth is that overly enthusiastic advocates of hypnosis have contributed to the controversy by making exaggerated claims about it. For example, it just presses the credibility of most open-minded scientists too far when it is seriously proposed that a person can be hypnotically age-regressed back to a previous life or that hypnosis can be used to "astrally project" the subject to different places, even to different worlds. The legitimate claims made about hypnosis are weird enough, and even they have elicited skeptical responses ranging from smile through smirk to snarl. To claim "supernatural" powers for hypnosis can make the difficult job of gaining scientific respect for the phenomenon almost impossible (Hilgard, 1971a). And, indeed, there have been long periods in history when the scientific study of hypnosis has simply ground to a complete halt.

At this moment in history, however, hypnosis is enjoying something of a renaissance: more research of higher quality is being done now than ever before; several books on hypnosis have recently been published (E. R. Hilgard, 1965; J. R. Hilgard, 1970; Gordon, 1967; Fromm & Shor, 1972; Barber, 1969, 1970; Barber, Spanos, & Chaves, 1974; Moss, 1965; Shor & Orne, 1965; Lassner, 1967; Sarbin & Coe, 1972); and hypnosis is gaining general acceptance into medical, dental, and psychological circles as it never has before. For example, the American Society for Clinical Hypnosis and The Society for Clinical and Experimental Hypnosis are two professional organizations that concern themselves exclusively with the clinical use and experimental investigation of hypnosis. Each society has an annual convention, sponsors workshops on hypnosis, and publishes a quarterly journal of interest to clinicians and/or scientists involved with hypnosis.

Several converging factors have led to this renewal of interest in hypnosis. Classical behaviorism is fast losing its hold on North American psychology, and there is an awakening to the importance of cognition and subjective experience as legitimate domains of inquiry. This recrudescence of subjectivity in science reflects a cultural trend in which "consciousness raising" has become a catch phrase and is achieved not only by diligent discussion but by meditation, drugs, novel therapeutic techniques, biofeedback, Eastern religions, and rock music—to name only a few roads to Rome.

Partly to accommodate this emphasis on subjective experience, there has been a concomitant liberalization of what counts as "objectively real" in science. Verbal reports, for example, are considered far more seriously today as an index of genuine internal experience than they were ten years ago. And philosophers of science have recently accorded more formal recognition to the subjective roots of scientific endeavor (for example, Kuhn, 1962; Polanyi, 1958; but see also Scheffler, 1967). It has even been seriously proposed in a prestigious scientific journal that certain external realities can only be perceived under an altered state of consciousness—induced either by drugs or by other means (Tart, 1972).

Just where the pendulum will stop its swing toward subjectivity is difficult to say. Certainly the field of hypnosis has profited from this liberalization, but too much salt in the stew can quickly make it unpalatable. As Shor (1972) has rightly phrased it, "The fundamental problem in hypnosis research is the necessity of maintaining at the same time both caution and conviction" (p. 36). Lightly salting hypnosis with cautious conviction is what I hope to accomplish in this book.

The book begins cautiously indeed, questioning the very reality of hypnosis. This may seem an odd way for an advocate to begin a book about hypnosis, but it stems from a decision, early made, that the skeptical view should be aired early and forcefully. Skeptics may be more receptive to what I say in later sections of the book if their doubts are dealt with openly at the outset. For the credulous, whose belief in hypnosis often borders on the mystical, an initial dose of skepticism helps to lay the groundwork for a more reasoned and reasonable understanding of hypnotic phenomena. I hope that before the book is over the credulous will have been rescued from superstition and the skeptics from self-righteousness. Those open-minded readers who are simply curious about hypnosis need not feel forsaken, since the early chapters deal with classical hypnotic phenomena as portrayed in some timeless experiments of both older and more modern eras.

Although the book begins cautiously, it is my conviction that hypnosis is virtually a window into the mind. Often the window is smudged and dirty with artifacts and exaggerated claims; but even through a glass darkly we are beginning to see forms of thinking, perceiving, and feeling that are barely hinted at in more conventional lines of inquiry (see especially E. R. Hilgard, 1973a, 1974). Eventually— and in the not too distant future, I suspect—research on hypnosis will begin to be assimilated into a more general theory of cognition far more probing and satisfying than any now existing. Conversely, the findings from experimental work in cognition and perception will also enhance our understanding of hypnosis.

In writing this book, I have made no attempt to survey all the literature in the field; today that would be an almost impossible task. What I have tried to provide is an intellectual framework in which hypnotic phenomena can be understood. The framework is, of course, one that I find congenial, and it undoubtedly has heavily influenced the research selected for exposition. However, I have not ignored research that challenges my biases, nor have I tried to duck the really tough issues that confront current investigators in the field.

Throughout the book I have attempted to keep technical language to a minimum. Some excursions into statistical issues have been impossible to avoid completely, but I have done my best to present them in a simple, straightforward manner. On occasion, the sophisticated reader may find it convenient to skip over some elementary statistical concepts that are aimed at the novice. This is especially true in Chapter 5.

There is one point, also treated in Chapter 5, that I would like to mention briefly here in order to aid the reader's comprehension of earlier chapters. Becoming hypnotized is not an all-or-nothing proposition. While some people are able to achieve deep hypnosis without difficulty, and others seem intractable to hypnosis, many more people are only moderately hypnotizable. Just why these differences in hypnotic ability exist is not entirely clear, although I will later have some things to say about the origins and development of hypnotic talent. In any event, the differences in persons' hypnotic ability (or hypnotic susceptibility, as it is more frequently called) can be measured by various scales designed for that purpose. These scales involve actually hypnotizing a person, administering several suggestions, and seeing how many of the suggestions the person "passes." The more suggestions passed, the more hypnotically susceptible the person is.

A final word: I have tried very hard to present some complex issues as simply as possible, but without simplifying the complexities. Consequently, the reader new to psychology in general and to hypnosis in particular may find parts of the book challenging—but, I trust, rewarding. It is my hope that anyone who has a genuine itch to know about hypnosis will find this book a satisfying scratch. It is also my hope that investigators of hypnosis who have been scratching for some time will find in this book something that extends their reach.

1.
Is Hypnotic Behavior Faked?

Many readers of this book probably view hypnosis as an unquestionably authentic phenomenon in which a deeply entranced subject acts on the almost irresistible suggestions of a hypnotist in an automatic and automaton-like manner. This more or less *credulous view* of hypnosis has never had the unequivocal support of the scientific community, and in the last 10 or 15 years it has been attacked as seriously misguided (for example, Barber, 1969; Sarbin & Coe, 1972). In assaulting this credulous view, recent investigators have often conveyed, wittingly or unwittingly, the suggestion that there is something phony or put-on about hypnosis, that hypnotized subjects may be deceiving the hypnotist and even, perhaps, themselves. This *skeptical view* of hypnosis has a venerable tradition that is due, ironically, to the dramatic effects that are sometimes produced in hypnotized subjects. How can mere words—suggestions tendered by a hypnotist to his subject—make a person see things that aren't there, forget things he just heard, be insensitive to pain and unable to smell ammonia? It all seems to stretch credibility too far.

A similar skepticism has also infected our concept of hysteria, a psychological disorder that has a historic connection with hypnosis. According to Szasz (1964), hysteria has been regarded as a sort of "counterfeit illness," in which the "patient himself did not know that he was simulating. Hysteria was thus viewed as unconscious malingering" (p. 46). The symptoms of hysteria are very similar to some of the phenomena that can be suggested in hypnosis, such as blindness, deafness, paralysis, and the inability to feel painful sensations. As a matter of fact, a famous French neurologist named Jean Charcot was (erroneously) convinced that hypnosis was a pathological condition of the nervous system restricted to hysterical patients.

The point is that in neither hysteria nor hypnosis are the phenomena in question caused by some bodily breakdown. Instead, they seem to represent an instance of "mind over matter"; that is, the primary cause of the condition seems to involve a system of thoughts or ideas that has untoward influence over bodily functioning and experience. In hysteria, the basis for the problematic behavior is psychodynamic. For example, the patient might convert anxiety/conflict about an impending marriage into a temporary leg paralysis. In hypnosis, the words of the hypnotist engender peculiarities in experiencing and behavior.

Thus, there seems to be something "mental" about the origins of hypnotic and hysteric behavior. And in matters scientific, phenomena that depend on mentalistic explanations are sometimes thought to be not quite respectable. Consequently, if hysteric disorders or hypnotic phenomena need some sort of mentalistic explanation, the phenomena become as unreal and insubstantial as the mind itself is presumed to be.

A Historical Precedent

Perhaps it would be helpful by way of illustrating this point to turn the clock back to 1784. America had recently been victorious in its revolution against England, and Benjamin Franklin, one of the aging heroes of that altercation, was serving as ambassador to France. Franklin was a man honored in America and on the Continent for his scientific as well as his political acumen. Consequently, he was appointed by the king of France, along with several other scientists (including the famous chemist Lavoisier), to investigate the phenomena of mesmerism, or what we now call hypnosis.

For the previous five years, Franz Anton Mesmer had been capturing the imagination of Paris, so to speak, with his marvelous magnetic powers. He had repeatedly conducted seances during which he induced convulsive seizures called crises, which ostensibly had a benign and healing effect on the body. In an atmosphere of heavily draped rooms and soft music, patients would hold onto metal bars extending from a wooden tub, or baquet. The baquet was filled with water, ground glass, iron filings, and, presumably, electricity or magnetism. It was claimed that the action of magnetic fluid centered in the baquet somehow realigned imbalances in a person's magnetic equilibrium and led to bodily cures of one kind or another. There can be no question that some rather dramatic moments were achieved in Mesmer's Parisian salons; patients visited by crises would frequently be carried to a special padded room where they convulsed in relative safety. There *were* many questions, however, regarding the explanation of these dramatic effects.

Mesmer fully believed that the cause of the crisis was a form of physical magnetism, and he was anxious to have his magnetic theory of mesmerism vindicated by the scientific establishment of the day. On several occasions he had requested that a commission be established to study his practices. These requests met with little success. Ironically, one of the main reasons that finally led the king of France to take action was "a secret [police] report that some mesmerists were mixing radical political ideas in their pseudoscientific discourses" (Darnton, 1970, p. 62).

The royal commission headed by Franklin performed a number of experiments with patients treated by Charles Deslon, Mesmer's right-hand man. Members of the commission provided Deslon with a number of physically ill persons, but they were not appreciably helped by his application of mesmerism. Patients that Deslon himself provided seemed to be helped more, but on members of the commission themselves mesmerism had virtually no effect whatsoever.

Even more discrediting were some of the controlled observations that were set up to test Mesmer's claims. One of the most famous experiments took place in Franklin's garden at Passy. Deslon mesmerized an apricot tree there, claiming that anyone who touched it would be affected. Deslon was waved away from the tree to prevent his signaling the subject, a 12-year-old boy. The subject was led blindfolded out of the house and taken to four unmagnetized trees, one after another. "At the first tree the boy perspired and coughed. At the second he felt a pain and stupor in his head. At the third he complained of an increasing headache and said he was getting closer to the magnetic tree, though he was further from it than ever. At the fourth tree he fainted. They carried him to a grass plot where Deslon revived him" (Van Doren, 1938, pp. 715–716).

Evidence of this kind led the commissioners to conclude that "imagination without magnetism produces convulsions, and that magnetism without imagination produces nothing." They further concluded "on the question of the existence and utility of magnetism that there is no proof of its existence, that this fluid without existence is consequently without utility, and that the violent effects observed in public clinics are to be attributed to the touching, to aroused imagination, and to that mechanical imitation which leads us in spite of ourselves to repeat that which strikes our senses" (as quoted in Pattie, 1967, p. 21).

What should be noted here is that the commission did *not* say that the mesmeric phenomena lacked authenticity. What the commission did state unequivocally was that magnetism, the presumed cause of mesmerism, was nonexistent and that the crises and convulsions ordinarily produced by Mesmer and his followers were really the result of an inflamed imagination. Unfortunately, the judgment that mesmerism depended upon imagination was tantamount to saying that it was imaginary (that is, not real), since in that day and age the only "real" things were those that could be physically observed.

Why was this so? In the 1700s the scientific establishment was very aware of its recent escape from the clutches of medievalism, in which all sorts of supernatural explanations were invoked to explain all manner of phenomena. Consequently, the scientific establishment was skeptical about accepting as "real" anything that didn't have some clear place in the natural order of things. For example, in 1769—only 15 years before the commission on mesmerism—a similar investigative body of the French Academy (also including Lavoisier) proclaimed that meteorites did not exist. In effect, they argued that since meteorites were presumed to be heavenly bodies and heaven did not exist, meteorites did not exist either (Paneth, 1948-1949). Thus, both the commission on meteorites and the one on mesmerism virtually discounted a phenomenon because the *explanation* of the phenomenon was viewed as inadequate. The consequences of both decisions were disastrous. Museums all over Europe, beholden to the authority of the French Academy of Science, began to throw their precious meteorites away. And mesmerism as an acceptable phenomenon virtually went underground for more than half a century. Only in the middle of the 19th century did mesmerism re-emerge, and with a new name—hypnosis.

Stage Hypnosis

Skepticism about hypnosis persists in some quarters to the present day. In part this attitude results from the association of hypnosis with the stage, particularly with stage magic. A magician has a sort of license to fool people, to create illusions. The audience enjoys being fooled and, in fact, sanctions the magician to fool them. Magic is a kind of temporary and permissible defection from "reality" that is perpetrated by the magician and enjoyed by the audience. Since stage hypnosis looks so much like other kinds of magic, it is easy to assume that here, again, all is not what it appears to be; that some kind of illusion is being perpetrated for entertainment's sake; that, in short, the audience is being "put on."

According to an article by Meeker and Barber (1971), this perception of stage hypnosis has more than a grain of truth in it. Although some of what stage hypnotists do may involve legitimate hypnosis, a great deal of it is evidently an illusion. One stage magician quoted by Meeker and Barber even goes so far as to state:

> To the serious minded student of hypnotism who wishes to produce a hypnotic show for entertainment purposes, it is recommended that he forget all about trying to be a legitimate hypnotist, and turn to the little known secrets of the profession .... [T]he hypnotic show must be faked, at least partially so, to hold audience interest, and be successful as an entertainment feature [Nelson, 1965, as quoted by Meeker & Barber, 1971, p. 64].

Just what are these "little known secrets of the profession"? Meeker and Barber suggest that in part these secrets involve cooperation between the hypnotist and his subject. "For instance, if the stage performer wants [a subject] to sing like Frank Sinatra (or to crow like a rooster), he may whisper to his most extraverted *S*, 'Please give the audience a good act of singing like Sinatra (or crowing like a rooster)'" (Meeker & Barber, 1971, p. 65).

Another gambit involves utilizing "hypnotic tricks" that look much harder than they really are. For example, it is possible for most people to suspend their bodies from head to heel between two chairs. Yet, most people think that this feat must be very difficult indeed, and, when they see it performed on the stage by a subject who is supposedly hypnotized, they believe that the person can do it only *because* he is hypnotized.

Meeker and Barber mention many other tricks of the trade, the most dramatic of which involves actually rendering a person unconscious by stopping the flow of blood to the head. This technique, which involves pressing on the carotid arteries, is especially effective with people who have proven stubborn and challenging to the hypnotist and who need convincing in a straightforward and completely compelling fashion. (It should be noted that this technique is dangerous, especially with medically unsound subjects, and that under no circumstances should it be used as a parlor game.)

I have spent some time talking about stage hypnosis because many people have derived their chief impressions of hypnosis from stage (and perhaps staged) demonstrations of it. For these individuals, skepticism about hypnosis is not only understandable but, as we have seen, warranted.

Another potential basis for a skeptical attitude toward hypnosis involves first-hand communications with former hypnotic subjects who claim to have faked hypnosis on one occasion or another. A famous example of apparently successful chicanery involves the humorist and novelist Mark Twain. As a boy, Twain volunteered to be a hypnotic subject for a stage hypnotist. The latter was apparently successful in inducing a deep trance, which Twain in fact dissembled. At one point, Twain even tolerated people sticking needles through his flesh; although this caused him excruciating pain, he successfully suppressed all outward expressions of discomfort. Everyone in the audience was quite impressed with the performance, and Twain was never able to convince his mother in later years that he had faked the whole episode. She had *seen* her son accept the needles without evident pain, and that was more convincing to her than his own belated testimony to the contrary (Neider, 1959).

The Case of Uniocular Blindness

There are few hypnotists who haven't heard second-hand reports about subjects claiming to have fooled them. One of the best-known instances of a scientist apparently being fooled by a good hypnotic subject was a case reported by Pattie (1935).

Pattie had suggested to a young woman that one of her eyes was blind. The subject was then given a variety of tests to see whether she in fact behaved like a one-eyed person. For example, the experimenter wrote the subject's name in green and red letters and then held a red filter over the "good" eye. Now, red letters viewed through a red filter would be invisible, and under these conditions a truly one-eyed person would be able to see only the green letters. If, despite the suggestions for uniocular blindness, the subject could still see with both eyes, the red letters would be visible to the eye with no filter over it. Under these test conditions, the subject said she saw only the green letters, suggesting that she could not see the red letters with her "blind" eye. The experimenter thus concluded that hypnotic suggestion had in fact rendered the subject blind in one eye.

However, this test for uniocular blindness turned out to be inadequate. When the subject was presented with a multicolored display with a red filter over her "good" eye and a green filter over her "blind" eye, the situation was much more challenging, and the subject demonstrated that she could in fact see with both eyes. This raised the question of how the subject had managed to fake one-eyed blindness so convincingly on all but the final test.

Through long and rather arduous questioning, the experimenter gradually determined that the subject had actually done "homework" to learn just how to fake one of the tests. Thus, it appears on the face of it that a really good hypnotic subject will go considerably out of his or her way to fool the hypnotist. Moreover, it seems that the faking component of hypnotic behavior may be considerable, and Pattie's findings have often been invoked to cast doubt on the genuineness of hypnotic phenomena in general.

However, a close reading of Pattie's case of uniocular blindness reveals some rather interesting features that raise questions about whether the young lady was consciously pretending blindness pure and simple. For it seemed evident in the subsequent questioning that the subject had genuinely forgotten that she used a ruse or two to achieve "blindness" of one eye. Moreover, the recall of her homework and of her other "tricks" took place only while she was hypnotized and only with a great deal of conflict and emotional upheaval. Some direct quotes from the report are most convincing in this regard.

> I first asked her [that is, while awake] if she had been conscious of faking any tests; she said no. When I asked if she believed that her eye had been actually blind, she said "It *was* blind" [p. 238].

Pattie then hypnotized the subject. Subsequently he

> persuaded her to remember, recovering a little bit at a time, but evidently a very great conflict was going on; she clenched her fists, tossed about in the chair, and showed a great deal of agitation in her vocal and facial expressions

.... She began crying at one point and continued to be tearful, in spite of my efforts to quiet her, for ten or more minutes [p. 238].

Even as the subject began to recall some of the devices she had used to "fake" blindness,

> She continued to be emotionally worked up, putting her head on the arm of the chair and beginning to cry with renewed force. I asked why she was crying; she said, "I don't know. It is something I can't remember." After a few moments of further crying, tossing about, and clenching her fists, she said suddenly that the memories had come back, that she had practiced—at home .... At the time, she could not understand why she was doing this work and thought that perhaps she was becoming more interested in psychology. After this "home-work," she had forgotten all about it [pp. 238-239].

After the subject was awakened,

> The emotional disturbance manifest in the trance, which lasted about 45 min., left traces ... after waking. She then complained of dizziness, faintness, "swimming movements" of objects around her (though her eyes were perfectly steady), and headache. In addition, she expressed some apprehension about her condition [p. 240].*

Clearly, it is an oversimplification to state that the subject "faked" uniocular blindness and just let it go at that. In a real sense, the girl herself evidently didn't realize the extent of her deception, and the recovery of this fact caused her a great deal of emotional discomfort. Maybe in another sense she "faked" blindness, but something quite different from conscious, purposeful deception was going on. Thus, we should draw a careful distinction between a person's conscious cooperation with a stage hypnotist who requests him to crow like a rooster and the young lady's "unconscious cooperation" with Pattie's suggestions for uniocular blindness. It is differences like this that make hypnotic phenomena so much more interesting than simple compliance with instructions.

Perhaps the reader is beginning to appreciate that hypnotic phenomena may force certain unusual distinctions in our thinking. For example, the distinction between purposefully faking blindness and unconsciously doing so seems to be an important one, yet the whole notion of unconscious faking is rather puzzling. Ordinarily one thinks of faking as something done intentionally and with full realization. Nevertheless, I seem to be suggesting that in hypnosis there can be falsification without realization—a sort of self-deception in which the subject himself remains more or less unaware of the welter of factors contributing to his or her behavior. I will expand on this possibility later on in the book and show how it tends to contravene the "faking" hypothesis of hypnosis. For now, however, we might pursue the possibilities presented by viewing hypnotic behavior as somehow faked or "put on."

The Simulating Paradigm

Martin Orne, one of the most ingenious current investigators of hypnosis, once conducted a study in which he lectured on hypnosis to a class and informed his students (falsely) that dominant arm catalepsy was a concomitant of hypnotic trance (Orne, 1959). (A cataleptic arm is stiff and difficult to move or bend.) Actual demonstrations of this phenomenon were staged for maximum impact on the audience. Another (control) class received a similar lecture on hypnosis without the information regarding dominant arm catalepsy. Subsequently, members from the two classes were hypnotized. Of the nine subjects from the experimental group, seven showed spontaneous (that is, unsuggested) evidence of catalepsy, whereas none of the nine subjects from the control classroom did.

Here we are confronted with a problem. Did the seven subjects purposefully put one over on the hypnotist, or were their expectations of catalepsy implicitly translated into a genuine experience of it? Did the subjects stiffen their arms purposefully and voluntarily, or did their arms become cataleptic of their own accord? To a large extent, we are placed in the position of having to believe the subjects' accounts of what actually happened. Of course, if a subject *were* trying to fool the experimenter in the first place, it can be argued that his subsequent account that his arm stiffened all by itself may simply reflect a continuing effort to deceive the experimenter. In other words, what the person says about his hypnotic behavior may be no more credible than his original behavior. What to do?

Orne (1959) came up with a rather ingenious solution to this dilemma: why not explicitly ask nonhypnotized subjects to fake hypnosis and see how their behavior compares with the genuine article? If one can observe differences between real and simulated hypnosis, then it becomes difficult to argue that truly hypnotized subjects are simply faking.

In Orne's so-called "simulating paradigm," an experimenter first interviews a soon-to-be simulating subject and instructs him to fake hypnosis with a hypnotist who doesn't know whether the subject is genuinely hypnotized or not. Furthermore, the simulator is informed that the hypnotist will stop the experiment if and when he sees through the deception. So, as long as the hypnotist permits him to continue, the subject knows he is simulating hypnosis successfully.

It is of course important to make sure that the simulating subject does not inadvertently become hypnotized during the induction procedure. This is more or less guaranteed by employing as simulators only subjects who are unsusceptible to hypnosis. (As we shall see in Chapter 5, people differ considerably in their ability to be hypnotized. Consequently, whether or not a person becomes hypnotized depends more upon his or her degree of hypnotic ability than upon any mysterious "power" of the hypnotist.) Since only unsusceptible subjects are employed as simulators, they cannot be hypnotized, and we have reason to accept their subsequent hypnotic-like behavior as simulated instead of genuine.

How successful are simulators in fooling the hypnotist under these specially contrived circumstances? The answer is: very successful, as indicated in the following rather dramatic example.

There has been a long-standing controversy regarding whether a person would actually perform antisocial acts under hypnosis that he would not perform while awake (Orne, 1972a; Kline, 1972; Barber, 1961). Some early studies by Rowland (1939) and Young (1952) suggested that deeply hypnotized subjects would throw fuming nitric acid into the face of a research assistant and pick up a poisonous snake with their bare hands. In replication of these experiments by Orne and Evans (1965), five out of six hypnotized subjects indeed performed both antisocial actions just as other hypnotized subjects had in the earlier studies. In addition, subjects in the Orne and Evans investigation also picked a penny out of the acid with their bare hands before throwing the acid at the assistant. However, six out of six simulators also yielded to all three of the antisocial suggestions! In other words, subjects who simulated hypnosis behaved in the same antisocial fashion as the hypnotic subjects did.

Perhaps the reader is curious about just how many persons—both subjects and research assistants—survived these rather arduous experiments. Happily, everyone, because there were built-in safeguards to protect the participants from the consequences of their actions. A virtually invisible curved glass separated the snakes from the subjects, and the "nitric acid" thrown at the assistant was actually a harmless but identical-looking substitute for the real acid from which the penny had previously been fetched. In the experiment in which the subject pulled a penny from nitric acid, a quick dousing of the subjects' hands in water prevented any damage to their skin. Of course, the subjects were not informed of these safeguards in advance.

What do these experiments indicate?

Since simulated hypnosis looks so much like its genuine counterpart, Orne seems to have painted himself into a corner. In attempting to show that unique characteristics of genuine hypnosis would be evident over and above those of simulated hypnosis, he instead appears to have lent credibility to the assertion that hypnotic subjects are simply faking. As we shall see in a moment, the simulator paradigm does *not* permit this conclusion. Nevertheless, in summarizing his own personal reaction to the simulating subjects, Orne does state that, "as a clinician who had worked extensively with hypnosis, I never doubted that it would be easy for me . . . to recognize those [subjects] who were, in fact, simulating. It came as a complete surprise as well as a considerable blow to my fantasies of omniscience to find that [subjects] were actually able to deceive me" (Orne, 1971, p. 189).

Before looking at other examples of the simulator paradigm, we should consider just what it can and cannot tell us about hypnosis. The behavior of subjects who are simulating hypnosis is based on certain cues inherent in the experimental setting (including the hypnotic suggestions) and on their knowledge and expectations of hypnosis. Orne (1959, 1962b) has called these factors the *demand characteristics* of the situation. Hypnotic subjects are influenced in their behavior *both* by these demand characteristics *and* by any unique contribution of being hypnotized—for example, the trance state. Consequently, if differences occur between hypnotic and simulator subjects, we should be able to conclude that there is something to hypnosis over and above the purposeful use of demand characteristics to fool the hypnotist. As the experiment on antisocial behavior demonstrates, however, comparison of hypnotic and simulated behavior need not lead to observation of differences in overt behavior. Thus, we are no further along than we were initially; we can't be sure beyond any shadow of a doubt that hypnotic subjects aren't also "faking it." On the other hand, it is important to emphasize that finding no difference between simulator and hypnotic subjects does *not* allow us to conclude positively that hypnotic subjects are merely faking. It just may be that under the particular experimental circumstances, it is impossible for any unique behavioral manifestation of hypnosis to emerge. A rough analogy may help. We cannot tell which of two cars is capable of going faster when they are both following a prescribed 30-mph speed limit; the test conditions make any firm conclusions about their top speed impossible.[1]*

Are there any substantive grounds for resisting a conclusion that hypnotic behavior is simply a pretense of some sort? The answer to this question depends upon how seriously one is willing to take subjects' phenomenological reports. Simulated and genuine hypnosis can look the same to an onlooker, but what subjects in these two conditions *say* about their experiences differs radically. For example, simulated subjects experience themselves as purposefully making the suggested behavior happen, whereas genuinely hypnotized subjects often experience the same behavior as somehow happening to them. Simulating subjects often try to "second-guess" what the hypnotist expects of them, whereas

---

*Numbered footnotes may be found at the end of each chapter.

genuinely hypnotized subjects deny that the hypnotist's expectations influenced their behavior (Orne, 1959).

As I noted earlier, however, it is conceivable (although unlikely) that hypnotic subjects are not being entirely truthful in what they say about their experiences. It would be helpful therefore to have an index of behavior that is not so vulnerable to falsification as a verbal report. One experiment conducted by Gray, Bowers, and Fenz (1970) tried to do just that by attempting to demonstrate objective differences in genuine and simulated hypnosis that would correspond to the alleged differences in subjective experiences. In this experiment, heart rate was recorded as hypnotic subjects attempted to experience, and simulator subjects attempted to fake, a negative hallucination. *Four* red dots, each about four inches in diameter, were projected onto a wall. All the subjects were then asked to see only *three* dots when they opened their eyes. The subjects were to keep their eyes closed until the end of a slow countdown from ten to one. The data that concern us are the heart rates during this countdown.

By the end of the countdown, there were pronounced differences in the heart rates of hypnotic and simulating subjects. Nine out of ten hypnotic subjects had demonstrated heart-rate increases over an earlier baseline, whereas eight out of ten simulators had shown heart-rate decreases. Incidentally, all subjects *said* they saw only three dots, so only the relatively subtle shift in heart rate discriminated the genuine from the simulating subjects.

It is of course important to know that objective differences between hypnotic and simulating subjects are obtainable. Yet, one might ask whether there is any interpretation of the data that lends further interest to them. Ordinarily, increased heart rate is presumed to signify an increase in the organism's level of arousal. Thus, in the study under discussion, the data suggest that during the countdown, the simulators became less aroused (because their heart rate decreased) and the hypnotic subjects became more aroused (because their heart rate increased). This interpretation is somewhat puzzling, however, because there is no clear reason why simulating hypnosis should create a state of decreased arousal. After all, by the end of the countdown, simulators should have been more concerned than ever about what to expect and how to behave when they opened their eyes. Intuitively it seems that heightened concern of this kind should be accompanied by increased arousal.

Perhaps a more illuminating explanation of the heart-rate findings emerges out of the work of John Lacey (1967). Lacey suggests that heart rate is responsive to the subject's psychological orientation to the environment. If the subject becomes vigilant for situational cues, heart rate should decelerate; if he instead tries to reject or filter environmental input, heart rate should increase. Lacey (1967) and others (Lacey, Kagan, Lacey, & Moss, 1963; Bowers, 1971a) have demonstrated these heart-rate effects many times. What is interesting for our purposes is how nicely this interpretation of heart rate fits the findings in question. For it is the genuinely hypnotized subjects who are trying to reject part of the environment (that is, negatively hallucinate), and their heart rate does indeed go up. The simulators, on the other hand, are engaged in a problem-solving endeavor in which they must be vigilant for any external cues that will aid them in their attempts to fool the hypnotist. This vigilant, reality-testing orientation should, according to Lacey, produce heart-rate deceleration; and this is, of course, precisely what happens. Thus, the most fundamental rhythm of the body—heart rate—may reveal whether a person is negatively hallucinating or only pretending to do so.

Are there experimental conditions in which these subjective differences can be translated into overt behavioral differences? Here, again, the answer is yes. One rather extended example will suffice here, and others will follow throughout the book.

Posthypnotic behavior involves the enactment of hypnotic suggestions *after* the subject has resumed a normal waking state. For example, the awakened subject may scratch his ear whenever the experimenter gives a prearranged signal and do so unaware that he is following a posthypnotic suggestion given earlier while he was hypnotized. It is possible, however, that posthypnotic suggestions are enacted only when the subject thinks someone is evaluating his responsiveness. This possibility was tested by Fisher (1954) in a classic experiment on posthypnotic behavior. He suggested to each of 13 subjects that they would scratch their ears whenever they heard the word "psychology." Upon awakening, and during an initial test period when it was obvious that the experimenter was recording ear-scratching behavior, all 13 subjects scratched their ears in response to the cue word. However, the experimenter then modified the atmosphere of the interview setting by implying that the experiment was over. He did this by talking about the fact that a posthypnotic suggestion had been given, that it had been effective, and that, in general, the experiment had been a success. During this second period most subjects stopped scratching their ears in response to the word "psychology." Finally, the experimenter reinstated the expectancy that the experiment was still in progress by saying "I'm going to hypnotize you once again and remove the suggestion I gave you. I'm sure you wouldn't want to go around scratching your ear indefinitely" (Fisher, 1954, p. 504). During the third period that ensued, 11 out of the 13 subjects began to scratch their ears again. In other words, the subjects' ear-scratching behavior was turned on and off by the subjects' perception of whether the experiment was on or off. This result contrasts rather dramatically with the credulous view that hypnotic subjects invariably respond in a literal and compulsive fashion to posthypnotic suggestions.

Because Fisher's study seemed to foster skepticism about the validity of hypnotic phenomena, it was later replicated with several important additions (Orne, Sheehan, & Evans, 1968). These authors maintained that Fisher's subjects may have interpreted the initial posthypnotic suggestions as meaning that they would scratch their ears in response to the cue word *"as long as the experiment [was] in progress"* (Orne et al., 1968, p. 190). If this is what happened, then the subjects' nonresponsiveness to the cue word during the experiment-off period may not mean much. The authors argued that "if such a restriction to the experimental context was implicit in Fisher's suggestion, it is premature to conclude from his study that a posthypnotic response can be elicited only in that context" (Orne et al., 1968, p. 190).

Orne and his co-workers got around this problem by employing a posthypnotic suggestion to the effect that for the *next 48 hours* subjects would scratch their ears whenever they heard the cue word "experiment." For genuinely hypnotized subjects, the time-definite quality of these suggestions would presumably be effective in all contexts, not just in those perceived as experimental. In effect, Orne reasoned that the ear-scratching behavior of genuine hypnotic subjects should be more or less automatically triggered by the prearranged signal, regardless of when or where it occurred. By contrast, ear scratching in the simulator subjects should *not* be automatically triggered by this signal; instead, it should be more or less intentionally performed in order to communicate to any onlookers the appearance of a posthypnotic response. Thus, if no one were scrutinizing the simulator's behavior, there would be no reason for him to perform in this way. For example, a simulator sitting alone in his own room has no reason to scratch his ear if he hears a radio announcer utter the word "experiment." In the same situation, a hypnotic subject should scratch his ear if the 48-hour time-definite suggestion is really effective. Thus, hypnotic subjects, unlike simulators, should behave in accordance with the 48-hour suggestion *whether or not* they perceive their behavior to be under scrutiny. To put the matter another way, if simulators do *not* scratch their ears in accordance with the time-definite suggestions, it is because they do not think their behavior is being monitored. This is a very useful feature of the simulating paradigm, for, if a condition can be found in which simulators do not fake hypnosis, it must be because they do not view this particular circumstance as a test situation. It is precisely under the (apparently) nontest conditions that the presence of genuine posthypnotic behavior is most convincing; for then it is obviously not behavior simply calculated to please the experimenter and satisfy the demands of the situation. Instead, it is a more or less automatic response to an indwelling suggestion to respond to the triggering signal.

Practically speaking, of course, one cannot observe subjects while they are alone in their room to see if they will rub their ears in response to a radio announcer's use of the word "experiment." But, reasoned Orne and his associates, there may be other, slightly less private circumstances that simulators will not perceive as evaluative in nature. The authors felt that simulators might be caught off guard, so to speak, if a laboratory secretary delivered the critical cue word to the simulator before or after an actual experimental session. The procedure was as follows.

Each of the subjects seen in the experiment was provided with a hypnotic induction together with posthypnotic suggestions stating that "during the next 48 hours whenever he heard the word 'experiment' his right hand would rise up to touch his forehead." In addition, subjects were told to forget the suggestions (Orne et al., 1968, p. 192). The hypnotic induction and posthypnotic suggestions were administered both to subjects highly susceptible to hypnosis and to low-susceptibility subjects who had previously been asked to simulate hypnosis. After the subjects were given suggestions to awaken, they emerged from the laboratory. Each subject was then met by the secretary, who "confirmed the time for which he was scheduled 'to come for the next part of the *experiment*'." She then asked "whether it would be all right to pay him 'now for today's *experiment* and for the next part of the study tomorrow.'" Finally, when the subject returned the next day, the secretary asked "Are you here for Dr. Sheehan's *experiment*?'" (Orne et al., 1968, p. 192). In other words, the secretary actually delivered the cue word *"experiment"* three times in circumstances that permitted the recording of the subjects' responses to the cue word in this (apparently) nonexperimental context.

We can look first at how the simulating subjects behaved in this situation. Each of the 13 simulating subjects had three opportunities to respond to the secretary's use of the word "experiment." Thus, there was a total of 39 opportunities for the simulating subjects to respond to the cue word. Yet, the simulators responded to the cue word only on three occasions, or 7.7% of the time.

In contrast, the 17 genuine posthypnotic subjects had a total of 51 opportunities to touch their foreheads, and did so on 15 occasions, or 29.5% of the time. In other words, the genuine posthypnotic subjects touched their foreheads more than three times as often as simulators did. If we look at just the six most hypnotizable individuals (that is, those passing all the items of a hypnotic susceptibility scale), the difference between genuine and simulated posthypnotic behavior is much more dramatic. These six subjects touched their foreheads 13 out of 18 possible times in response to the cue word "experiment." In other words, the best hypnotic subjects touched their foreheads 70% of the time in response to the cue word—nine times as often as the simulating subjects. What is important to recall about these results is that the hypnotic subjects followed the posthypnotic suggestions under circumstances that are evidently not perceived as evaluative. The fact that simulators by and large did not respond to the secretary's off-hand use of the word "experiment" means that there were few contemporaneous demand characteristics to do so. Despite the evident absence of contextual demands to respond posthypnotically, the genuinely hypnotic subjects tended to do so—suggesting that they were indeed responding unconsciously to the previously delivered posthypnotic suggestions. These results imply that there is something far more pervasive and subtle to hypnotic behavior than voluntary and purposeful compliance with the perceived demands of the situation. Moreover, it suggests that the "faking hypothesis" is an entirely inadequate interpretation of hypnosis. In the next three chapters, I will try to document this point further by showing how genuinely hypnotized subjects experience suggested phenomena as subjectively convincing.

Footnotes

[1]Perhaps a note about the drawbacks of the simulating paradigm should be entered at this point. Simulating subjects ordinarily differ from genuine hypnotic subjects in two ways: (a) they are low instead of high in susceptibility, and (b) they receive simulating instructions, whereas the genuine subjects, of course, do not. Consequently, any outward differences in genuine and simulated hypnosis cannot be unambiguously assigned to the presence of hypnosis in the genuinely hypnotized subjects. For this and other reasons, Orne calls the simulator subjects a *quasi-control* group. Their function is to provide a check on the adequacy of the experimental procedures and not, strictly speaking, to serve as a comparison group by which to determine the effect of hypnosis. The logic of the simulator paradigm is somewhat complex, and cannot be spelled out in any greater detail here. The reader who wishes to pursue the matter further is referred to the following articles: Orne (1962b, 1969, 1970, 1971, 1972b), Sheehan (1971, 1973), Bowers (1973a).

2.
Are Hypnotic Effects Genuine? Hypnotic Analgesia

In this and the next two chapters, I will concentrate on two related but importantly different questions: (a) Does a deeply hypnotized person experience the suggested state of affairs as subjectively convincing? (For example, do suggestions for deafness make it seem to the subject that he cannot hear?) (b) Are the suggested state of affairs and its physically real counterpart alike in all particulars? (For example, is suggested deafness *exactly* the same thing as actually being deaf?)

It is important to treat these questions separately, since the answers to them may well be different. For instance, it would be a mistake to assume that a hallucinated rose is not subjectively real to a deeply hypnotized person simply because the neurophysiological events underlying the hallucination may be subtly different from those that accompany seeing an actual rose. Any such difference may be more salient and significant to the experimenter than to the person viewing a real or hallucinated rose.

Similarly, if a real and a suggested state of affairs have different behavioral effects, the experimenter may unduly magnify their importance in evaluating the subjective experience of a hypnotized subject. For example, subjects who negatively hallucinate a chair (that is, do not see a chair that is actually present) will nevertheless avoid running into it if asked to walk around the room (Orne, 1962a). The experimenter may take this as evidence that the person actually sees the chair. The hypnotic subject, on the other hand, may insist that he really didn't see the chair. If we are interested primarily in the phenomenology of the deeply hypnotized subject, we have to decide whether it is his avoidant behavior or his testimony that more accurately reflects his experience.

In general, we have to be very cautious about the kind of evidence we accept as relevant to the subjective experience of a hypnotized subject. It is not always easy to decide whether a demonstrable difference between an actual and a suggested state of affairs reflects important differences in how these events are experienced or whether it simply reflects differences in how similar experiences are achieved (or both).

Ultimately, of course, a person's experience is a very private event. We can feel only our own pain; another's pain we can only imagine and infer. Consequently, we may never know for sure whether we are correct in evaluating another person's subjective experience. But if we are clever and persistent, we ought to be able to reduce the likelihood of error in such evaluations. This and the next two chapters are thus devoted to an examination of how various investigators have persisted in determining just what the subjective effects of hypnotic suggestions are. To accomplish this goal, we will look at three major hypnotic phenomena: hypnotic analgesia, posthypnotic amnesia, and visual and auditory effects suggested in hypnosis.

Some Preliminary Considerations

An analgesic ameliorates or eliminates pain. Most analgesics are chemical preparations, ranging from aspirin, the analgesic most frequently used for minor aches and pains, to morphine and codeine derivatives, employed for serious pain. Hypnotic analgesia, on the other hand, is a psychological technique for reducing or eliminating pain. Clinically, it has long been used with some success in obstetrics and dentistry (Kroger, 1963), as well as in some intractable diseases like terminal cancer (Erickson, 1966). Indeed, one of the most remarkable pages in the history of hypnosis concerns the clinical use of hypnosis to ameliorate surgical pain.

James Esdaile was an English surgeon who practiced medicine in India between 1845 and 1851. Having learned about mesmerism from a Scottish surgeon named Elliotson, Esdaile became one of its leading advocates and practitioners. During the time he was in India, he performed about 1000 operations, 300 of them involving major surgery. He became particularly adept at removing enormous scrotal tumors, sometimes weighing in excess of 50 pounds. An account of one such operation follows.

> Oct. 25.—Gooroochuan Shah, a shop-keeper, aged 40. He has got a "monster tumor," which prevents him from moving; its great weight, and his having used it for a writing-desk for many years, has pressed it into its present shape. His pulse is weak, and his feet oedematous [swollen with fluid], which will make it very hazardous to attempt its removal; . . . He became insensible on the fourth day of mesmerizing, . . . two men held up the tumour in a sheet, pulling it forward at the same time, and, in the presence of Mr. Bennet, I removed it by a circular incision, expedition being his only safety. The rush of venous blood was great, but fortunately soon arrested; and, after tying the last vessel, . . . he awoke. The loss of blood had been so great that he immediately fell into a fainting state. . . . On recovering he said that he awoke

while the mattress was being pulled back, and that nothing had disturbed him. The tumour weighed eighty pounds, and is probably the largest ever removed from the human body. I think it extremely likely that if the circulation had been hurried by pain and struggling, or if shock to the system had been increased by bodily and mental anguish, the man would have bled to death, or never have rallied from the effects of the operation. But the sudden loss of blood was all he had to contend against; and, though in so weak a condition, he has surmounted this, and gone on very well [Esdaile, 1957, pp. 221-222].*

Although the clinical use of hypnotic analgesia has provided many people with relief from pain, clear and compelling experimental evidence of the phenomenon has been difficult to obtain. Part of the problem may derive from subtle differences between clinical pain and pain that is experimentally induced (Beecher, 1959). People who are suffering clinical pain come to the therapist for their own good reasons. People who serve as subjects in experimental studies on hypnotic analgesia come to the laboratory less for their own reasons than for the investigator's. The subjects arrive in a pain-free state and are exposed to painful procedures under psychological conditions that hopefully minimize the pain. Their patterns of motivation cannot help but be different from those of clinical patients, and these motivational differences may be quite important in effecting analgesia.

Another reason why laboratory evidence of hypnotic analgesia has been hard to obtain may derive from the peculiar nature of pain itself. Consequently, we must turn to some of these problems before launching our examination of hypnotic analgesia.

The Problem of Pain

For the person experiencing it, there is nothing very complicated about pain: it simply hurts. However, the scientific study of pain is beset by all sorts of problems. There is no specialized pain organ as there are, for example, specific organs of sight and hearing. Moreover, there is no specific kind of stimulation, such as light or sound, that is inherently pain producing. Pain comes in a variety of sizes and shapes—dull aches; stabbing pains; deep, throbbing pain; and so on. Although there are theories of pain (Beecher, 1959; Melzack & Wall, 1965; Melzack, 1973), the exact mechanisms by which stimulation is translated into pain are not totally clear. Nor is it altogether clear why various painkillers, like aspirin or morphine, work.

The problem of understanding pain is complicated even further by some of its lesser-known anomalies. Phantom limb pain can be excruciating even though the person no longer posseses the hand or foot

*From *Hypnosis in Medicine and Surgery,* by J. Esdaile. 1957, Julian Press, Inc. Reprinted by permission.

in which he experiences the pain. In referred pain, the person experiences pain in a location removed from the site of stimulation. In delayed pain, the person experiences pain considerably after the offset of a painful stimulus. Certain rare people have a congenital incapacity to feel pain. Other people suffer more or less continuous pain even though there is no evident physical basis for it. A recent television documentary devoted to pain presented a case study in which the victim of a motorcycle accident continued to experience intractable (phantom limb) pain despite the fact that a progressive series of surgical operations had eliminated every neural pathway and center deemed necessary for the experience of pain (see Hackett, 1967). Millions upon millions of dollars are spent each year to eliminate or minimize pain; and yet pain persists. All of which is to say that pain is a very puzzling phenomenon.

The study of pain is further complicated by certain methodological problems. What shall we take as evidence of another person's pain? Several pain indices suggest themselves. First of all, we usually expect a person to experience pain in the presence of a stimulus that would ordinarily produce pain in us. The person's reflexive withdrawal from such a stimulus is additional evidence that it hurts. If we can observe tissue damage at the site of stimulation, we can be even more confident that the person experienced pain. When the application of an ordinarily painful stimulus is accompanied by psychophysiological activity such as increased heart rate, there is some additional evidence that the person in fact experienced pain. Finally, if the subject says he experienced pain, we usually believe him.

The problem is that none of these pain indicators is absolutely foolproof. Pain can certainly occur in the absence of any apparent stimulus (for example, phantom limb pain), and people are sometimes insensitive to a pain-inducing stimulus (for example, when drugged). Physiological responses are affected by a variety of things— unexpectedness and suddenness of stimulus onset, anxiety, and so on. Consequently, psychophysiological activity may be a response to pain, but it may also be a response to some other feature of a pain stimulus. As far as tissue damage is concerned, it is sometimes not even noticed by the victim until someone calls it to his attention. Finally, verbal reports of pain (or their lack) are subject to falsification. The pain avowed by victims of automobile accidents sometimes disappears with unseemly haste once the insurance claim is paid. Moreover, genuine pain can be disavowed. Consider the heroic denial of pain by the young man who inadvertently picks up a steaming hot plate of peas while dining at his girl's parents' for the first time.

As some of the preceding examples suggest, circumstances sometimes provide a reason for seriously distorting the otherwise straightforward relationship between the experience of pain and the report of it. On the other hand, the potentially distorting effects of circumstances may not constitute a real problem in the clinical or experimental study of hypnotic analgesia. After all, if there are no reasons for the subject to falsify his experience of pain, his pain reports should correspond to this experience. The question therefore boils down to this: in the study of hypnotic analgesia, does the experimental or clinical context provide a reason for subjects to deny the experience of pain? One investigator of hypnosis has answered this question affirmatively. He states that

> The motivation for denial of pain is present in the clinical hypnotic situation. The physician who has invested time and energy hypnotizing the patient and suggesting that pain will be relieved expects and desires that his efforts will be successful, and by his words and manner communicates his desires and expectations to the patient. The patient in turn has often found a close relationship with the physician-hypnotist and would like to please him or at least not to disappoint him. Furthermore, the patient is aware that if he states that he suffered, he is implying that the physician's time and energy were wasted and his efforts futile. The situation is such that even though the patient may have suffered, it may be difficult or disturbing for him to state directly to the physician-hypnotist that he experienced pain and it may be less anxiety-provoking to say that he did not suffer [Barber, 1970, pp. 211–212; see also Barber, 1963; Sarbin & Coe, 1972, p. 136].*

Although the above quotation is concerned with the clinical use of hypnotic analgesia, similar considerations might well enter into the experimental study of it. In other words, if we start with the assumption that patients or subjects report and "behave" pain when they have no reason to hide it, we must contend immediately with the possibility that the very presence of a physician or experimenter may constitute a reason for denying felt pain.

As I shall later indicate, this problem may not be as formidable as it first appears. Investigators, however, have implicitly acknowledged the problematic status of pain reports by seeking an index of hypnotic analgesia that seems less vulnerable to purposeful distortion than subject's verbal report, and, almost invariably, they have settled on some psychophysiological measure such as the galvanic skin response (GSR)[1] or heart rate. Now, as we have already seen, the presence of a psychophysiological response can reflect a variety of things besides pain, such as suddenness of stimulus onset. The *absence* (or at least the minimization) of any such response in the presence of an ordinarily painful stimulus, however, would be fairly convincing evidence that hypnotic analgesia is effective in reducing or eliminating pain. In one way or another, it is this kind of evidence that many investigators of hypnotic analgesia have sought. Although some of this work on hypnotic

---

analgesia occurred before 1960 (Shor, 1967, reviews these studies), the best work in the area has appeared since that date.

Hypnotic Analgesia and Physiology

The first such study that we shall consider is one performed by Sutcliffe (1961). It is a complex study, only part of which need concern us here. The author selected a sample of subjects high and low in hypnotic susceptibility and assessed their GSR to each of six conditions. We will pay particular attention to the 16 high-susceptible subjects who were allocated to either a hypnotic or a control condition and who received or did not receive four electric shocks during the experimental treatment. (All subjects were familiarized with the shock before actually participating in the experiment.)

There are two ways in which little or no GSR might be evoked: by the presentation of a nonpainful stimulus and by the presentation of an (ordinarily) painful stimulus to a person who in fact cannot feel it (that is, is analgesic). Consequently, Sutcliffe compared the GSR of analgesic subjects receiving a buzzer-shock combination with the GSR of analgesic subjects receiving only the nonpainful buzzer. His argument was that if hypnotic analgesia were really effective in eliminating pain, then the analgesic subjects in the buzzer-shock group should react just like their control counterparts receiving only the buzzer. Sutcliffe was also interested in comparing the GSR of analgesic and nonanalgesic subjects receiving a shock. Here he argued that if hypnotic analgesia were really effective in eliminating pain, the GSR changes in the analgesic subjects should be much lower than those in the nonanalgesic control group.

Table 2-1 presents some of the results of this study. This table shows that subjects receiving the buzzer-shock combination showed much greater GSR change than subjects who received only the buzzer. Even among the analgesic subjects, those who received shock were much more GSR responsive than those who did not. In fact the analgesic subjects receiving shock generated slightly more GSR change than did the shocked control subjects who were not in the analgesic condition. The lowest GSR change of all occurred in the control subjects who neither expected nor received shock.

If the GSR does in fact measure pain, it looks very much as if the analgesic subjects were experiencing the electric shock as painful. On the other hand, we have already seen that the GSR can be responsive to many characteristics of a painful stimulus besides the pain per se, so we should not immediately jump to any conclusions about the significance of the GSR responses in these subjects. And, as a matter of fact, the four subjects in the shock-analgesic condition denied feeling any pain, despite the fact that they were quite as GSR responsive to the shock stimulus as

Table 2-1. Mean changes in GSR expressed as log conductance change (all subjects are highly susceptible to hypnosis; $N = 4$ in each cell)

	Buzzer-nonshock	Buzzer-shock
Hypnosis with suggestions for analgesia	8.7[a]	19.4
Control condition	3.3	18.1

[a] In this condition, subjects were led to expect that shock would in fact be delivered simultaneously with the buzzer. In fact, however, no shock was given.

From "'Credulous' and 'Skeptical' Views of Hypnotic Phenomena: Experiments on Esthesia, Hallucination, and Delusion," by J. P. Sutcliffe, *Journal of Abnormal and Social Psychology*, 1961, 62, 189-200. Copyright 1961 by the American Psychological Association. Reprinted by permission.

subjects in the nonanalgesic condition. In other words, the verbal testimony of subjects in the shock-analgesic condition reflected the suggested state of affairs, whereas their bodily reaction (GSR) reflected the stimulus state of affairs.

According to Sutcliffe, it is impossible to decide on the basis of this evidence whether the hypnotic analgesic subjects misperceived the situation or simply misreported it. This suspension of judgment is reasonable only if the conflicting GSR and verbal report are given equal status as pain indicators. However, I have already suggested that there are some serious difficulties with the autonomic indicators of pain, and the next study casts even further doubt upon their adequacy.

Bowers and van der Meulen (1972) compared the heart rate and GSR of seven dental patients, each of whom had two caries repaired. One tooth was drilled and filled under chemical analgesia; the other (bilaterally symmetrical) was restored under hypnotic analgesia. Since chemical analgesics are widely believed to be effective in eliminating pain, one might expect that the use of a chemical analgesic would eliminate autonomic indicators of pain. However, the data clearly indicated that both heart rate and the number of GSRs increased dramatically during the drilling period with chemical as well as hypnotic analgesia. Across all subjects, the type of analgesia utilized made no difference in the physiological responsiveness of subjects during this crucial period. In other words, *if* physiological reactivity is viewed as an index of pain, *then* chemical and hypnotic analgesias are equally ineffective in controlling dental pain. Obviously, there is something wrong with this conclusion, since the effectiveness of chemical analgesics is not under question. The explanation may be found in the rather ominous sound of the drill, which probably arouses the subjects and elevates their heart rate and GSR whether or not they feel pain. Again we see that so many things besides pain can influence physiological measures that we must exercise extreme caution in simply inferring pain from physiological reactivity—a caution that must apply to both the evaluation of hypnotic analgesia and the evaluation of chemical analgesia.

Incidentally, in that same dental study, there were interesting differences in the physiological reactivities of subjects reporting no pain and subjects reporting at least some pain. For example, in the hypnotic analgesia condition, the heart-rate increase from a baseline period to the drilling period was twice as great for the three subjects reporting *no* pain than for the four subjects who reported at least some pain. In the chemical analgesic condition, two subjects reporting *no* pain showed twice as much increase in GSR activity as the four subjects reporting at least some pain. (One subject was excluded from this comparison, because he had been inadvertently administered an analgesic containing adrenalin.) Moreover, there was no difference in heart rate between subjects reporting pain and those reporting none. Granted, the number of subjects involved in these comparisons was too small to permit sweeping generalizations; nevertheless, there is little comfort in these findings for the assumption that physiological reactivity is inevitably proportional to felt pain.

A third study was somewhat more successful in the use of psychophysiological indices to assess pain. Barber and Hahn (1962) deviated from most previous research about hypnotic analgesia in their choice of a painful stimulus. Instead of employing a brief, episodic stimulus such as electric shock, they utilized the so-called cold-pressor test. Specifically, these investigators immersed the subject's left hand for three minutes in water that was just above the freezing point (2° C). This procedure produces not only a very cold hand but a very painful one, and it is a pain that increases over most of the three-minute period of immersion. Thus, the cold-pressor technique induces pain that is more protracted than electric shock and is, at least in this respect, closer to clinical pain.

Barber and Hahn tested four different groups of subjects; all of the subjects had previously scored in the upper 25% on a scale of waking suggestibility. The four groups were in the following conditions: (a) a hypnotically suggested analgesia condition (in which a 20-minute hypnotic induction was followed by suggestions that the subject's left hand would become numb and lose all sensation); (b) a waking imagined analgesia condition (in which subjects were highly motivated to imagine that the water was pleasant and comfortable); (c) an uninstructed condition; and (d) a control condition (in which uninstructed subjects immersed their hand in room-temperature water). All the subjects were asked after each of the three minutes of the cold pressor how their hands felt (on a scale ranging from cool to very painful). As might be imagined, the subjects in the uninstructed control condition found the room-temperature water quite comfortable and not at all painful. By contrast, the uninstructed subjects whose hands were placed in the cold water found it painful. Both the hypnotic- and the waking-analgesic groups rated the water as uncomfortable (but not painful). So, whether or not subjects were hypnotized, analgesic suggestions seemed to be partially effective in reducing the pain of the cold pressor; but neither the hypnotic nor the waking analgesia procedure was completely effective in eliminating pain.

Before presenting the psychophysiological evidence of this study, two points should be noted: (a) For the first time, we have evidence that a nonhypnotic technique is as effective as a hypnotic one in modifying a person's report of subjective experience. (In Chapter 6, we will further explore whether or not the formal induction of hypnosis is necessary to produce effects ordinarily associated with hypnosis.) (b) Unlike Sutcliffe, Barber and Hahn did not get complete denial of pain by the subjects in hypnotic analgesia condition. This may mean that Barber and Hahn were less successful in inducing analgesia than Sutcliffe, but it may also mean that cold-pressor pain is more difficult to eliminate than the pain of electric shock. Perhaps of greater interest is the fact that subjects who were hypnotically analgesic were willing to acknowledge discomfort. Earlier I asked whether the subjective reports of hypnotic subjects reflected their actual experience or, rather, their need to please the hypnotist. Acknowledgement of discomfort by subjects who are supposed to be hypnotically analgesic is presumptive evidence that they are in fact reporting what they feel. If the subjects were only interested in pleasing the hypnotist, why wouldn't they simply deny feeling any pain whatsoever? Perhaps hypnotic subjects' reports of subjective experience are credible after all.

Does the physiological evidence in the Barber and Hahn study corroborate the findings of verbal testimony? To evaluate the physiological reaction to the cold-pressor test, four different measures were employed: muscle potential,[2] respiratory irregularity, heart rate, and GSR. The pattern of findings was somewhat complex, but in general both the subjects under hypnotic analgesia and those under waking-imagined analgesia showed less change in muscle potential and respiratory irregularity than did the uninstructed subjects. However, the changes in heart rate and GSR were virtually the same for all three of these groups, and they all differed significantly from the changes that took place in the subjects in the control group who immersed their hands in warm water. In other words, whether a person responded physiologically to the stimulus state of affairs (water of 2° C) or to the suggested state of affairs (the water will be pleasant) depended upon the particular physiological measure being employed.

As Barber and Hahn note, the two measures that are responsive to the suggested state of affairs (forehead muscle potential and respiratory irregularity) are under greater voluntary control than the two measures that are responsive to the stimulus state of affairs (heart rate and GSR). This fact raises the possibility that subjects might have voluntarily inhibited their physiological reactions to a painful state of affairs on those indices for which it was possible to do so. The more voluntary control a person has over a response system, the easier it may be for him or her to fake nonresponsiveness to it. For this reason, the more involuntary a physiological indicator is, the more persuasive it is when it remains unresponsive to an ordinarily painful stimulus. It is this kind of evidence that has recently been generated at Stanford's Laboratory of Hypnosis Research.

Under the direction of E. R. Hilgard, the Stanford Laboratory of Hypnosis has been in the forefront of hypnosis research since 1957. Some of the many contributions made by this laboratory will be presented throughout the remainder of this book, but none is more arresting than the work on hypnotic analgesia (Hilgard, 1967, 1969a, 1971b; Lenox, 1970; Sachs, 1970; Hilgard, Morgan, Lange, Lenox, Macdonald, Marshall, & Sachs, 1974; Hilgard, Ruch, Lange, Lenox, Morgan & Sachs, 1974).

The Stanford work investigating hypnotic analgesia involved preliminary studies on the relationship of pain reports and blood pressure changes on the one hand and two different means of producing pain on the other. One such means we are already familiar with—the cold-pressor test. Unlike Barber and Hahn's subjects, however, those in Hilgard's lab immerse the forearm (instead of just the hand) into circulating ice water. The fact that the water is circulating means that the warmth of the arm itself cannot create local increases in the water temperature. This procedure is extremely painful, and under ordinary circumstances subjects can only stand it for 20–40 seconds instead of the three minutes characteristic of the subjects in Barber and Hahn's study.

The Stanford laboratory also employs ischemic pain in its investigations. Ischemic pain is produced by placing a blood pressure cuff on the arm of a subject and pumping it so full of air that it blocks the flow of blood to the hand. This tourniquet arrangement does not hurt at first, but by 10 minutes or so pain is beginning to build, and by 20–40 minutes it is usually unbearable.

Before presenting the Stanford findings on subjects who were hypnotically analgesic, it is worthwhile to present some of the findings obtained with ordinary waking subjects. The two chief measures of pain employed in these studies were a subjective report of pain and a blood pressure index. As far as the subjective report is concerned, subjects were periodically asked to rate how much pain they were experiencing—a report of 0 indicating no pain, and a rating of 10 indicating pain so severe that the subject would like to discontinue his or her participation in the experiment. (Since subjects were urged to continue on in the experiment even beyond this point, reports of pain could exceed 10.)

The blood pressure index was employed because various investigations had established it as a more reliable measure than heart rate (Lenox, 1970). Figures 2-1 and 2-2 show how both subjective report of pain and blood pressure increase at about the same rate in cold-pressor pain and in ischemic pain. These findings suggest that for normal waking subjects, pain rating and blood pressure are responding to increases in pain as a function of time in the painful situation. This very sensible finding is buttressed by many others that we will not go into here. All in all, the findings suggest an orderly and consistent relationship between stimulus duration and intensity on the one hand and verbal reports and physiological indices of pain on the other.

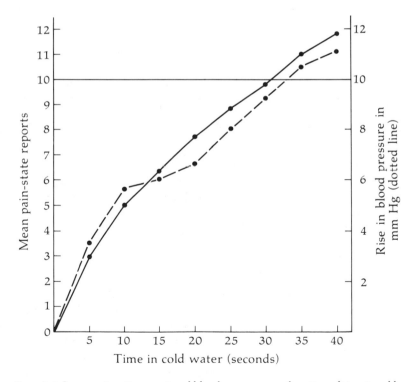

Figure 2-1. Increase in pain report and blood pressure as a function of time in cold pressor (0° C). Adapted from "Pain as a Puzzle for Psychology and Physiology," by E. R. Hilgard, *American Psychologist*, 1969, *24*, 103–113. Copyright 1969 by the American Psychological Association. Reprinted by permission.

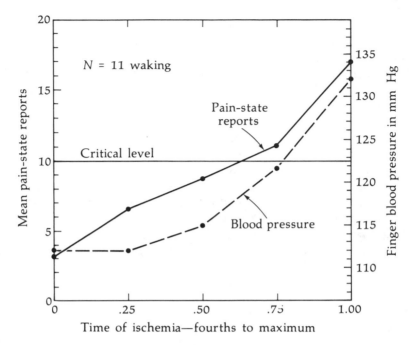

Figure 2-2. Pain reports and blood pressure as a function of time in ischemia. (The tourniquet was removed when pain became intolerable, which varied from 12 to 32 minutes for these 11 subjects. Hence the time to intolerable pain was divided into fourths for purposes of obtaining the means that are plotted.) From "Pain as a Puzzle for Psychology and Physiology," by E. R. Hilgard, *American Psychologist,* 1969, 24, 103-113. Copyright 1969 by the American Psychological Association. Reprinted by permission.

The question is, of course, what happens to these nice, straightforward relationships when hypnotic analgesia is introduced. If the subjective experience of pain is actually minimized or eliminated by hypnotic analgesia, increases in stimulus duration and intensity should not lead to corresponding increases in subjective pain and blood pressure.

One way of approaching this problem is to find a few highly susceptible subjects who are also very responsive to suggestions for hypnotic analgesia. Then, while these subjects are hypnotically analgesic, their blood pressure can be monitored under conditions that ordinarily engender extreme pain. If these subjects neither report pain nor demonstrate the increases in blood pressure that ordinarily accompany severe pain, we have as good evidence as one could wish that hypnotic analgesia is genuinely effective in eliminating pain.

Lenox (1970) reported a study that employed this general strategy. Eight selected subjects were exposed to ischemic pain under both waking and hypnotic analgesia conditions. As indicated in Figure 2-2, in ischemia the mean pain rating and the blood pressure increased during the waking state as a function of time. During the analgesic condition, however, most of the subjects reported no pain whatsoever, and, as Figure 2-3 shows, their blood pressure hardly increased at all. Furthermore, their blood pressure remained relatively low considerably beyond the point in time at which the same subjects in the waking condition found the pain so unbearable that they had to discontinue their participation in the experiment.[3]

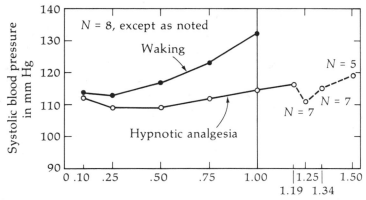

Ischemia based on 1.00 as maximum time in waking

Figure 2-3. The mean systolic blood pressure response in mm Hg to ischemia during waking and hypnotic analgesia conditions. From "Effect of Hypnotic Analgesia on Verbal Report and Cardiovascular Responses to Ischemic Pain," by J. Lenox, *Journal of Abnormal Psychology,* 1970, 75, 199–206. Copyright 1970 by the American Psychological Association. Reprinted by permission.

I have previously claimed that the *absence* of a physiological response to conditions ordinarily regarded as painful would constitute rather telling evidence that no pain was experienced. The evidence from these eight subjects, highly selected for their hypnotic susceptibility and for their responsiveness to analgesic suggestions, seems rather strong support for the proposition that hypnotic procedures *can* dramatically alter the subjective experience of a deeply hypnotized individual. Unfortunately, there is a serious flaw in the study, which compromises its value as a controlled investigation. Hypnotic analgesia was always evaluated on a day after the subjects' waking exposure to ischemia, and the subjects had a good deal of practice on the ischemic task between the waking and the hypnotic-analgesic test sessions. (This last point is not made entirely clear in Lenox's published account.) Consequently, the impressive absence of blood pressure increases during the second (hypnotic) test session may be due as much to subjects' interim practice as to suggestions for analgesia per se. Despite this problem, the study suggests that, for one reason or another, selected subjects can minimize or eliminate physiological signs of pain even in the presence of a stimulus that usually occasions extraordinary pain. Such an outcome of course confirms the verbal reports of analgesic subjects who express no experience of pain.

Although the evidence above was based on ischemic pain, the Stanford researchers have also utilized cold-pressor pain. They have done so on subjects selected for their hypnotic susceptibility (but *not* for their demonstrated responsiveness to suggestions for hypnotic analgesia). Figure 2-4 shows that subjects in the hypnotic analgesic condition reported much less pain over a 40-second period than these same subjects did either in a waking state or when hypnotized without receiving analgesic suggestions. (Incidentally, the correlation of hypnotic susceptibility and pain reduction due to analgesic suggestions seems to be about .48 *whether or not* the suggestions are delivered to waking or hypnotized subjects [Evans & Paul, 1970; Hilgard, Ruch, et al., 1974].)

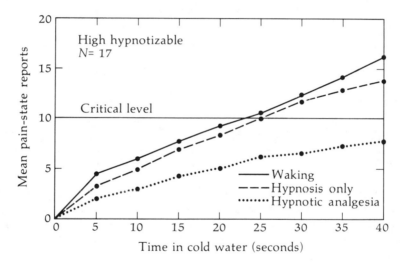

Figure 2-4. Pain as a function of time in water of 0° C in waking state and following attempted hypnotic induction without analgesia instructions and with analgesia instructions. From "Pain as a Puzzle for Psychology and Physiology," by E. R. Hilgard, *American Psychologist*, 1969, *24*, 103–113. Copyright 1969 by the American Psychological Association. Reprinted by permission.

It is important to note in Figure 2-4 that, even in the analgesic condition, the verbal reports of pain increase in a systematic and orderly way as a function of time in the cold-pressor test. This lawful pattern of pain reports lends them a credibility that, it might be argued, is absent in the isolated reports of pain used in other experiments on hypnotic analgesia. In other words, if multiple reports of pain are lawfully related to each other and to the duration of the painful stimulus, each report gains credibility precisely because it fits into an observable pattern. One isolated report of pain may not be as persuasive, simply because it lacks a context of patterned relationships. However, once verbal reports of pain are established as reliable, even isolated pain reports take on the lustre of credibility and cannot simply be dismissed as fabrications.

Quite surprisingly, the blood pressure of the subjects exposed to the cold-pressor test was *higher* in the hypnotic analgesic condition than it was in either the waking state or the hypnosis alone condition. This outcome is of course opposite to that found for analgesic subjects in the ischemic condition, and it is not clear why this reversal occurred. Perhaps the mental condition produced by hypnotic analgesia interacts with the suddenness and coldness of the cold-pressor test to effect these blood pressure increases. Whether or not this explanation is correct, hypnotically analgesic subjects do show much different blood pressure responses to ischemic and to cold-pressor pain. We have already seen in the Barber and Hahn (1962) investigation that different physiological measures differ in their responsiveness to a cold-pressor test. Thus, one pretty safe conclusion from these studies is this: whether or not a painful event registers in the physiology of a hypnotically analgesic subject depends upon (a) the nature of the pain stimulus employed and (b) the kind of physiological response monitored.

At the beginning of this chapter, I entertained the possibility that reports of no pain by hypnotic analgesic subjects may be purposeful falsifications aimed at pleasing the hypnotist. In order to evaluate this possibility, I presented experiments that have attempted to employ indices of pain that are less falsifiable than verbal testimony. I also discussed how, after a great deal of very hard work, investigators have sometimes found the kind of evidence they were looking for. Along the way, however, we have discovered that physiological measures of pain are very problematic in their own right. Moreover, the fact that hypnotic analgesic subjects do report pain in an orderly and systematic fashion (see Figures 2-3 and 2-4) does suggest that subject testimony cannot automatically be written off as prevarication calculated to please—even when the subjects report no pain whatsoever. Indeed, Hilgard has stated in no uncertain terms that "there is no physiological measure of pain which is either as discriminating of fine differences in stimulus conditions, as reliable upon repetition, or as lawfully related to changed conditions, as the subject's verbal report" (1969a, p. 107). It is, of course, a source of satisfaction to know that physiological indices and verbal reports can correspond in indicating no pain in analgesic subjects. However, in those cases where verbal report and physiology do not agree, the verbal account is probably the truer indication of the subject's experience.

Some Genuine Problems

In a curious sort of way, the attempt to "validate" hypnotic analgesia physiologically has deflected scientific attention away from some genuine perplexities inherent in the phenomenon. By way of introducing these problems, let us return briefly to the study by Sutcliffe (1961). The reader will recall that in this study some hypnotic analgesic subjects, when exposed to a buzzer-shock condition, invariably showed GSR responses comparable to those of their waking counterparts. One of the analgesic subjects responded to the shock with a characteristically large GSR change, but, in addition, her whole body jumped. When questioned about her reaction, the subject said "I don't feel anything, but *she* seems uncomfortable" (Sutcliffe, 1961, p. 194). Very curious. Why this use of a third-person pronoun to refer to one's own reaction?

Consider next a brief report by Kaplan (1960). A 20-year-old college student was hypnotized several times and eventually demonstrated what has historically been called "automatic writing." In other words, the subject's right hand developed the ability to "write anything it wanted to, not subject to the control or restrictions of the 'conscious' personality" (Kaplan, 1960, p. 567). When hypnotic analgesia was suggested for his left hand, and the hand was subjected to (ordinarily) painful pin pricks, the subject seemed oblivious to what had happened and apparently experienced no pain at all. Nevertheless, as soon as the pin pricks were administered, the subject's *right* hand began to write "Ouch, damn it, you're hurting me" (p. 568).

Both of these examples suggest that subjects who are hypnotically analgesic register pain at some level, even though it may not be represented in ordinary conscious experience. Moreover, the pain "leaks" evidenced in these two accounts confirm clinical experience with both hypnotic and chemically induced analgesia. For example, some of Esdaile's Indian patients would writhe around and moan while their tumors were being removed, yet later on they reported that they had felt nothing. And in 1846, when a dentist named Horace Wells attempted to demonstrate for the first time the anesthetic properties of nitrous oxide, his patient groaned. Although the patient later reported feeling nothing, the professional audience thought they had witnessed a dental "put-on," and they jeered and hissed Wells off the stage of the operating amphitheater. The subsequent success of nitrous oxide as an anesthetic proved Wells right and his detractors wrong, but not in time to prevent poor Wells from committing suicide.

In general, then, we seem to be confronted with a situation in which clinical patients (or experimental subjects) are helped dramatically by analgesia in its various forms; at the same time, however, such subjects can effectively communicate (in one way or another) their appreciation of pain. Very recently, the Stanford group has tried to unravel some of these perplexities.

In an important theoretical paper that presents some preliminary evidence on this issue, Hilgard (1973a) reports a replication of the Kaplan (1960) finding with automatic writing. For example, one hypnotically analgesic subject whose hand and arm were immersed in circulating ice water reported no pain and remained calm during the entire duration of what would have ordinarily constituted a harrowing ordeal. Yet, while she was insisting verbally that she felt no pain, "the dissociated part of herself was reporting through automatic writing that *she felt the pain just as in the normal nonhypnotic state*" (Hilgard, 1973a, p. 398). Hilgard dubbed this clandestine communication system the "hidden observer" and began to study its functioning. The first formal investigation of this "secret" system of communication has recently been published (Knox, Morgan, & Hilgard, 1974).

These investigators selected eight highly susceptible subjects who had demonstrated an ability to engage in "automatic talking," a variant of automatic writing, in which the hidden observer says (instead of writes) things that remain unavailable to the subject's conscious awareness. (If the reader thinks such an eventuality is impossible *in principle*, he should consider for a moment the person who talks in his sleep, with no conscious awareness or memory of having done so.)

Each subject was seen for three sessions, one on each of three days. On the first day, subjects were exposed to ischemic pain in a normal waking condition and generally familiarized with the experimental procedure. On the second day, half of the subjects were hypnotized and administered ischemic pain while protected by suggestions for analgesia; the other half of the subjects received ischemic pain while hypnotized, but without the benefit of analgesic suggestions. On the third day, the subjects reversed their second-day conditions.

On both the second and third days of their participation in the experiment, all the subjects received the following hypnotic suggestions:

> When I place my hand on your shoulder, I shall be able to talk to a hidden part of you that knows things are going on in your body, things that are unknown to the part of you to which I am now talking. The part to which I am now talking will not know what you are telling me or even that you are talking ... [p. 842].*

In all three days of the experiment, the subjects were asked, after the first minute, to make ordinary ("open") reports of pain and suffering; the request was repeated at two-minute intervals during the ischemic condition. On the last two days of the experiment (when the subjects

*From "Pain and Suffering in Ischemia," by V. J. Knox, A. H. Morgan, and E. R. Hilgard, *Archives of General Psychiatry*, 1974, *30*, 840–847. Copyright 1974, American Medical Association. This and all other quotes from this source are reprinted by permission.

were hypnotized), subjects'"hidden" reports were also obtained. In order to get these reports, the hypnotist placed his hand on the subject's shoulder immediately after each open report and requested a second (hidden) pain and suffering report. As in previous Stanford investigations, an analgesic subject's report of pain consisted of calling out a number from 0 (no pain) to 10 or above (exceedingly painful).

The results of this investigation expressed the level of reported pain and suffering at the subject's eighth minute of involvement in ischemia, since all hypnotized subjects persisted at least this long, whether or not they had received analgesic suggestions. As Table 2-2 shows, under the ordinary, open-report conditions, there was a clear decrement in pain

Table 2-2. Mean pain and suffering reports for hypnotized subjects under various treatment and report conditions

	Pain		Suffering	
	Open report	*Hidden observer*	*Open report*	*Hidden observer*
With analgesia	1.0	8.0	0.4	6.2
Without analgesia	9.9	10.2	7.8	8.6

From "Pain and Suffering in Ischemia," by V. J. Knox, A. H. Morgan, and E. R. Hilgard, *Archives of General Psychiatry,* 1974, *30,* 840–847. Copyright 1974, American Medical Association. Reprinted by permission.

and suffering from the condition of hypnosis alone to that of hypnotic analgesia. This result replicates those of many previous investigations showing that subjective reports of pain are minimized or eliminated under conditions of hypnotic analgesia. What is novel about this study is the subjects' "hidden observer" reports, which disclose that, when the hypnotized subjects have received analgesic suggestions, they report almost as much pain and suffering as they do under nonanalgesic conditions. The authors comment: "These results suggest that at some hidden level the pain and suffering are fully processed essentially as in the nonanesthetic condition" (Knox et al., 1974, p. 844). This does *not* mean, however, that the effects of hypnotic analgesia are suspect. Resistance to such an unwarranted extension of these findings is justified in light of reports by participants in the investigation. One subject said:

> The hidden observer and the hypnotized part are both *all of me,* but the hidden observer is more aware and reported honestly what was there. The hypnotized part of me just *wasn't aware* of the pain [p. 845].

Another subject said:

> In hypnosis I kept my mind and body separate, and my mind was wandering to other places—not aware of the pain in my arm. When the hidden observer

was called up, the hypnotized part had to step back for a minute and let the hidden part tell the truth. The hidden observer is concerned primarily with how my body feels. It doesn't have a mind to wander, and so it hurt quite a bit. When you took your hand off my shoulder, I went back to the separation, and it didn't hurt anyone, but this separation became more and more difficult to achieve [p. 846].

Yet another subject phrased the situation as follows:

As time went on, the hidden observer was telling me more and more clearly that my arm was hurting. Toward the last I felt that it was going to take over and say, "This is ridiculous, it's going too far, I'm getting hurt!" It became very adamant and said, "You know there is pain there even though you don't feel it." The hidden observer feels that at times I'm dull—not too perceptive. Toward the end it wanted to break out, but the hypnotized part just wouldn't give up [p. 846].

The "double consciousness" revealed in these comments will be expanded later on in this book. Suffice it to say here that these are not the comments of people who are trying to conceal something from the investigator. Instead, the subjects are trying hard to convey some genuine if confusing aspects of their experience.

Some skeptics will doubtless leap upon these findings as evidence that hypnotic analgesia is not genuine. Such skepticism is of course no stranger to hypnotic phenomena in general and to hypnotic analgesia in particular. For instance, Esdaile and other devotees of mesmerism were openly ridiculed in the *Lancet*, a famous British medical journal, and in other scientific publications. For example, in response to one case study of surgery performed under mesmerism, it was "asserted that the patient was an imposter who had been trained not to show pain" (Rosen, 1946, p. 537). Esdaile's response to this kind of criticism might be considered definitive. He stated:

... I have *every month* more operations of this kind than take place in the native hospital in Calcutta a year, and more than I had for the six years previous. There must be some reason for this, and I only see two ways of accounting for it: my patients, on returning home, either say to their friends similarly afflicted, "Wah! brother, what a soft man the doctor Sahib is! He cut me to pieces for twenty minutes, and I made him believe that I did not feel it. Isn't it a capital joke? Do go and play him the same trick; you have only to laugh in your elbow, and you will not feel the pain." Or they say to their brother sufferers,—"look at me; I have got rid of my burthen (of 20, 30, 40, 50, 60, or 80 lbs., as it may be), am restored to the use of my body, and can again work for my bread: this, I assure you, the doctor Sahib did when I was alseep, and I knew nothing about it;—you will be equally lucky, I dare say; and I advise you to go try; you need not be cut if you feel it." Which of these hypotheses best explains the fact my readers will decide for themselves [Esdaile, 1957, pp. 218–219].*

Case rested.

*From *Hypnosis in Medicine and Surgery,* by J. Esdaile. 1957, Julian Press, Inc. Reprinted by permission.

Footnotes

[1]The GSR is a measure of the skin's resistance to an electric current. Ordinarily, a relaxed subject displays high resistance; an anxious or aroused subject, a low resistance. Moreover, the GSR ordinarily responds to sudden stimulation with a precipitous decrease in resistance. Sometimes the change in GSR is reported in conductance instead of resistance units. Decreases in resistance reflect an *increase* in conductance. The GSR reflects the activity of sweat glands.

[2]Muscle potential is a measure of the electrical activity accompanying muscular movement.

[3]Incidentally, three low-susceptible subjects who were asked to simulate hypnotic analgesia and exposed to ischemic pain were completely unable to inhibit either their gross behavioral signs of discomfort or their blood pressure response to ischemia (Lenox, 1970).

3.
Are Hypnotic
Effects Genuine?
Posthypnotic Amnesia

In 1783, a shepherd boy mesmerized by the Marquis de Puysegur engaged in sleepwalking and later had no memory of it. Since somnambulism is another word for sleepwalking, and since some early forms of hypnosis resembled sleepwalking, hypnosis came to be considered a kind of artificial somnambulism, and the forgetting of the somnambulistic events was presumed to be one of its chief characteristics. Since Puysegur's time, views of hypnosis have of course changed. Among other things, the forgetting of trance events (that is, posthypnotic amnesia) is no longer considered an inevitable feature of a hypnotic episode, although highly susceptible subjects are often responsive to suggestions for posthypnotic amnesia. It is mainly with *suggested* forgetting that we will concern ourselves here, and not with the relatively rare spontaneous forgetting manifested by Puysegur's shepherd boy.

Forgetting "X" Is Different from Never Having Known "X"

One of the distinguishing characteristics of suggested posthypnotic amnesia is that it is reversible; the person can recover the forgotten material (Cooper, 1972; Nace, Orne, & Hammer, 1974). This recovery is usually engendered by a signal from the hypnotist. For example, when giving the suggestions for posthypnotic amnesia, the hypnotist might say something like "You will not be able to remember anything at all of these hypnotic experiences until I tell you 'Now, you can remember everything.'" When later on the hypnotist repeats this signal to the now waking subject, the latter suddenly remembers—often with apparent amazement—what he had forgotten up to that moment.

Skeptics sometimes question whether posthypnotic amnesia truly makes a subject forget anything. For example, one prominent investigator has stated that "it appears possible that . . . practically all instances of suggested amnesia may be characterized by a motivated unwillingness to verbalize the events to the experimenter or to the hypnotist" (Barber, 1969, p. 215). This "motivated unwillingness to verbalize" includes everything from outright refusal to mention what the subject remembers perfectly well to active efforts by the subject not to remember. In the latter form, posthypnotic amnesia is often experienced as a disinclination to think about the forgotten events. Amnesic subjects often say such things as "I know if I really tried to remember I could"; "It's like a thin curtain separates me from what I've forgotten. All I'd have to do is draw the curtain, and I'd remember"; "I just keep thinking of other things so that I can't remember."

Outside the context of hypnosis, it is sometimes true that persons actively avoid thinking about things that distress or disturb them. The injunction to "forgive and forget" suggests the possibility of purposefully putting memories out of one's mind. We might, for the sake of exposition, call this *volitional forgetting;* it is the kind of forgetting that Barber (1969) seems to suggest is generally characteristic of posthypnotic amnesia.

On the other hand, we have all experienced what it's like to forget where we put something that we want desperately to find. Consider the plight of the fellow who is already ten minutes late for an appointment. He cannot find his glasses, without which he cannot even drive his car. Where the heck did he put them? In a fit of frustration, he slams the desk top with his fist, knocking the telephone directory askew. And lo— underneath the directory—are his glasses. *Now* he remembers what happened. He was putting on his socks in the bedroom when he had remembered to make an important telephone call. He had gone to the telephone on the desk, taken off his glasses to read the directory (since he was nearsighted and read without them), and put them on the desk top. When he had found the number he needed, he had put the book on top of the desk (that is, on top of the glasses) and made the call. Just as he was hanging up, the doorbell had rung; it was a buddy who wanted to return a book, but who then stayed to talk to our hero while he finished dressing. The general effect of this sequence of events was, of course, to make him forget where he had put his glasses. This is all very ordinary. What is extraordinary, however, is how readily sequences like this come to mind *after* finding lost objects. We may as well call this *nonvolitional* forgetting, since it is this kind of forgetting that people experience as involuntary and resistant to conscious and deliberate efforts to recover "X," the forgotten material. The problem here is in the retrieval of relevant information, not in its absence from the memory store. In posthypnotic amnesia, however—and this is a very important point—no matter how nonvolitional the forgetting of "X" may be, it is *not* equivalent to never having known "X" in the first place. Several experiments make this point quite clearly.

Goldstein and Sipprelle (1970) selected from 72 subjects 33 who demonstrated an ability to experience hypnotic amnesia.[1] These subjects were then divided into three groups, only two of which concern us here: those who were hypnotized and given suggestions to forget previously learned material and those who were told to *pretend* they had forgotten previously learned material. The "previously learned material" consisted of a sequential pattern of poker chips (blue, white, white, white, blue, white, blue, blue, white, blue) that the subjects had successfully reproduced three times in a row during learning trials.

The authors argued that if hypnotic amnesia was like total ablation of memory (that is, if it was like never having seen the pattern of poker chips), the errors the subjects made should have been totally random. If a person had in fact never learned the pattern of poker chips, then in each and every one of the ten available positions he had a 50-50 chance of being correct in selecting either the blue or the white chip (in the same way that a coin flip has a 50-50 chance of coming up heads or tails). Since each subject in the experiment had three separate amnesia trials, there were 3 x 10, or 30, individual occasions in which subjects could be either correct or incorrect in selecting a blue or a white chip. On a chance basis, of course, the truly naive subject would be in error 50% of the time (that is, 15 times out of 30). The pretend group in fact made an average of 13.5 errors—that is, very close to a chance performance. The hypnotic-amnesia subjects, on the other hand, made an average of only seven errors. The performance of these subjects far exceeded chance level and clearly suggested that they remembered a great deal, even though they may have experienced themselves as having forgotten what they implicitly knew.

Incidentally, the experience of having forgotten what one implicitly knows is not at all uncommon. For example, consider the multiple-choice exam (each question containing four alternatives). Even on the subset of questions for which the testee subjectively feels he is simply guessing, the likelihood is high that he will get more than 25% correct answers. People often know more than they can consciously remember.

One of my recent studies (Bowers, 1975) has produced findings very similar to Goldstein and Sipprelle's. Highly susceptible subjects were given posthypnotic suggestions to pick one of a pair of paintings (either a portrait or a landscape) that was associated with a 4-digit index number containing the numeral 7. In other words, the subjects were instructed to respond automatically to the presence of the number 7 by selecting paintings associated with it. Posthypnotic amnesia was then suggested for these instructions so that the subjects would not realize or remember the role of the number 7 in triggering their choice of paintings. After the end of the experiment (the nature of which need not concern us here), subjects were asked a long series of questions. Among other things, these questions were designed to determine whether the subjects were in fact amnesic for the instructions regarding the number 7. Subjects who evidenced memory for the number 7 and its role in their selection of paintings were eliminated from further consideration. Nineteen subjects remained, who, on the basis of this very probing inquiry procedure, were judged to be amnesic. Nevertheless, when these subjects were asked to circle a number from 1 to 9 that they *might* have been looking for, 10 out of 19 circled the number 7. Thirty-six control subjects received no prior directions regarding the number 7, and only six of these subjects later circled this number. Thus, truly naive subjects circled the number 7 one-sixth of the time, whereas posthypnotic-amnesia subjects circled 7 more than half the time. Clearly, what the posthypnotic subjects had consciously forgotten did have an influence on their choice of a number to circle. It is interesting to note that most of these amnesic subjects experienced their circling of the number 7 as a guess or rationalized their choice by saying "it's a lucky number" or "it's my favorite number." In other words, they experienced their choice of the number 7 in pretty much the same way as the six control subjects who picked the number 7. The difference is, of course, that for the amnesic subjects the explanation was spurious, even though they did not consciously appreciate that fact.

Both the study by Goldstein and Sipprelle (1970) and the one by Bowers (1975) are very clear demonstrations that posthypnotic amnesia is not equivalent to never having known something in the first place. However, it does not follow from these findings that there is something phony or put-on about posthypnotic amnesia.

Pretending to Forget?

A study by Bowers (1966), for example, argues that in hypnotic amnesia we are not dealing with some kind of faked forgetting. Subjects in his investigation generated a series of sentences while under the posthypnotic suggestion to begin each sentence with the pronoun "I" or "we." They also received the posthypnotic suggestion to be amnesic for these "I-we" instructions. Simulating subjects were told to behave *as if* they had received this same posthypnotic suggestion while deeply hypnotized. As expected, both real and simulating subjects typically generated sentences beginning with "I" and "we."

Then the experimenter gave all the subjects a false explanation of the experiment, took off his white lab jacket, and turned off the tape recorder—which had been running in full view of the subjects. Each of these explicit maneuvers was planned to help convince the subjects that the experiment was over. As in our previous discussion about the simulator paradigm, the experimenter tried to convey the appearance that the subjects' behavior was no longer being monitored and that, consequently, it was okay to stop simulating amnesia. In a very casual manner, the subjects were then asked whether or not they would be willing to talk to a graduate student whose dissertation plans were similar in method to the present investigation, and who therefore might find it helpful to get a subject's-eye view of the experiment. The subjects were told that they were not obliged to help the graduate student but that it wouldn't take long and that their aid would be greatly appreciated. All the subjects volunteered to be interviewed by the graduate student, whose real purpose was to probe for the subjects' memory of "I" and "we." In response to the interrogator's apparently casual but actually standardized set of questions, 13 out of 13 simulating subjects acknowledged their use of "I" and "we" in generating sentences, which suggests that the situational demands to maintain the *appearance* of amnesia had been successfully nullified.

Yet, despite this successful removing of any implicit situational demands to appear amnesic, 8 out of 14 genuinely posthypnotic subjects failed to recall their earlier use of "I" or "we." The behavior of the simulators during the postexperimental interrogation suggests that there was no reason to withhold such information if it were consciously available. Consequently, the failure of hypnotic subjects to mention their previous use of "I" and "we" suggests that this information was not consciously available to them—that is, that they had genuinely, if temporarily, forgotten it. To put it another way, the Bowers (1966) study argues against interpreting posthypnotic amnesia as a conscious attempt to conceal what is consciously remembered. Incidentally, the interrogator in the Bowers study did not know in advance which of the subjects he was interviewing was hypnotic and which was simulating, so he could not subtly bias the outcome of the results in a direction favorable to the hypothesis being tested (Rosenthal, 1966).

I have argued that posthypnotic amnesia is not the same as never having known something, nor is it simply faked forgetting. Another study by Williamsen, Johnson, and Eriksen (1965) sheds further light on these points. One of the goals of these investigators was to determine whether the extent of amnesia depended at all upon how it was assessed. To answer this question, a direct measure of recall and a relatively subtle, indirect one were employed. Williamsen and his co-workers argued that it was just possible that posthypnotic amnesia would be more clearly manifested if tested directly rather than indirectly.

Ten high-susceptible subjects were tested in a hypnotic condition, and ten subjects served as a control group. All the subjects learned the following six words: butter, dark, soft, king, slow, and cold. The subjects in the hypnotic condition learned the words while hypnotized, whereas the control subjects of course did not. The hypnotic subjects, after learning the words, were given posthypnotic suggestions to forget the words. The control subjects were given no such instructions; their presence in the study was simply to serve as a check on normal forgetting. A second experimenter (who didn't know which were the experimental subjects and which were the controls) evaluated amnesia in four different ways, only two of which will be mentioned here.

Subjects were first asked to recall as many words as they could from the list they had learned. The first row in Table 3-1 shows that, on the average, control subjects recalled more than four times as many words as the posthypnotic subjects. Statistically, this difference is quite signifi-cant. The second row of data in Table 3-1 indicates what happened after the termination of the amnesia at the end of the experiment and shows that the previously hypnotized subjects now recalled many more words than they did earlier. The increase from 1.3 to 4.6 words remembered is statistically significant. On the other hand, the average recall of 4.6 words by the posthypnotic subjects after termination of amnesia is not significantly less than the 5.4 words remembered by the control subjects. In other words, the posthypnotic subjects recalled far fewer words than the control group only *before* the termination of the amnesia; after this point, the two groups recalled the words almost equally well. This part of the Williamsen investigation demonstrated experimentally our previous statement that posthypnotic amnesia is reversible.

Table 3-1. A direct test of amnesia (simple recall of words) by high-susceptible subjects before and after a recall signal

	Experimental (posthypnotic) subjects	Control subjects
Before recall signal	1.3	5.4
After recall signal	4.6	5.4

From "Some Characteristics of Posthypnotic Amnesia," by J. A. Williamsen, H. J. Johnson, and C. W. Ericksen, *Journal of Abnormal Psychology,* 1965, 70, 123–131. Copyright 1965 by the American Psychological Association. Reprinted by permission.

Another test of amnesia utilized by these investigators was less direct than the simple recall of words. The partial-word test involved projecting 12 words one at a time on a screen in front of the subject. Six of these words were the experimental words already listed; the remaining six control words were the following: long, table, sour, woman, water, and high. Various letters were deleted from both the experimental and the control words as they were projected on the screen. For example, one of the experimental words may have been projected as b--t-r (butter); a control word might be projected as –i–h (high). The subjects were to guess what the words were and report their solution as soon as possible. The number of correct solutions and the time per solution (response latency) served as the dependent measures.

It was reasoned that the control subjects would be more successful in solving the experimental words than the control words, since they had just learned the former but not the latter. The situation with genuinely posthypnotic subjects might be quite different, however. If posthypnotic amnesia was equivalent to never having been familiarized with the words, the amnesic subjects should have been equally inept at solving the experimental and the control partial words. This turned out *not* to be the case, as the data in the upper half of Table 3-2 indicate. The first column of data in this table indicates that posthypnotically amnesic subjects solved three times as many experimental words as they did control words—a statistically significant difference. Both the posthypnotic and the control subjects solved more than half the experimental words and only one-sixth of the control words. This means that *both* groups of subjects were three times more successful in solving experimental words than they were in solving control words. Clearly, even when posthypnotic subjects were amnesic for previously learned (experimental) words (as indicated by the recall test), these words were much easier to recognize even in partial form than the nonlearned (control) words.

Table 3-2. An indirect test of amnesia (partial-words test) by high-susceptible subjects

	Experimental (posthypnotic) subjects	Control subjects
Mean number of solutions		
Experimental words	3.5	4.6
Control words	0.9	1.0
Mean latency in seconds (time per guess)		
Experimental words	15.7	10.5
Control words	23.4	23.8

From "Some Characteristics of Posthypnotic Amnesia," by J. A. Williamsen, H. J. Johnson, and C. W. Ericksen, *Journal of Abnormal Psychology*, 1965, 70, 123–131. Copyright 1965 by the American Psychological Association. Reprinted by permission.

The latency data convey a similar message. If posthypnotic amnesia for the experimental words is equivalent to never having been familiarized with them, then the amnesic subjects should take as long to solve the experimental partial words as to solve the control partial words. The data in the lower half of Table 3-2 indicate that this was clearly not the case. On the average, the hypnotized subjects took 7.7 seconds less time to solve the experimental words than to solve the control words—a statistically significant difference. Control subjects, instead, took a mean of 13.5 seconds less time to solve the experimental words than to solve the control words—a finding that is also significant. It is true that the hypnotized subjects did take an average of 5.2 seconds more than the control subjects to solve the experimental words. This difference suggests some effect of amnesia on an indirect test of memory, but the effect is not statistically significant. It would thus seem that, whether or not persons are amnesic for previously learned words, these words take much less time to recognize in partial form than words not learned in the experimental context.

To summarize, when a direct measure of forgetting was employed (that is, simple recall), the hypnotic amnesia group seemed to have less access to previously learned material than control subjects, at least until amnesia was terminated. On an indirect measure of amnesia (partial words), the hypnotic and control subjects performed equivalently; there was no measurable effect of amnesia for the posthypnotic subjects.

It might be tempting at this point to make some unwarranted conclusions regarding the relative adequacy of the direct and indirect measures of amnesia used in this experiment. For example, it might be argued that the indirect measure of amnesia was somehow a better or more faithful index of what the hypnotic subjects actually remembered. This argument would likely coalesce around the notion that the recall task was a transparent measure of forgetting and that, consequently, subjects might wittingly or unwittingly fake amnesia on it (much as Pattie's subject faked uniocular blindness). The partial-words technique, on the other hand, is less obviously a test of forgetting, and it would make it more difficult for subjects to appear amnesic without really being so. Since the partial-words test seems relatively invulnerable to faking, performance on it may represent what the subject really remembers—or so the argument might go.

This line of reasoning limps rather badly when forced to walk very far. In the first place, we have learned to be skeptical about the faking interpretation of hypnosis. Even when it is possible for hypnotic subjects to falsify their experience, it does not appear that they ordinarily do so. Moreover, the Bowers (1966) study described earlier should have put the notion of faked forgetting to rest. Finally, another phase of the Williamsen study contains evidence that demolishes the argument that the indirect measure of amnesia is better than the direct one because it makes it more difficult for subjects to fake amnesia.

Williamsen and his co-workers also tested simulator subjects in addition to the hypnotic and waking control subjects. The response of these simulator subjects can give us a very good idea whether or not it is possible to appear amnesic on the partial-words task; if the simulators tend to guess very few of the experimental words and take a relatively long time to make their responses, then the partial-words task is fakable. This is precisely what happened. On the partial-word task, simulators solved an average of only 1.6 experimental words as compared to 1.9 control words; that is, on the six partial experimental words, the simulators behaved as if they had not been previously familiarized with them. Similarly, on the latency measure it took as long for the simulators to guess the experimental words as to guess the control words (24.5 and 22.7 seconds, respectively).

Clearly, the partial-words test is not so subtle that it offers no clue regarding how to appear amnesic on it. If simulators can successfully fake amnesia on this indirect test of memory, so could hypnotic subjects, *if that is what they were interested in doing.* The fact that genuine hypnotic subjects did not behave on this task like their simulating counterparts argues against viewing their behavior as motivated by the desire to appear amnesic. And, if the desire to *appear* amnesic is discredited as the dominant motivation of posthypnotic subjects, then their behavior on the direct recall measure can be viewed as a relatively straightforward index of real forgetting.

But, the reader may ask, why do direct and indirect measures of amnesia render such disparate records of forgetting? How can a subject "really forget" on a direct measure of amnesia, and not forget at all on an indirect measure? The easiest way of dealing with this conundrum is to appreciate the fact that recalling a temporarily forgotten name is much more difficult than simply recognizing it. Moreover, two people who have momentarily forgotten a name will both recognize it immediately when reminded; yet they may well differ in the amount of time it takes them to recall the name without help. Psychologists have long realized that different ways of evaluating memory can yield different results, and they often take pains to employ several measures of memory in their investigations. Forgetting is multifaceted, and different measures reveal different aspects of the phenomenon. In the present case, posthypnotic amnesia seems to make the *recall* of a word quite difficult; however, it seems to leave relatively unaffected the *use* of the word as a response.

There are many aspects of the Williamsen study that we have not reported. For example, in addition to testing subjects highly susceptible to hypnosis, the investigators also tested low-susceptible subjects in various treatment conditions. The results of those comparisons reveal the importance of individual differences in hypnotic susceptibility—an issue we will cover in some detail later on in this book. One thing that we might just mention now, however, is that the findings of the Williamsen study were replicated in essential details by Barber and Calverley (1966). These investigators enlarged upon the earlier study by testing subjects who were exposed to suggestions for amnesia without first receiving a hypnotic induction. Such subjects seemed to be at least as amnesic as posthypnotic subjects and in some cases more so—a result suggesting that inducing hypnosis may be less important in achieving suggested effects than is generally assumed. In Chapter 6 we will explore this issue in some detail. What should be emphasized at this point is that the subjective reality of suggested effects is separable from the issue of whether a traditional hypnotic induction is necessary to produce such effects. These are complex issues that deserve our careful consideration; handling one problem at a time will make for greater clarity. As far as hypnotic amnesia is concerned, we have argued that (a) it is not faked forgetting, (b) it is not equivalent to never having known something in the first place, and (c) it is more evident as a phenomenon when measured by direct recall than when evaluated by indirect means. Whether these findings are unique to hypnosis, whether a hypnotically induced altered state of consciousness is necessary in producing them, and whether individual differences are important in furthering our understanding of amnesia and other hypnotic phenomena are questions we can only introduce here and defer for later consideration.

Forgetting as Disorganized Retrieval

Before concluding our discussion of posthypnotic amnesia, one other line of inquiry needs to be presented. I have shown that, subjectively, persons can experience posthypnotic amnesia in a variety of ways, from a disinclination to think about "forgotten" material to the inability to recover it even when thoroughly motivated. Even in the latter case, however, the problem seems to be one of *retrieval* of stored information. If the material were forgotten because it wasn't stored or registered in the first place, then the reversibility of posthypnotic amnesia would be impossible. The fact that hypnotic amnesia consists of a breakdown in the retrievability of memories is certainly supported by the subjective experiences of amnesic subjects. Whether or not they are simply disinclined to seek out the forgotten item or whether their active and concerted mental search fails to turn up the missing memory, both conditions imply that there is something there to find. In our example of the person who misplaced his glasses, he knew that he had put them somewhere and that when he found them he would probably remember having put them there—a much different feeling from that of not knowing the whereabouts of, say, a stolen article. Since it is retrieval of stored information that seems to be impaired in posthypnotic amnesia, it might be instructive to compare the process of information retrieval in subjects who are amnesic with the process of retrieval in subjects who are not. In other words, it may be interesting to determine whether differences in *how* something is remembered are as revealing as differences in *how much* is remembered.

The work that we will now review was conducted by Evans and Kihlstrom (1973; Kihlstrom & Evans, 1971). These investigators noted that memories ordinarily have a contextual "tag" that makes them easier to recover. For example, if the fellow who misplaced his glasses had remembered that he was just putting on his socks when it occurred to him to make the telephone call, he may well have remembered where his glasses were. Indeed, one of the most important contextual tags for remembering is the sequence, or ordering, of events. People who write Christmas messages to friends usually reconstruct the year's events in chronological order, at least in part, because that is the easiest way to remember everything important. Evans and Kihlstrom reasoned that if amnesia obscured or otherwise jumbled the sequential tagging of events, it might be more difficult to retrieve items from the memory store.

In order to test this notion, the investigators cleverly exploited the sequence of suggestions administered on a scale of hypnotic susceptibility (see Chapter 5), in which one of the last items was a posthypnotic suggestion to forget the earlier items in the scale. After the subject is awakened, posthypnotic amnesia is tested by asking subjects to remember the various suggestions they had received during the course of the hypnosis scale. The fewer items recalled, the more effective the amnesia is. (Of course, normal forgetting may also account for a few unremembered items.)

The way of discerning whether or not sequential tagging has remained intact is to compare the order in which items are remembered with the order in which they were administered. A simple correlation (*rho*) between the orders in which items are administered and recalled will do the trick statistically: the higher the correlation, the greater the match between order of item recall and order of item administration. Thus, in this investigation, a statistically significant, positive correlation represented an *ordered* retrieval; all other correlations reflected *random* retrieval. The hypothesis is, of course, that if posthypnotic amnesia somehow jumbles the contextual (in this case, sequential) tags for memory, then whatever items amnesic subjects remember should be recalled out of sequence; that is, their recall should reflect random retrieval. Subjects who were not amnesic should display instead an ordered process of retrieval.

The *rho* correlations calculated for each of 168 subjects were categorized with respect to (a) type of retrieval—ordered (significant and positive) or random—and (b) the hypnotic susceptibility of the subject— high or low. Table 3-3 shows the results of this analysis. The findings clearly suggest that high-susceptible subjects remember events out of correct order to a much greater extent than low-susceptible subjects. A closely related finding is that 34 out of 40 low-susceptible subjects recalled the initial item in the scale first, whereas only 8 out of 23 high-susceptible subjects recalled the initial item first (X^2 = 16.41, $p < .001$).

Table 3-3. Retrieval order and hypnotic susceptibility

Retrieval	Susceptibility Low	High
Ordered	22	3
Random	18	20

$$X^2 = 13.04; \, p < .001$$

Adapted from "Posthypnotic Amnesia as Disrupted Retrieval," by F. J. Evans and J. F. Kihlstrom, *Journal of Abnormal Psychology,* 1973, *82,* 319–323. Copyright 1973 by the American Psychological Association. Used by permission.

It might be objected that these differences reflect relatively enduring differences in styles of remembering by subjects high and low in susceptibility and not retrieval disruptions in subjects who are momentarily amnesic. However, "after amnesia had been lifted, there did not seem to be a differential effect of hypnotizability on the order of retrieval" (Evans & Kihlstrom, 1973, p. 320). This finding suggests that it is an amnesic condition, not simply differences in susceptibility, that accounts for the data in Table 3-3. It is true, of course, that high-susceptible subjects are more *able* to experience suggested amnesia than low-susceptible subjects, which undoubtedly accounts for the fact that only high-susceptible subjects showed so little ordered retrieval.

To summarize this chapter, I have argued that posthypnotic amnesia is experienced as a real inability to remember and that genuine forgetting does take place, at least on direct measures of memory. I have also argued that really forgetting something in amnesia is not equivalent to never having known about it in the first place. The forgotten material is stored in the brain, but the subject's access to it is very limited. And, as we have seen, the retrieval problem exemplified in posthypnotic amnesia may result from a temporary disruption of cognitive organization—an organization that usually provides the basis for an orderly retrieval of stored memories.

Footnotes

[1]This study is somewhat unusual in that it demonstrated forgetting in subjects while they were hypnotized, not posthypnotically.

4.
Are Hypnotic Effects Genuine? Auditory and Visual Effects

Hyppolite Bernheim (1837-1919), one of the most revered names in the history of hypnosis, reported the following incident in his classic book *Hypnosis and Suggestion in Psychotherapy:*

> I recently hypnotized a remarkably intelligent young girl, . . . who was not in the least flighty and whose good faith I can guarantee. I made her see an imaginary rose when she waked up. She saw it, touched it, and smelt it. She described it to me. Then, knowing that I might have given a suggestion, she asked me if the rose was real or imaginary. "It is perfectly impossible for me to tell the difference," she said. I told her that it was imaginary. She was convinced of this, and in spite of it was certain that by no effort of the will could she make it disappear [p. 40].*

Although this degree of subjective convincingness can occasionally be realized with hypnotically induced hallucinations, it is unusual. Hilgard (1965) found that only 3% of unselected subjects passed the hallucination item on one of the Stanford Susceptibility Scales (see Chapter 5). On this particular item, a white Christmas-tree light is lit on one end of an oblong box, and the subject is to hallucinate another light at the other end of the box. Of the 19 subjects who hallucinated the light successfully, only 8 could not tell which light was real and which was hallucinated. Evidently, hypnotic hallucinations can be quite convincing, but, at least in their most fully realized form, they are relatively rare.

Even in those relatively rare instances of truly convincing hallucinations, differences between the perception of real and hallucinated objects are easily shown. Bernheim, for example, neatly demonstrated that a prism doubled the image of a real object but not of a hallucinated one. Bernheim (1964) concludes:

The hallucinatory image may be as distinct, as bright, and as active to the subject as reality itself, but, borne entirely in the subject's imagination, he sees it as he conceives it, as he interprets it, as conscious or unconscious memory brings it up again in the sensorium. It is a psychical cerebral image and not a physical one. It does not pass by the peripheral apparatus of vision, has no objective reality, follows no optical laws, but obeys solely the caprices of imagination" [pp. 103–104].*

It would be difficult to improve upon this statement, written close to 100 years ago. There has, of course, been a great deal of research since that time, which has fleshed out our understanding of hypnotically induced hallucinations. An attempt will be made to convey with a few quick strokes the essence of some more recent findings and render a more complete account of one particular study. If the reader is interested in a more complete review of the literature on suggested alterations in vision and audition, he is referred to Sutcliffe (1960) and Barber (1964a, 1964b).

Auditory Effects

Hallucinations can be either positive or negative. Positive hallucinations involve seeing or hearing something that is not objectively present; negative hallucinations involve *not* perceiving something that is present. One way of testing a negative auditory hallucination is, for example, to compare its effects with those of organic deafness. This is exactly what one team of investigators did (Malmo, Boag, & Raginsky, 1954). Two highly susceptible subjects were selected from a larger group of 35 on the basis of "their marked suggestibility and the ease with which hypnotic deafness was induced during the first trial session" (p. 305). These subjects, after having been hypnotized and given suggestions for deafness, were presented with ten loud three-second tones at one-minute intervals. The subjects' muscle tension in response to the tones and their reports of the experience were measured. Only one of the subjects denied hearing any sounds during hypnotically induced deafness, and I will confine my remarks to her. This subject clearly showed muscle-potential reactions to the first signal and much lessened reactions on the other nine trials.[1] In the organically deaf subject, there were no muscle-potential reactions to the noise. Thus, a negative hallucination for auditory stimulation is apparently not the same as actually being deaf—a proposition similar to the one already advanced in our discussion of posthypnotic amnesia.

Incidentally, one additional feature of this experiment deserves to be mentioned. In the first chapter, we noted how hysteric symptoms bore a

*From *Hypnosis and Suggestion in Psychotherapy: The Nature and Uses of Hypnotism,* by H. Bernheim. Copyright 1964 by University Books. Reprinted by permission.

certain similarity to hypnotic phenomena. Malmo and his co-workers (1954) also tested an hysterically deaf subject in their experiment. Like the hypnotic subject, the hysterical patient, Anne, showed a distinct muscle reaction to the first stimulus but lessened reactivity to subsequent stimulation. When questioned later, Anne denied hearing anything but did add that "she had felt pain in her head 'as if something hit me on the head.'" She then stated "'It felt as if the top of my head were going to blow off'" (Malmo et al., 1954, p. 314). In fact, Anne was so disturbed by the events that she wept. This reaction is somewhat reminiscent of the reaction I discussed in Chapter 1, manifested by the hypnotic subject in Pattie's experiment who had "faked" uniocular blindness (Pattie, 1935). There was, however, no similar emotional outburst by the hypnotic subject in the Malmo investigation.

Although this study clearly distinguished organic from hypnotic or hysteric deafness, the authors did not deny the impact of "psychological" deafness. They speculated that hysteric and hypnotically induced deafness is "the result of a defence mechanism which prevents sound from reaching consciousness" (Malmo et al., 1954, p. 315). All in all, both hysteric and hypnotic deafness seem to involve registration of auditory input at some level, but not one consciously experienced as sound. We have already seen that hypnotic analgesia too can eliminate pain at a conscious level of experience—pain that is nevertheless registered at a lower level of analysis. I will develop this multilevel model of perception and experience in later chapters of this book.

Although the conscious experience of sound may be eliminated by hypnotically induced deafness, objective effects of auditory stimulation remain. This point is particularly well made by studies investigating whether hypnotically induced deafness would minimize the speech disturbances ordinarily engendered by delayed auditory feedback (Sutcliffe, 1961; Kline, Guze, & Haggerty, 1954; Barber & Calverley, 1964a; Kramer & Tucker, 1967; Scheibe, Gray, & Keim, 1968). Delayed auditory feedback involves talking into a tape recorder that is especially outfitted to play back the speaker's words a fraction of a second after they are spoken. In most persons, this delayed feedback causes a serious breakdown in speech, which includes stuttering, slurring, mispronunciations, slowed speech, and so on. Now, if a person is rendered deaf to the sound of his own voice, he should not be distracted by it as it is recycled back into his ears. In all investigations employing this technique, however, hypnotically suggested deafness did *not* eliminate the speech disturbances due to delayed auditory feedback, although most of the subjects reported being deaf. As Sutcliffe points out, "it is the real state of affairs rather than the subjective experience that determines the subject's objective behavior. ... there remains, however, the puzzling discrepancy between the subjects' reports of hallucination and the evidence of their objective performance" (Sutcliffe, 1961, p. 197).

Visual Effects

The same kind of conclusion pretty much holds true for hypnotic suggestions of visual effects, as convincingly demonstrated by Miller, Lundy, and Galbraith (1970). These investigators hypothesized that a hallucinated green filter would be as effective as a genuine one in permitting subjects to read numbers that would be invisible unless filtered. The pale-green numbers were projected onto a field of bright red light, which effectively masked the numbers unless the red background was turned black via a green filter placed in front of the subject's eyes. Although all ten subjects used in the investigation were highly susceptible and trained in hallucinating various colors, and although they successfully hallucinated the presence of a green filter in front of their eyes, in no case did the hallucinated filter permit a subject to identify the number being superimposed on the red field. In all cases, the number was visible when an actual green filter was employed.

The authors of the investigation correctly point out that their findings do not invalidate the genuineness of visual hallucinations. They do, however, establish the limits of such hallucinations to effect genuine optical changes. Clearly, Bernheim (1964) was right: hallucinations do not follow optical laws.

A persistent skeptic might ask, even at this point, whether subjects aren't just saying they hallucinated—that in effect, they are faking hallucinations. A study by Bowers and Gilmore (1969) indicates that subjects who simulate hallucinations say very different things about what they see than do hypnotic subjects. Genuine hypnotic subjects maintain their reports of hallucinations even in contexts where such reports are not implicitly demanded. Simulators, on the other hand, change their reports of hallucinations drastically from one context to another, depending upon demand characteristics of the situation.

It is probably just as well, however, that we do not have to rest our case on the reality of hypnotically suggested visual effects with a comparison of genuine and simulated hallucinations. In an unusual set of investigations, Graham and Leibowitz (1972) have demonstrated beyond any reasonable doubt that visual acuity can be improved through hypnotic suggestions. In their first experiment, these investigators compared in each of three separate sessions the acuity of nine highly susceptible subjects first under waking conditions and then under hypnotic conditions. While the subjects were hypnotized,

> specific suggestions were given to feel completely relaxed, refreshed, and alert, to concentrate on the muscles around and behind the eyes and notice them becoming as relaxed and weightless as the rest of the muscles in the

body. It was explained that the degree of relaxation attained would affect the muscles which controlled the lens, thus changing the focus of the eye and permitting clearer vision [Graham & Leibowitz, 1972, p. 173].*

Figure 4-1 indicates the improvement of acuity from waking to hypnotized conditions in subjects with different degrees of nearsightedness (myopia). As is easily seen, the improvement in acuity was greatest for the three most myopic individuals, only moderate for the three slightly myopic individuals, and virtually nonexistent for the three normal-sighted individuals. Figure 4-1 also demonstrates that visual acuity improved as a function of the number of sessions.

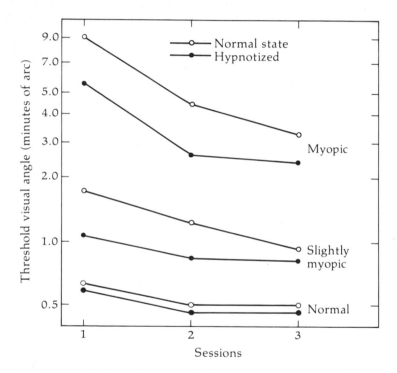

Figure 4-1. Threshold resolution angle (in minutes of arc) attained by the experimental groups in the waking and hypnotic conditions in Experiment I. From "The Effect of Suggestion on Visual Acuity," by C. Graham and H. W. Leibowitz, *International Journal of Clinical and Experimental Hypnosis*, 1972, *20*, 169–186. Copyrighted by The Society for Clinical and Experimental Hypnosis, July 1972. Reprinted by permission.

While hypnotized, the subjects received posthypnotic suggestions to the effect that their improved visual acuity would transfer to the waking state. When later examined in an optometrist's office (that is, not in the

*From "The Effect of Suggestion on Visual Acuity," by C. Graham and H. W. Leibowitz, *International Journal of Clinical and Experimental Hypnosis*, 1972, *20*, 169–186. Copyrighted by The Society for Clinical and Experimental Hypnosis, July 1972. This and all other quotes from this source are reprinted by permission.

laboratory where the experiment was conducted), the subjects who had initially been most myopic showed considerable improvement in their visual acuity in comparison with an earlier eye examination.

It seems clear that suggestions for improved acuity given to highly susceptible, deeply hypnotized subjects can improve myopic vision. Various control groups employed in the study discounted the possibility that the improvements were due to motivational or practice factors. However, it is not clear whether the subjects improved because they were highly susceptible to hypnosis or because they had actually been hypnotized. In other words, would highly susceptible subjects show similar suggested improvements in visual acuity even though they were not hypnotized? It is to this question that the authors addressed themselves in their second experiment.

Six myopic subjects susceptible to hypnosis and five myopic subjects insusceptible to hypnosis were compared to determine the extent to which their vision improved as a function of pertinent *waking* suggestions. These suggestions stressed the importance of relaxation, and both groups were asked to practice eye muscle relaxation between the three experimental sessions. Figure 4-2 presents data from this experiment. As can easily be seen, the insusceptible subjects did not show improvements in visual acuity from pre- to postrelaxation trials, whereas susceptible subjects did. This improvement did not transfer to the optometrist's

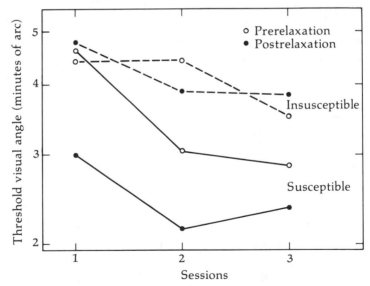

Figure 4-2. Threshold resolution angle (in minutes of arc) attained by the hypnotically susceptible and insusceptible groups in Experiment II when tested without hypnosis in the laboratory. From "The Effect of Suggestion on Visual Acuity," by C. Graham and H. W. Leibowitz, *International Journal of Clinical and Experimental Hypnosis,* 1972, *20,* 169–186. Copyrighted by The Society for Clinical and Experimental Hypnosis, July 1972. Reprinted by permission.

office; however, no specific suggestions for such transfer had been given to the subjects.

This second study shows that the induction of hypnosis per se is not necessary to improve visual acuity; what is necessary is that the subject be susceptible to hypnosis. Moreover, the degree of improved acuity is a function of how nearsighted the subject is in the first place; suggestions for improved acuity cannot make a normal-sighted person see even better.

The investigators performed one more experiment, aimed at determining how suggested improvements in acuity were achieved. They suspected that, because of relaxation of the eye muscles, the lens accommodated better for distance vision. Employing a novel laser technique that simultaneously assessed lens accommodation and visual acuity, Graham and Leibowitz found that lens accommodation was *not* the basis for improved visual acuity. They did, however, replicate their earlier finding that suggested improvement in vision was directly proportional to the degree of myopia—that is, the more nearsighted a person, the greater the improvement.

The findings of this last study leave unexplained the mechanism by which the suggested improvements in acuity take place. As the authors put it,

> Whatever the mechanism, it cannot be fitted neatly into the traditional schema of a causal relationship among factors in the peripheral visual anatomy. ... Ultimately, investigation of the more central components of the system may lead to therapeutic techniques of greater effectiveness [Graham & Leibowitz, 1972, p. 184].

Summary

Throughout these last three chapters, I have presented data that show that hypnotically suggested phenomena have a subjective reality that cannot be explained away as faking. Deeply hypnotized subjects often experience the suggested phenomena as subjectively compelling, even when careful assessment clearly indicates that the subjects do respond to the *objective* state of affairs.

If I have embraced the idea that hypnotic phenomena are genuine (in the sense of genuinely altering a person's perceptions and subjective experience), I have repeatedly ignored or hedged on another important issue—namely, the difference between being hypnotized and being susceptible to hypnosis. In the last study on visual acuity, for example, we discovered that the induction of hypnosis was unnecessary to produce improved vision; waking suggestions sufficed, so long as they were delivered to subjects susceptible to hypnosis. Clearly, the role of individual differences in hypnotic susceptibility is an exceedingly important one; so is the phenomenon of waking suggestibility. We cannot further delay consideration of these important issues, and it is to them that we now turn.

Footnotes

[1]The fact that the muscle potential reactions lessened as a function of trials might at first blush suggest that the subject was becoming more successful in consolidating the negative hallucinations for the tone. Actually, however, this decline in responsiveness represented a habituation response to repeated stimulation. Even in the waking state, the subject showed a similar decline, although habituation was not quite so rapid.

5.
Stability and Change in Hypnotic Susceptibility

Until the psychological character of mesmerism was fully recognized, it was widely believed that Mesmer and his followers had special (and secret) *magnetic* powers. Other investigators, such as the Marquis de Puysegur, shifted the emphasis from the mesmerist's *magnetic* powers to the mesmerist's superior *will* power to explain the effectiveness of the phenomenon. Modern cartoon characterizations of hypnosis perpetuate these early "power-of-the-hypnotist" notions. Perhaps the reader recalls seeing such caricatures: with a menacing extension of fingers during each successive thrust of the hand, the hypnotist simply overwhelms the hapless victim. This ritual hand thrusting reflects early notions that nervous or magnetic energy is radiated off the fingertips, subduing the subject by virtue of the hypnotist's superior power (cf. Shor, 1972). Since the mesmerist's "power" was taken for granted, it was difficult to notice individual differences in subjects' susceptibility to mesmerism. After all, if the mesmerist's "power" was genuine, why should it not be universally effective?

The early tendency to overlook or underemphasize individual differences in "mesmerability" was also made possible by the self-selection of persons seeking mesmeric treatment. This nonrandom procedure of subject selection was almost a guarantee that most patients being seen by early mesmerists believed (or at least hoped) that they would be subject to the power of the mesmerist. As we now know, such positive expectancies can be an extremely important factor in treatment effectiveness (Rosenthal, 1966; Shapiro, 1971; Evans, 1974a, 1974b).

In this context, it is worth repeating that one element that counted heavily against such "power" theories was Deslon's inability to mesmerize members of the Franklin committee or other patients selected by the committee rather than by Delson himself. Individual differences in "mesmerability," such as those found by the Franklin committee, thus became presumptive evidence that characteristics of the subjects (their beliefs, hopes, imagination, and so on) were far more important to an understanding of mesmerism than any supposed secret power of the mesmerist.

As we shall soon see, modern investigations have established beyond any doubt that people differ considerably in their hypnotic susceptibility. Yet, in a curious way, vestiges of a "power" theory of hypnosis remain. The power in question is no longer invested in superior magnetic or willful properties of the hypnotist but, rather, in the power of the psychological environment to modify hypnotic performance. A particularly important advocate of this modern "power" view of hypnosis is T. X. Barber, whose emphatic environmentalism has helped call attention to the situational influences affecting hypnotic performance. At the same time, however, Barber's views have diverted attention from the continuities and stabilities in hypnotic susceptibility that even Barber recognizes but does not systematically incorporate into his generalizations about hypnosis (Barber, 1969).

It will be one task of the present chapter to present what I believe to be a more balanced view of hypnotic susceptibility. We will ask how and to what extent it is possible for hypnotic susceptibility to be a relatively stable characteristic of a person and yet be subject to change as a result of natural or experimentally induced events. Perhaps this question can be answered in a preliminary sort of way by realizing that change and stability presuppose each other. To put the point somewhat aphoristically, nothing in nature is unchanging; yet, everything in nature continues to be more like itself than like anything else.

We shall begin our discussion of hypnotic susceptibility with an account of its stability.

The Measurement of Hypnotic Susceptibility

In science, a considerable portion of time is devoted to the construction of measuring instruments that permit precise observation of nature. In the physical sciences, the problem of measurement is sometimes fairly easy. For example, some unit of length is adopted as a conventional standard, and measured distances are expressed in that unit or in multiples and submultiples of it (meters, kilometers, centimeters, and so on). In the social sciences, to establish units of measurement is often more problematic. How does one measure a person's hypnotic susceptibility, for example? Since there is, of course, no physical scale appropriate to its measurement, we must seek instead a pertinent psychological scale or "yardstick."

The first such susceptibility scales were somewhat intuitive and unsophisticated (cf. Hilgard, Weitzenhoffer, Landes, & Moore, 1961, pp. 1-7); but recently some very sophisticated instruments have been devised to measure hypnotic susceptibility (see Hilgard, 1965). Basically, investigators select a variety of suggestions historically associated with hypnosis and present them one by one to a person who has received a standardized hypnotic induction. The more items he or she passes, the more hypnotically susceptible the person is said to be.

Some of these items are much more difficult to "pass" than others. For example, to a hypnotic suggestion that an extended arm is getting heavier and heavier, most people (about 90%) respond by lowering their arms at least a little. On the other hand, relatively few people (about 20%) can respond satisfactorily to a suggestion that they are unable to smell a bottle of household ammonia held directly under their nose. When several of these items are combined and presented in exactly the same (that is, standardized) fashion to a large, randomly selected group of subjects, a few people will be responsive to nearly all the suggestions, no matter how difficult; another few will be unresponsive to nearly all the items, no matter how easy. These extremely responsive and unresponsive subjects are of course the ones who are respectively high and low in hypnotic susceptibility. Most of the subjects tested in this fashion will be neither very high nor very low in hypnotic susceptibility, but will instead pass most of the easier items and few of the really difficult ones—thereby manifesting a moderate amount of hypnotic susceptibility.

Although this account tends to oversimplify the actual procedures and outcomes of this line of research, in principle it represents fairly accurately how individual differences in hypnotic susceptibility are initially identified. I say "initially" because without some additional evidence we cannot say for certain whether hypnotic susceptibility is an enduring and stable characteristic of a person. Conceivably, a person can be high in hypnotic susceptibility one day and virtually unsusceptible the next day, just as his or her mood can change dramatically from day to day. On the other hand, if hypnotic susceptibility is a fairly stable characteristic of a person, he or she should achieve about the same score (that is, pass approximately the same number of items) when measured on two successive occasions with a particular susceptibility scale. Or, to put the case slightly differently, if a group of people are twice administered a scale of hypnotic susceptibility, those who score high on the first test should also score high the second time around, and those who score low the first time should also score low the second time. This means that, if hypnotic susceptibility is a reasonably stable characteristic, a person should maintain about the same relative position on the first and on the second test.

The extent to which people in fact maintain the same relative position from one test to the next one can be expressed with a correlation coefficient (symbolized as r). A perfect correlation of unity (or one) would probably be obtained by recording the heights of pupils in a classroom on two successive days, since there would be virtually no discernible change in the heights of the students being measured. For a variety of reasons, a perfect correlation is seldom expected in measuring psychological (as opposed to physical) characteristics, and psychologists are generally satisfied if they can devise measuring scales having a test-retest correlation between .70 and .95. In effect, the extent to which this test-retest correlation departs from 1.0 is the extent to which people change their relative positions[1] from the first to the second testing.

When the time separating the two testings is not too great, the resulting correlation is called a reliability coefficient. If this coefficient turns out to be very low, it is not clear whether the phenomenon being measured is very changeable from day to day or whether the measuring instrument is inadequate—like an elastic yardstick that unpredictably stretches and shrinks from one day to the next. If, on the other hand, the reliability coefficient is high, it is an indication of two important things: (a) whatever is being measured has at least short-term stability, and (b) the measurement device yields reliable and consistent results (like a nonelastic yardstick).

The test-retest correlations for scales of hypnotic susceptibility are quite satisfactory, since they range up to .90+, depending upon the particular scale employed (Hilgard, 1965). Thus, we have our first evidence that hypnotic susceptibility is at least stable enough to demonstrate high test-retest reliability.

This evidence for test-retest reliability suggests that a person's susceptibility *score* on the same test taken twice remains about the same. It is important, however, to distinguish between a person's hypnotic susceptibility and the score he or she achieves on a particular susceptibility scale. Presumably, this score is accounted for, to some considerable extent, by the person's hypnotic susceptibility. But it is also true that the particular score achieved is a function of the difficulty level of the items specific to that scale. A person of moderate susceptibility (as judged clinically) would likely have a fairly low score on a susceptibility scale composed mostly of very difficult items (hallucinations, amnesias, and so on) and a fairly high score on a scale consisting mostly of easy items (eye closure, hand lowering, and so on).

In light of these considerations, it seems reasonable to ask whether there is a way of determining the extent to which a person's performance (score) on a scale of hypnotic susceptibility is due to stable characteristics of the person on the one hand and to the specific items comprising the scale on the other. One way of approaching this problem is this: if hypnotic susceptibility is a stable characteristic of the person, then people should maintain the same *relative* position on a variety of scales comprised largely of *different* items, that is, the highest scorers on one scale of susceptibility should also be the highest scorers on another scale—

regardless of the specific scores achieved (that is, items passed) on either scale. This relative stability of hypnotic susceptibility can again be expressed as a correlation coefficient, but since it expresses the relationship between people's performances on different susceptibility scales, the correlation is no longer a test-retest reliability coefficient.

Table 5-1 characterizes the susceptibility scales now commonly used;

Table 5-1. A brief characterization of some commonly used scales of hypnotic susceptibility

1. Stanford Hypnotic Susceptibility Scale, Forms A and B (SHSS: A and B) (Weitzenhoffer & Hilgard, 1959). These individually administered 12-item scales (the two forms are essentially interchangeable) were the first ones whose psychometric properties were thoroughly explored. They are relatively easy scales, with a preponderance of motor items (such as, "your hand will get heavy and fall") and only a few items calling for profound perceptual-cognitive distortions, such as posthypnotic amnesia. Because these scales are relatively undemanding, they are used for the initial contact with a subject in order to determine his susceptibility in a preliminary sort of way.
2. Stanford Hypnotic Susceptibility Scale, Form C (SHSS: C) (Weitzenhoffer & Hilgard, 1962). This 12-item individually administered scale is essentially an upward extention of the SHSS: A and B. It is a considerably more difficult scale, since it includes a far greater proportion of items requiring perceptual-cognitive distortions. For example, one item suggests that the subject will be unable to smell household ammonia. This scale is frequently used to assess the limits of susceptibility. A person passing all 12 items is very susceptible indeed.
3. Stanford Profile Scales, I and II (SPS: I and II) (Weitzenhoffer & Hilgard, 1967). These scales are very difficult, and items included in them sample most of the historical domain of hypnosis (hallucinations, age regression, and so on). The purpose of the test is to identify specific areas of hypnotic skills in a person—to determine his or her hypnotic profile, so to speak. The 9-item scale is individually administered, but, unlike the other Stanford scales, each item can be scored from 0 to 3 instead of on a simple pass-or-fail basis. A perfect score of 27 is of course very rare, and anything close to it means that the person is highly competent in all aspects of hypnosis.
4. Harvard Group Scale of Hypnotic Susceptibility (HGSHS) (Shor & Orne, 1962). This scale is a translation of the SHSS: A for group administration—a very convenient feature, since it saves considerable time in the identification of subjects high and low in hypnotic susceptibility. Generally, however, it is advisable to verify a person's HGSHS score with an individually administered scale.
5. Barber Suggestibility Scale (BSS) (Barber, 1969). This 8-item individually administered scale is constructed so that it can be used either with or without a prior hypnotic induction. Also, it takes subjective experiences into account, and not just behavioral responses to suggestions.

Table 5-2 reports the correlations between the various scales. As Table 5-2 shows, these correlations range from a low of .58 to a high of .82 and average about .70. These correlations are somewhat lower than the test-retest reliability coefficients, which tend to range from .80 to .90+. In effect, the *difference* between the test-retest reliability coefficient and the correlation between two different susceptibility scales represents the extent to which a person's performance on one of the scales is a function of the particular items comprising it rather than the person's relative ability to become hypnotized. Although the difference between same-scale and cross-scale correlations cannot simply be ignored, the fact that it is typically small is important. It suggests in fact that, on any particular scale of hypnotic susceptibility, the person's performance (relative to others) is not an accidental consequence of the specific items employed but reflects instead a comparatively enduring characteristic of the person being tested—namely, his or her hypnotic susceptibility.

Table 5-2. Correlations among various, frequently used scales of hypnotic susceptibility

	SHSS:C	SPS:I	SPS:II	HGSHS	BSS
SHSS:A	.82	.64	.62	.74	.63[a]
SHSS:C		.71	.72	.59	.58
SPS:I			.78		

[a] Correlation based on 10 of 12 items from the SHSS:A.
Table compiled from Hilgard, 1965; Bentler and Hilgard, 1963; Evans and Schmeidler, 1966; Ruch, Morgan, and Hilgard, 1973, 1974.

For purposes of exposition, the above analysis has overlooked certain complexities that should at least be mentioned here. First, although there does seem to be a general talent, or skill, for hypnotic responsiveness, it is also true that there are specific skills for experiencing, or behaving in accordance with, specific suggestions. For example, some subjects are particularly adroit at experiencing posthypnotic amnesia but are totally unable to hallucinate. These suggestion-specific "talents" detract somewhat from a conceptualization of hypnotic susceptibility as the degree of *general* responsiveness to hypnotic suggestions (Hilgard, 1965). This state of affairs is analogous to that found in the domain of intelligence, in which special abilities (for example, mechanical or mathematical) can be differentiated from general intelligence.

A second caveat to be introduced here and elaborated later is this: it has been a useful pretense to assume that a person's *score* on a particular scale of hypnotic susceptibility is a function of only two things—his or her relatively stable hypnotic suscept-*ability* on the one hand and the specific scale items on the other. As we shall see later on in this chapter, a susceptibility score is also a function of a variety of other things, such as the subject's motivation, expectancies, desire to please the hypnotist, and so forth. The addition of these other factors tends to complicate the situation, but it does not fundamentally alter the fact that hypnotic ability *per se* is a relatively enduring characteristic of the person, which, more than anything else, determines how well a person does on a particular scale of hypnotic susceptibility. More of this later.

Now, it is time to point out that all the previous statements regarding the "relative stability" of hypnotic susceptibility—and the studies on which the statements are based—have been subject to an important limitation. In the investigations showing the high test-retest and cross-test correlations of hypnotic susceptibility, the susceptibility scales were administered on two occasions that were pretty close together in time. Therefore, we have good evidence for the short-term stability of hypnotic susceptibility. But what about the proposition that a person who is high in susceptibility one year may be low in susceptibility the next? In other words, is there any evidence that there is long-term stability as well?

The answer is yes. For example, a recent investigation by the Stanford laboratories (Morgan, Johnson, & Hilgard, 1974) reports that 85 persons were administered a hypnotic-susceptibility scale twice—once when they were undergraduates at Stanford and then again ten years later, after they were well launched on a career. Despite this passage of time and the accumulation of personal experiences, the correlation between the two administrations was .60 (.57 for women; .62 for men). Subjects' average score changed hardly at all; indeed, "the hypnotic susceptibility score, for most Ss, did not change more than a point or two in spite of different [hypnotists] and a different testing situation" (Morgan et al., 1974, p. 251). Thus, we have fairly impressive evidence for the long-term stability of hypnotic susceptibility in adults.

An earlier study reported by Cooper and London (1971) also examines the stability of hypnotic susceptibility over time. Their study differs from that by Morgan and her associates (1974) in two important ways: it was conducted with children, aged 5 to 16 (instead of young adults), and the longest interval between testings of any particular child was two (instead of ten) years.

The fact that children were employed in this investigation means that the *development* of hypnotic susceptibility was more at issue than the stability of hypnotic susceptibility in adults. Hence, we can expect two kinds of developmental patterns to emerge from such a study: first, the closer in time the measurements, the higher their correlations; second, the older the child, the higher the correlations from one year to the next.

These developmental patterns are easily seen when expressed in terms of physical growth. We expect the correlation of height between two consecutive years (say, ages 5 and 6) to be higher than the correlation of height between the ages of 5 and 7. In effect, this tendency for correlations to decrease with the amount of intervening time reflects the fact that differential growth rates in different children have more opportunity to reflect the changes in the *relative* heights of the children in question. However, as children approach their final adult height, they increasingly maintain the same height in relation to one another. This increased "sameness" in relative height from one year to the next is reflected in higher correlations for older than for younger children.

The data in Table 5-3 largely confirm these developmental patterns with respect to hypnotic susceptibility. The table shows that, regardless of age, the correlation between the one-*week* retest scores and the first-session scores is higher than the one-*year* retest scores and the first-session scores. And with one minor exception, the two-year scores correlate less with first-session scores than do the one-year retest scores. Moreover, the older the children when tested for the first time, the higher the correlations with first-session scores. The major exception to this latter trend is the correlation of .46 in the two-year retest of 13- to 16-year-olds. The fact that this correlation is much below the .62 of the 9- to 12-year-olds suggests the importance of adolescence as a "flummox" factor. It is an age during which many otherwise regular growth patterns show all sorts of curious and idiosyncratic trends. It is not surprising that patterns of hypnotic susceptibility reflect these trends.

Table 5-3. Susceptibility correlations across various periods of intervening time in children of various ages

Age of subject at first session	One-week retest	One-year retest	Two-year retest
5–8 years	.76	.41	.34
9–12 years	.74	.58	.62
13–16 years	.80	.63	.46

From "The Development of Hypnotic Susceptibility: A Longitudinal (Convergence) Study," by L. M. Cooper and P. London, *Child Development*, 1971, 42, 487–503. Copyright © 1971 by the Society for Research in Child Development. Reprinted by permission.

The data from the London and Cooper (1971) study indicate that, within certain age ranges, hypnotic susceptibility is reasonably stable. Since the authors did *not* test the *same* children a decade apart (say, at ages 6 and 16), we can only guess what the results of that testing would have been. It is fair to say that the correlations between hypnotic susceptibilities assessed at ages 6 and 16 would be positive but low, and surely nothing like the *r* of .60 reported for adults tested two times a decade apart (Morgan et al., 1974). In other words, it would be next to impossible to predict the hypnotic ability of an adolescent knowing only his susceptibility at age 6.

In sum, we know that hypnotic susceptibility remains fairly stable in children over relatively short periods of time (a year or two) and also that it remains reasonably stable in adults over long periods of times. But it is also true that hypnotic susceptibility does not show genuinely long-term stability in children until they begin to approach late adolescence.

Natural Changes in Hypnotic Susceptibility

So far we have concerned ourselves with the question of the stability of an individual's hypnotic susceptibility over time. And as we have seen, this stability has been cast in terms of an individual's performance *relative* to other people. Although it may not be immediately apparent to the reader, this particular notion of stability is consistent with the possibility of pronounced changes in the subjects' *average* susceptibility scores obtained during two or more testings. This point is illustrated in Table 5-4, whose hypothetical data show the susceptibility scores of ten individuals tested on two occasions. Notice that the *average* susceptibility score increases by 3 points from first to second testing, yet the correlation between these two sets of scores is 1.0. Now, of course, this hypothetical outcome is empirically unlikely, but it does make the point that even perfect *relative* stability of subjects' hypnotic performances (that is, a correlation coefficient of 1.0) is consistent with rather dramatic changes in subjects' average scores from one testing occasion to another. This is an important point, since it means that claims for the modifiability of hypnotic susceptibility are not necessarily prejudicial to claims for its stability.

One way to illustrate this last point empirically is to examine change in hypnotic susceptibility as it occurs "naturally" over time—that is, without the help of experimental interventions designed specifically to increase susceptibility. Evidence for the change of hypnotic susceptibility with age can then be balanced against the evidence already submitted for the impressive stability of hypnotic susceptibility over time.

Table 5-4.

Subject	Score on first testing	Score on second testing
1	9	12
2	8	11
3	8	11
4	7	10
5	7	10
6	6	9
7	5	8
8	5	8
9	3	6
10	2	5
	$\overline{X} = 6.0$	$\overline{X} = 9.0$
	$r = 1.0$	

Morgan and Hilgard (1973) tested a total of 1232 subjects ranging from 5 to above 40 years of age. Then they grouped these different subjects into ten age categories, each with a span of four years. Thus, subjects aged 5 to 8 comprised one category, subjects aged 9 to 12 comprised the next category, and so on. Figure 5-1 shows a gradual decline in the average susceptibility after the ages of 9 to 12, when susceptibility seems to be at its highest. Earlier, less formal investigations (such as Bernheim, 1964) are largely in agreement with this finding that hypnotic susceptibility "peaks out" just before adolescence and declines thereafter (cf. Gordon, 1972).

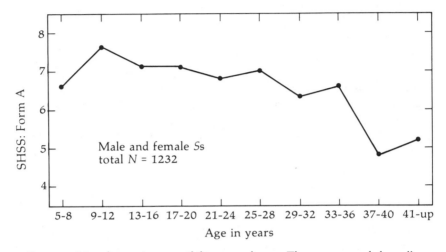

Figure 5-1. Mean hypnotic susceptibility scores by age. The scores recorded are all from individual hypnotic tests. From "Age Differences in Susceptibility to Hypnosis," by A. H. Morgan and E. R. Hilgard, *International Journal of Clinical and Experimental Hypnosis,* 1973, *21,* 78–85. Copyrighted by The Society for Clinical and Experimental Hypnosis, April 1973. Reprinted by permission.

What these findings confirm is that a person's responsiveness to hypnosis is not fixed and unchanging throughout life. The experiences involved in growing up and growing old substantially alter one's responsiveness to hypnosis—a state of affairs perfectly consistent with the possibility of there being genetic determinants of hypnotic susceptibility (Morgan, 1973; Morgan, Hilgard, & Davert, 1970). Just exactly what causes these changes in hypnotic responsiveness is not clear, although certain provisional guesses are implicit in some recent efforts to enhance susceptibility experimentally. It is to some of these efforts that we now turn.

The Experimental Modification of Hypnotic Susceptibility

Personal growth. We shall first look at a couple of studies investigating the impact of personal growth on susceptibility. Tart (1970a) was the first investigator to do research in this area. He tested the hypnotic susceptibility of seven resident fellows at Esalen Institute before their training program began and again nine months later, when it was nearly finished. The residential program emphasized personal growth as achieved in a variety of ways, such as sensitivity groups, gestalt therapy, biofeedback training, and so on. On an abbreviated 10-point scale of susceptibility focusing on overt behavior to various suggestions (SHSS:C), the subjects averaged 3.3 at the beginning of training and 5.3 at the end. On an experiential measure derived from the same scale, the pretreatment average was 43, the post-treatment average was 66 (out of a maximum of 116 points). The gains for both behavioral and experiential susceptibility scores were statistically significant. Nevertheless, a person's initial susceptibility level had a great deal to do with his or her final, post-treatment score, since the (rank order) correlation between these two administrations was above .80 for both the behavioral and experiential scales. On the basis of these data, Tart (1970a) suggested that the residential program encouraged the subjects "to overcome many of the inhibitions about experiencing, reporting, and acting on other [that is, altered] states of consciousness, and one consequence of this was increase in hypnotizability" (p. 264). Implied in this statement is the notion that socialization tends to inhibit the innate capacity to experience altered states of consciousness. This is perhaps one reason for the decline of susceptibility with age.

Perhaps because it was the first of its kind, Tart's study had some serious methodological flaws. The worst of these was the absence of an appropriate control group. The improvement in susceptibility that Tart attributed to the residential program *per se* may have been in fact due to being liberated for nine months from the daily demands of telephones, deadlines, competition, and so forth. Perhaps a control group given a nine-month all-expense-paid tour of the world would have shown similar enhancement of susceptibility.

A less exotic (and far less expensive) alternative was introduced by Shapiro and Diamond (1972), who found that a total of 26 hours of encounter-group experience emphasizing the importance of *inter*personal interactions significantly increased hypnotic susceptibility from an initial score of 7.7 to a score of 10.0. A similar group experience emphasizing *intra*personal communication demonstrated a nonsignificant increase in score from 4.5 to 5.6, which was comparable to the change shown by a nontreatment control group. On the basis of their results, the authors suggest that it is an increase in interpersonal trust that enhances hypnotic responsiveness, and not a reinstated ability to experience altered states of consciousness, as Tart (1970a) had argued. The importance of interpersonal trust to hypnotic responsiveness has long been known and recently confirmed by Roberts and Tellegen (1973). There is, however, no necessary contradiction between the views of Tart and those of Shapiro and Diamond. Perhaps interpersonal trust simply allows the subject being hypnotized to experience unusual, trance-like episodes without feeling threatened or suspicious. In any event, it is quite possible that interpersonal trust tends to diminish with the loss of youthful innocence and that this accounts for some of the decline in hypnotic susceptibility with age.

Sensory deprivation. In noting that the gains in hypnotic susceptibility due to personal-growth training are modest, it is important to keep in mind that such programs are not directed primarily at enhancing hypnotic susceptibility. One experimental attempt to do just that has been reported by Sanders and Reyher (1969). These investigators were impressed by the dramatic alterations in perception and thinking experienced by subjects undergoing sensory deprivation. The original studies of this genre were conducted at McGill University (Bexton, Heron, & Scott, 1954; Heron, 1957), and the basic findings of these by now classic investigations have been replicated many times. Essentially, people who are maintained in an environment of minimal stimulation begin to experience changes in body size and location, paranoid ideation, visual and auditory hallucinations, and, most particularly and pervasively, an inability to direct and guide their thinking (Zuckerman, 1964). Although the psychological effects of sensory deprivation vary somewhat as a function of the specific experimental conditions (Orne & Scheibe, 1964), there can be no doubt about the profound impact that such procedures typically have on human functioning.

Proceeding from a model of brain functioning developed earlier (Reyher, 1964), Sanders and Reyher (1969) argue, in effect, that both sensory deprivation and hypnosis lead to a lower level of adaptation—a level at which it is difficult for the subjects to direct and regulate their behavior and thinking. The reader can perhaps intuit this situation by remembering how impossible it is to guide the course of one's own dreams. Such dreams seem to have a life and direction of their own and are not guided by conscious purposes and goals, as are the person's waking thoughts and actions.

On the basis of such considerations, Sanders and Reyher (1969) argued that if persons were subjected to sensory deprivation, the point at which they began to lose the ability to think directively and adaptively would also be the point of increased susceptibility to the influence of hypnotic suggestions. In other words, the subjects would begin to experience suggested phenomena in the same passive way as they ordinarily experience their dreams (Bowers & Bowers, 1972).

The investigators tested these notions by placing female subjects, selected for their low susceptibility, into sensory isolation for up to six hours. The isolation chamber was a 12-by-12 cubicle that minimized the amount of light and sound reaching the subject. All subjects in the experimental group were informed that the purpose of the experiment was to test the effect of sensory deprivation on their ability to become hypnotized. Ten control subjects (also selected for their low hypnotic ability) were told that the experiment involved evaluating the effect of familiarity of surroundings on hypnotic susceptibility. The low-susceptible control subjects also stayed in the isolation chamber, but never alone and with plenty of stimulation provided by radio, magazines, and other means.

As the experiment progressed, the subjects were to report on their subjective experiences over an intercom system, so that the experimenter could detect when their thinking and perception began to deteriorate. Evidence of this deterioration included comments on peculiar bodily sensations and alterations in body image; evidence of restlessness, fear, anxiety, or anger; impairment in logicalness of thought and speech; and statements requesting contact with the experimenter. When subjects began to show evidence of deterioration (or after six hours, whichever came first), the experimenter began to induce hypnosis. For control subjects, the hypnotic induction began after four and a half hours, which was the average amount of time that the experimental subjects lasted before psychological impairment was evident and inducement of hypnosis begun.

When the hypnosis scale was completed, subjects were released and asked to return after a week for a final administration of a susceptibility scale in order to evaluate the durability of any changes in susceptibility that had been found at the end of the experiment.

Figure 5-2 shows that low-susceptible persons subjected to sensory isolation showed an increase in their hypnotic susceptibility of nearly 5 scale points over their pretest performance—a gain that had slightly increased when the subjects were tested again a week later. Since the control subjects showed virtually no increase in susceptibility, it appears that sensory deprivation per se has a profound impact on hypnotic responsiveness—just as theory had suggested.

It is not clear exactly why the change in susceptibility lasted for a week; after all, the subjects were not re-exposed to sensory deprivation upon their return to the laboratory; they were simply rehypnotized. Perhaps we have here an example of the "raindrop effect": the first drop of water down a windowpane facilitates the passage of the second one. After a psychological passage had been opened through their usual resistance to hypnosis, perhaps the experimental subjects found it easier to find this path again and follow it when provided with a subsequent opportunity to become hypnotized. In any event, it would certainly be interesting to know whether these gains were stably maintained over an even longer period of time. Conceivably, enduring features of the person's character and cognitive style will eventually recoup from their "defeat" by a sensory-deprivation experience; it is also possible that the

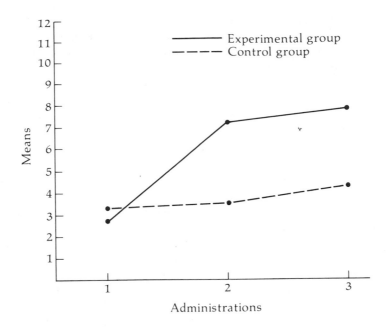

Figure 5-2. Mean SHSS scores for experimental and control groups. From "Sensory Deprivation and the Enhancement of Hypnotic Susceptibility," by R. S. Sanders and J. Reyher, *Journal of Abnormal Psychology,* 1969, *74,* 375-381. Copyright 1969 by the American Psychological Association. Reprinted by permission.

internal changes inspired by sensory deprivation will become permanently incorporated into the subject's personality. Although the question remains unanswered, other investigations (Wickramasekera, 1969, 1970) confirm the finding that at least temporary increments in hypnotic susceptibility flow from sensory isolation. So, there is some reason to believe that sensory deprivation can facilitate hypnotic experiences in subjects who ordinarily are recalcitrant to such experiences.

Psychotomimetic drugs. Since sensory deprivation has rather bizarre perceptual-cognitive consequences that seem to enhance hypnotic susceptibility, it is reasonable to expect that drug-induced alterations in cognition and thinking might have a similar effect (see Weitzenhoffer, 1953, p. 52, for some early work in this area). Several studies on this possible effect have been reported (Levine & Ludwig, 1965; Solursh & Rae, 1966; see also Diamond, 1974, p. 182), but we will concentrate on an investigation by Sjoberg and Hollister (1965) as the one best controlled and most revealing. In this study, each of 24 men between 21 and 40 years of age received a different psychotomimetic drug on each of four separate days, with a week's interval between sessions. The four drugs employed were LSD-25, psilocybin, mescaline, and a weighted combination of these three drugs such that each contributed about a third of the total effect. Since each subject received a different drug in each of three drug sessions (with order counterbalanced), the effects of different drugs on a 17-item suggestibility scale could be compared. Moreover, since all the subjects returned for a final hypnotic session one month after the last drug administration, the suggestibility-enhancing effects of drugs and of hypnosis could also be compared. It is important to understand that this investigation does *not* directly study the effects of drugs on hypnotic susceptibility. Rather, the experiment investigates whether and to what extent a person's ordinary, waking suggestibility can be enhanced by the ingestion of drugs and by the induction of hypnosis. Since subjects were administered a suggestibility scale both before and after drug ingestion (or hypnosis induction), a person's increase in suggestibility from the waking to the drugged (or hypnotic) state could be assessed separately for each session.

In addition, the investigators also administered a "Trance Indicator Score" both before and after trance or drug administration. This 17-item index was derived from subjects' introspective accounts of their subjective experiences, together with the outward signs of trance-like behavior as judged by the tester. Parenthetically, the reader might have noticed that this is the first time I have mentioned an index of trance that is separate from the measure of responsiveness to suggestions. I will elaborate on this distinction in Chapter 6.

The findings of the Sjoberg and Hollister study are presented in Table 5-5. These findings represent clear evidence that hypnosis and all

Table 5-5. Effects of drugs and hypnosis on suggestibility scores

| | Suggestibility scores | | | |
	Pretest	Post-test	Change	Probability level
Mescaline	3.333	5.500	+2.167	.005
LSD-25	3.625	5.167	+1.542	.025
Psilocybin	3.458	3.541	+0.083	NS
Combination	3.333	4.750	+1.417	.005
Hypnosis	2.792	4.667	+1.875	.005

| | Trance indicator score | | | |
	Pretest	Post-test	Change	Probability level
Mescaline	7.250	12.792	+5.542	.005
LSD-25	7.417	13.917	+6.500	.005
Psilocybin	7.375	9.167	+1.792	.025
Combination	7.917	11.459	+3.542	.005
Hypnosis	5.500	14.333	+8.833	.005

From "The Effects of Psychotomimetic Drugs on Primary Suggestibility," by B. M. Sjoberg and L. F. Hollister, *Psychopharmacologia*, 1965, 8, 251–262. Copyright© 1965 by Springer Verlag. Reprinted by permission.

drugs used in the experiment, except psilocybin, significantly increased the subjects' responsiveness to suggestions and their trance-like experiences. Thus, the findings confirm our expectancy that drugs have a considerable impact on our state of consciousness and on our suggestibility as well.

These tables are also revealing in another way. The reader will notice that in both parts of Table 5-5 the pretest scores for the hypnosis condition are considerably lower than the pretest scores for the drug condition. In one sense, this can be considered a methodological artifact. What happened is that subjects showed less pretest suggestibility and trance with each succeeding session—an effect that disappears when the LSD data, say, are averaged across different subjects taking that drug on different sessions. Since hypnosis was *always* administered last, the progressive lowering of pretest suggestibility and trance shows up clearly.

Even though it is possible to explain away the lower pretest scores of the hypnosis session, the fact remains that a limited history of drug taking did not enduringly enhance waking suggestibility and/or "tranceability." One might have expected that repeated exposure to psychotomimetic drugs would have had a facilitating effect in this regard; if anything, the reverse occurred. This negative finding for the durability of drug effects on waking suggestibility contrasts with other evidence showing the enhancement of hypnotic susceptibility by the contemporaneous ingestion of drugs (Fogel & Hoffer, 1962; Levine & Ludwig, 1965) and the enduring impact of sensory deprivation experiences on hypnotic susceptibility (Sanders & Reyher, 1969). Just what this pattern of conflicting evidence means is not entirely clear at this time.

Biofeedback. Another sort of experimental attempt to increase hypnotic susceptibility employs biofeedback training. This procedure involves electronically monitoring some body process (such as brain waves or muscle tension), amplifying this output, and converting it into an auditory or visual signal that is fed back to the subject. Since the feedback signal corresponds in frequency or intensity to the frequency or intensity of the body process being monitored, the subject is continuously informed about an aspect of his or her functioning that is ordinarily difficult to detect. For example, people are not usually aware of when they generate brain waves of about 7 to 13 cycles per second—the so-called alpha rhythm. Yet they can be made aware of their alpha production if the presence of alpha in their brain-wave pattern activates an auditory or visual signal that the subjects can hear or see. An important implication of this feedback principle is that, with practice, the subjects may learn how to keep the signal on for longer and longer periods of time, which is of course an indication that the subjects have also learned to voluntarily increase the amount of alpha in their brain-wave pattern.

The possibility of increasing alpha production through biofeedback becomes particularly exciting in light of evidence strongly suggesting that alpha production in waking-relaxed subjects is highly correlated with their hypnotic susceptibility (London, Hart, & Leibovitz, 1968; Nowlis & Rhead, 1968). If it is in fact true that people low in alpha production tend to be low in susceptibility and people high in alpha production tend to be high in hypnotic susceptibility, perhaps low hypnotic susceptibility can be improved by biofeedback training of alpha production. This possibility is especially tantalizing, since the subjective experiences accompanying alpha production tend to be detached, dreamy, "suspended" sorts of feelings (Kamiya, 1969) similar to those frequently reported by hypnotized subjects. Perhaps alpha feedback can help relatively unsusceptible subjects experience these hypnotic-like states that are otherwise rare for them.

An investigation conducted by Engstrom, London, and Hart (1970) was aimed at finding out just that, and a later report has recently appeared that revises and expands upon the original study (London, Cooper, & Engstrom, 1974). What follows is taken from this revised account. Twenty-six subjects were chosen from a much larger sample on the basis of both their low level of alpha production and their low-to-moderate level of hypnotic susceptibility. These subjects were then randomly assigned to an experimental group ($N = 19$) or to a control group ($N = 7$). All subjects were told that the study involved training in brain-wave control as a method of improving hypnotic susceptibility, and they were seen for six training sessions over a one-to-two-week period. However, only the experimental subjects received genuine feedback based on their ongoing electroencephalographic (EEG) activity. The control subjects received the tape-recorded signal of a single experimental subject who had shown a great deal of improvement over the six training sessions. The control subjects, of course, did not know that the signal they heard for increasing amounts of time had nothing to do with their own alpha activity. And, since the signal did not discriminate between a control subject's *own* alpha-on and alpha-off periods, it could not be used to learn how to increase alpha.

The results of this experiment were in keeping with past results and with the experimental hypotheses. In the first place, it replicated earlier findings by showing a high correlation between hypnotic susceptibility and alpha production ($r = .80$ for the experimental and .88 for the control group). For the experimental group, the measure of alpha production changed from an average of 27.26 in the pretest to 104.79 during the last training session—an increase significantly greater than that shown by the control group, whose alpha production increased from 33.00 to 74.00. (The unit of measure here is the mean seconds of alpha out of 240 seconds.) As far as hypnotic susceptibility was concerned, the mean score of the experimental group increased from a pretest score of 3.16 to a post-test score of 7.42. This gain was significantly greater than the (nonsignificant) change from 4.00 to 5.14 shown by the control group. In general, then, alpha-feedback training did increase the subjects' hypnotic susceptibility.

Although (and perhaps because) the findings regarding alpha production and hypnotic susceptibility represent an exciting development, they have not gone unchallenged. One criticism has been directed at the presumed impact of alpha feedback on alpha production (Paskewitz & Orne, 1973; Lynch, Paskewitz, & Orne, 1974). These critics do not dispute the finding that alpha production increases during the course of the training procedure, but they do not agree that biofeedback per se produces these gains. They support their claim with data showing that false feedback leads to alpha increases comparable to those engendered by true feedback. The authors argue that subjects in both feedback conditions began the experiment with their alpha levels inhibited by the unfamiliar milieu in which they found themselves; as the subjects became more comfortable and relaxed in the experimental setting, their alpha production increased.

Other investigators dispute the validity of the relationship between subjects' hypnotic ability and the amount of resting alpha they generate (Edmonston & Grotevant, 1975). Evans (1972), for example, argues that the apparent relationship between these two variables is an artifactual consequence of how the subjects were initially selected. It should be noted in passing that neither of these criticisms addresses itself to the observed increases in hypnotic susceptibility due to alpha training (London et al., 1974). And there is now additional evidence supporting the propositions that enhancement of alpha production can be due specifically to alpha feedback (Travis, Kondo, & Knott, 1974) and that hypnotic ability is associated with resting alpha (Morgan, Macdonald, & Hilgard, 1974). Clearly, however, there is a good deal more research to be done in this area before any final conclusions are warranted.

An experiment conducted by Wickramesekera (1973) helped to confirm the reasonableness of the theory that biofeedback can enhance hypnotic susceptibility. In this experiment, however, it was not alpha production that was at issue but muscle tension. The investigator saw six experimental and six control subjects for ten sessions of 30 minutes each. An electromyographic (EMG) record of muscle tension was employed, and the subjects were instructed to turn *off* an EMG-associated biofeedback signal that indicated the *presence* of muscle tension. Only the experimental subjects heard their *own* tension signals; the controls unknowingly heard the tape-recorded feedback of one experimental subject who showed considerably reduced tension over sessions.

The results of this training regimen are among the most dramatic in the literature. Subjects in the experimental group increased their susceptibility score almost 6 points, from a pretreatment average of 4.83 to a post-treatment average of 10.16. The control subjects showed virtually no improvement: their score went from an average of 5.00 before treatment to an average of 5.16 after treatment. These results are particularly impressive when compared with the more modest gains of 2 to 3 points that are typically reported by experimenters attempting to improve susceptibility.

One way of understanding Wickramasekera's findings is to consider the relationship of hypnosis and relaxation. Traditionally, the hypnotic induction involves, among other things, suggestions for progressive relaxation. Perhaps the EMG technique facilitates the subjects' ability to relax completely, thereby increasing their responsiveness to hypnotic suggestions as well. Wickramasekera also makes the novel suggestion that perhaps this trained reduction in tension also reduces the extent to which subjects are distracted by internal, body "noise," just as sensory deprivation reduces subjects' distractibility caused by external noise. He suggests that internal and external noise may very well reduce the effectiveness of verbal suggestions, thus implying, in effect, that reduction in distractibility is a prerequisite for the subject's focused concentration upon hypnotic suggestions.

Although there is undoubtedly some truth in it, this notion is not entirely consistent with an alternate proposal by As (1962a). This author suggests that highly susceptible subjects became oblivious or inattentive to irrelevant stimuli as a *consequence* of being absorbed in the cues and suggestions presented by the hypnotist. Whether such hypnotic absorption in verbal suggestions is a result or a cause of reduced distractibility is an issue to which we shall return in another context. It is enough to state at this point that highly susceptible subjects indeed seem to be less distracted by internal (Van Nuys, 1973) and external (Mitchell, 1970) "noise" than low-susceptible subjects.

Hypnotic training. Another sort of evidence that hypnotic susceptibility can indeed improve derives from experiments in which subjects are given practice and training in hypnosis. There is no question that most people, when exposed to hypnosis for the first time, go through a period of adjustment to the experience. Most of the time, anxieties and uncertainties are sloughed off, inaccurate stereotypes are discarded, and residual doubts or suspicions about the hypnotist are generally minimized. An engaging description of this process has recently been offered by Kidder (1972). She found that persons who originally had a skeptical attitude toward hypnosis gradually came to accept their responsiveness to suggestion as due to hypnosis—an acceptance that was subtly "negotiated" over three days of interacting with the hypnotist, and which probably enhanced the persons' susceptibility (although this latter point was not specifically established).

Until recently, however, little research has been done to enhance hypnotic susceptibility through hypnotic training beyond the point achieved after a few practice sessions. This is not too surprising considering that evidence for the stability of hypnotic susceptibility had wide acceptance and that, therefore, it seemed futile to try to improve upon it. Also, if experimenters were interested in working with highly susceptible subjects, it was much easier to select them, rather than train them. Consequently, unless an experimenter was specifically interested in modifying susceptibility, there seemed little point in doing so.

To be sure, there were clinical reports of improvements in hypnotizability achieved after literally hundreds of hours of persistent effort by the hypnotist (Erickson, 1965). And these reports, together with a growing realization that high susceptibility had certain potential advantages (for example, the control of pain), began to change the zeitgeist. Reports of the experimental modification of hypnotizability first appeared in the late 1950s (Pascal & Salzberg, 1959) and have been recently increasing to the point of warranting a couple of serious reviews of these efforts (Sachs, 1971; Diamond, 1974). Since we have already examined some of the extrahypnotic means of enhancing susceptibility, it is now time to consider how hypnosis itself can be used to modify hypnotizability.

There are two major kinds of studies to be considered here. The first emphasizes practice and training in hypnosis *per se;* the second focuses on alterations in the "atmospherics" of hypnosis—that is, subjects' expectancies and perceptions about hypnosis and the hypnotist. It is important to stress at the outset that these two sorts of approaches are quite different both in tactics and in outcome, although the distinction is sometimes blurred or completely overlooked.

There are several studies of the first kind (among them, Shor & Cobb, 1968; As, Hilgard, & Weitzenhoffer, 1963), but I will discuss the work of only three. In the first one (Cooper, Banford, Shubot, & Tart, 1967), six subjects were trained for 7 to 16 sessions, each lasting one or two hours. Since individualized training was the rule, the hypnotist was free to employ whatever training technique he wanted. Before and after training, different versions of the Stanford Profile Scales were administered to evaluate pre- and post-treatment performance. Each of these scales was administered by a different hypnotist, and *neither* of the hypnotists who evaluated an individual's hypnotic susceptibility was responsible for training the person. Five out of the six participating subjects showed increased susceptibility, the average increase across all subjects being 2.92. This is a statistically significant improvement ($t =$ 2.14, $p < .05$), but it is not a dramatic increase in practical terms, especially considering the effort involved in training each subject.

A study by Sachs and Anderson (1967) reported more pronounced increases in hypnotic performance. Unlike the authors of the previous study, these investigators gave each subject five or six hours of special training on items the person had missed or barely passed on the pretest. For example, subjects were given special exercises to become aware of sensory experiences accompanying a (suggested) weight at the end of their outstretched arm. The ten subjects participating in this experiment showed average increases of up to 6 points from pre- to post-testing. One might suspect the investigators of a little "cheating" to get their results, since it seems a bit odd for a hypnotist to evaluate treatment gains on the very test he or she had utilized in training the subject; the possibilities for biasing the outcome are considerable. However, the increases did generalize to a new hypnotist (giving the same scale) and to a different scale administered by the training hypnotist. Although these precautions do not offer complete immunity from biased outcomes, they do represent an improvement.

Other problematic features of this investigation are represented by the small number of subjects and by the lack of a control group. However, a subsequent study (Kinney & Sachs, 1974) rectified both of these problems and improved other features of the experiment as well. In this improved version, 20 experimental subjects showed significant gains of 4 to 4.5 points on the SHSS:C scale, whereas 10 untreated control subjects showed virtually no improvement at all. Although the experimental subjects had been trained on the C scale, the treatment effects generalized to another, more complex scale of susceptibility (the Stanford Profile Scale) and persisted one month later on both of these scales. The evaluation of pre- and post-test susceptibility in this experiment, unlike that in the previous one, was conducted by a person other than the training hypnotist to avoid a potential source of bias.

In sum, the evidence suggests that some increments in hypnotic susceptibility can be effected by practice and training in hypnosis per se. Nevertheless, the final scores tend to correlate highly with the initial scores. In the study by Cooper and his associates (1967), for example, a rank-order (rho) correlation of .94 was obtained between pre- and post-test scores. In other words, a person's initial susceptibility level tends to limit his or her final level of susceptibility, no matter how much practice and training the person may have had in between. As Hilgard (1975) has commented, "The hope of producing hypnotic virtuosos out of originally low scorers has not been fulfilled" (p. 27). This summary statement pretty much holds for all attempts to modify hypnotic susceptibility by whatever means.

One final comment should be made here about both the Cooper

(1967) and the Sachs and Anderson (1967) studies. The subjects employed in these investigations had considerable experience in hypnosis before being administered the pretest. This precaution makes it unlikely that subsequent gains demonstrated by the subjects were due to the removal of the uncertainties and apprehensions that often detract from initial hypnotic performances. In other words, the treatment gains were not "cheap"; that is, they were not likely due to an artifically low pretest baseline.

It is not so clear that this problem has been avoided in investigations focusing on the "atmospherics" of hypnosis. In general, these studies select two groups of subjects who are naive about hypnosis and differentially manipulate the perception, or set, of these subjects. This is accomplished by providing the experimental (but not the control) group with information about hypnosis, by increasing the perceived prestige of the hypnotist, by enhancing the subject's desire to be hypnotized, and so on (see Diamond, 1974, pp. 183–187, for a review of these studies). These maneuvers invariably provide a slight advantage to the experimental group. Therefore, it often seems that the experimental subjects are being treated in a way that optimizes their hypnotic performance by reducing the uncertainties and anxieties that generally accompany an initial encounter with hypnosis. By contrast, the control subjects are often provided less than optimal conditions.

If studies of this sort wish to conclude only that optimal conditions for hypnosis lead to a somewhat higher susceptibility *score*, then certainly the findings cannot be disputed. However, if these experiments are taken to imply that susceptibility per se has been enhanced, we begin to run into problems. It is worth dwelling a bit on this issue, since it reveals a general point that should always be kept in mind when the modification of hypnotic susceptibility is under consideration.

To begin with, recall the distinction, introduced earlier, between a particular hypnotic performance (that is, a score earned on a particular hypnosis scale) and the person's aptitude for hypnosis—his or her hypnotic suscept-*ability*. This distinction is important, for it implies that change in a person's susceptibility *score* does not necessarily reflect genuine changes in his or her hypnotic susceptibility. In order to do justice to this possibility, it is convenient to introduce a new concept, *plateau hypnotizability*.

This concept was initially defined as "the maximum hypnotic depth achieved in as many intensive hypnotic training sessions as the experimenter needed in order to feel confident that a stable plateau in the subject's hypnotic performance had been reached" (Shor, Orne, & O'Connell, 1966, p. 82). This definition implies (although it does not explicitly state) that a person's plateau level of hypnotizability reflects his or her "true" suscept-*ability*, whereas preplateau performances reflect an amalgam of this basic hypnotic ability and other extraneous factors that by and large detract from an optimal, or plateau performance. These extraneous factors can include all manner of attitudinal and affective variables, such as the subject's unfamiliarity with hypnosis, suspicions about the hypnotist's competence and integrity, faulty stereotypes about hypnosis, anxieties and apprehensions flowing from these uncertainties, and so on. The extent to which these extraneous factors are operative is the extent to which the resulting performance or score can be considered an *invalid* index of the subject's *ability* to be hypnotized.

It follows from these comments that fairly rapid increases in a person's preplateau susceptibility score may represent the steadily diminishing influence of extraneous factors affecting the subject's hypnotic performance. The eventual absence of these factors presumably permits a highly valid assessment of hypnotic suscept-*ability,* which is thereby revealed as a relatively stable characteristic of the person.

This formulation clearly suggests that it is easier to change a person's susceptibility score than it is to change his or her susceptibility per se. But it does not preclude changes in the latter. There is a problem here, however: we can never unambiguously attribute increases in a susceptibility score to genuine increases in a person's suscept-*ability,* since these increases might instead be attributable to further (if unexpected) reductions in performance factors extraneous to hypnotic ability per se (see, for example, Shor & Cobb, 1968). The possibility of this sort of endless waffling renders the notion of plateau hypnotizability somewhat problematic from a practical point of view. Conceptually, however, the notion embodies the important commonsense idea that some hypnotic performances are more valid indicators of suscept-*ability* than others; to abandon that idea would suggest that a person's hypnotic performance and his or her hypnotic susceptibility are synonomous and that changes in the former inevitably reflect genuine changes in the latter. But surely it is *possible* for a susceptibility score to be rendered relatively invalid by a subject's apprehensions, lack of cooperativeness, or even overzealousness (in attempting to please the hypnotist). It is precisely this possibility that the concept of plateau hypnotizability recognizes and preserves.

Perhaps the reason for this brief examination of plateau hypnotizability is now evident. We should be alerted to the possibility that reported increases of susceptibility *scores* do not automatically indicate corresponding increases in hypnotic susceptibility per se. We must judge in every case whether such increased scores might instead reflect an increasingly valid assessment of susceptibility, as extraneous factors like subject misinformation and anxiety are progressively reduced. This is a particularly important point to keep in mind as we evaluate the reports of susceptibility change due to manipulations of the atmospherics surrounding initial encounters with hypnosis. It seems fairly clear that such manipulations achieve their effects because of a reduction of extraneous factors that otherwise detract from hypnotic performance and not because of genuine increases in hypnotic suscept-*ability*. More generally, we can seriously question *any* study claiming to show improvements in hypnotic susceptibility if the investigator has not been careful to *start* with subjects who are already familiar and comfortable with hypnosis. Any gains reported with initially naive subjects are apt to be cheap—that is, a result of an artificially low pretest baseline.

Summary

We have seen that hypnotic susceptibility is a fairly stable characteristic of the person; but we have also seen that it is subject to age-related, developmental changes on the one hand and to experimentally induced modifications on the other. The latter modifications are not limitless, however, since subjects' initial level of susceptibility generally places a formidable constraint on their final level, no matter how much interim training they receive. Consequently, although moderately susceptible subjects may become highly susceptible with training, and low-susceptible subjects may become moderately so, no training or technique yet devised has regularly transformed initially unsusceptible subjects into highly hypnotizable ones. Thus, the "power" of the psychological environment to establish deep hypnosis is limited by the initial hypnotic abilities of the person being hypnotized.

Footnotes

[1]Obviously, one way subjects can maintain the same relative position from one testing occasion to the next is for each person to achieve exactly the same score on both occasions. However, as we shall see, even a perfect correlation is consistent with a change in subjects' average score. This is one reason why in this brief discussion of correlation we have emphasized subjects' *relative* positions rather than their absolute scores.

6.
Hypnotic Suggestibility and the Hypnotic State

From the point of view of an onlooker, there is no aspect of hypnosis more striking than the heightened suggestibility of a hypnotic subject. Indeed, this characteristic is so salient that hypnosis is frequently defined as a state of hypersuggestibility (see Weitzenhoffer, 1953; Bernheim, 1964; Hull, 1933).

Precisely because responsiveness to suggestion is such an overt, visible outcome of hypnosis, it is sometimes emphasized to the exclusion of another aspect of hypnosis less obvious to the spectator—the so-called hypnotic state or trance. Indeed, one possible consequence of identifying hypnosis with hypersuggestibility involves eliminating the notion of trance altogether (Sarbin & Coe, 1972; Barber, 1969, 1972). It is tempting to adopt this "tranceless" view of hypnosis, since the hypnotic state is largely experiential, and much harder for the onlooker to identify, than a clear behavioral response to a specific hypnotic suggestion. This relative "invisibility" of trance can thus be construed as tantamount to its nonexistence. My position, developed in this chapter, is that the dismissal of trance and/or trance induction as a trivial aspect of hypnosis is premature and ill-advised.

A second, and related, consequence of *equating* hypnosis with hypersuggestibility is that *all* instances of heightened suggestibility can become potential examples of hypnosis. This may seem to be a reasonable enough viewpoint, until one sees a soldier following the orders of a commanding officer to the point of suffering injury and even death. Somehow, the behavior of that soldier is not exactly what we have in mind when we talk about hypnosis (White, 1941). Among other things, the hypnotic subject, unlike the soldier, is under no particular threat of court martial or other sanction if he does *not* behave in the suggested manner. Quite to the contrary, the suggested behavior of the hypnotized person seems, to all outward appearances, remarkably uncoerced.

Moreover, research has shown that hypnotic responsiveness is not the same as conformity, gullibility, persuasibility, or other forms of compliance (Moore, 1964). These forms of compliance, just like soldierly submission to authority, simply lie outside the domain of hypnosis (Hilgard, 1973b).

We seem to have a problem here. Although hypnotic susceptibility generally leads to heightened responsiveness, evidently not all instances of heightened responsiveness to suggestion are properly conceived of as hypnotic in nature. This statement is not logically taxing; but, for some reason, logic is often difficult to keep firmly in mind when we turn to empirical inquiry. Consequently, it is worth examining in some detail how various instances of responsiveness to suggestion are relevant or irrelevant to our understanding of hypnosis.

The Task-Motivational Paradigm

In his many investigations of hypnosis, Barber and his colleagues have often employed what he calls a task-motivated control group. This group is typically instructed, in no uncertain terms, to behave in some particular fashion. In one study, for instance, (Barber & Calverley, 1964b) subjects were enjoined to hear (that is, hallucinate) a recording of "White Christmas" and to see (that is, hallucinate) a cat sitting on their laps. These subjects were then administered task-motivating instructions that stated, among other things:

> you did not do as well on [a pretest] as you really could. Some people think it is difficult to see an animal sitting on their lap or to hear a phonograph record playing, and therefore do not really try hard. However, *everyone is able to do this if they really try. I myself can do it quite easily, and all the previous subjects that participated in this experiment were able to do it when they realized it was an easy thing to do* . . . [p. 15, emphasis added].

Even the most casual inspection of the task-motivational instructions reveals that subjects receiving them are under very strong social pressure to report certain things, regardless of what they experienced.[1] It is not at all clear that similar pressures were operating on the hypnotic subjects; they were simply administered a standardized hypnotic induction and given suggestions to hear "White Christmas" and see a cat. From Barber's point of view, however, such differences in social pressure as may exist for these two sorts of subjects are unimportant. What does interest him is how similarly task-motivated and hypnotic subjects *behave*. In the hallucination study, for example, the two kinds of subjects did not differ in their *reports* of heightened (visual and auditory) hallucinations. This sort of null outcome leads Barber (1964a) to argue, on another occasion, that "it appears possible that standardized hypnotic induction procedures and brief task-motivating instructions produce heightened suggestibility in the same way: by motivating *S* to perform to the best of his ability on assigned tasks" (p. 206).

But things turn out to be more complicated than this. Bowers (1967) argued that the task-motivated subjects in the Barber and Calverley study reported more than they saw. He maintained that the subjects' testimony in effect corresponded more to external demands to *report* hallucinations than to a genuine experience of them (cf. Bowers & Gilmore, 1969). Bowers introduced the corrective of demanding an honest report from half the task-motivated subjects he tested. *After* these subjects tried to hallucinate "White Christmas" and a cat sitting on their lap, they were told by a different experimenter to report exactly what they had experienced—that, as far as the experimenter was concerned, the only helpful report was a truthful one. The *reports* of hallucinations by these subjects were much more modest than those by subjects in the standard task-motivated condition—that is, subjects whose reports were garnered without the corrective of an honesty demand. These latter subjects (and doubtless the comparable ones in the original Barber and Calverley study) were evidently falsifying their experience in order to satisfy the coercive demands of the task-motivational instructions.

Bowers did not run a hypnotic conditon in his experiment, so he could not examine the impact of honesty demands upon reports of auditory and visual hallucinations by hypnotized subjects. Spanos and Barber (1968), however, did just that. As in the Bowers study, these authors found that task-motivated subjects under honesty demands reported significantly less vivid (visual and auditory) hallucinations than task-motivated subjects who were not provided this corrective. But they also found that reports of heightened visual hallucinations by hypnotic subjects were *not* affected by demands for report honesty. Irrespective of report condition, what hypnotic subjects said was evidently what they "saw." And their reports of visual hallucinations considerably exceeded in vividness those reported by task-motivated subjects under honesty demands.

The data for the auditory hallucinations were more complicated, because the pertinent hypnotic suggestions did not significantly enhance them in the first place. Consequently, the honesty demand could not serve a corrective purpose. Incidentally, it is worth stressing that, in the absence of an honesty demand, task-motivated subjects *did* report heightened auditory hallucinations even though the hypnotic subjects did not. This outcome suggests that hypnotic subjects, unlike their task-motivated counterparts, do not modify their reports simply to satisfy experimental demand characteristics.

To summarize this line of investigation, strong task-motivational instructions can produce alterations in outward behavior and in experiential *reports*, but they are less likely to produce genuine alterations in perception and experience. However, it is precisely with alterations in perception and experience that hypnosis is primarily concerned. As Orne (1966) phrased it, "a subject is genuinely hypnotized not because he is willing to report certain things, but because his report really describes his personal subjective experience" (p. 724). Hypnosis is thus concerned with behavior and verbal report only insofar as they veridically reflect suggested (and unsuggested) alterations in a person's actual experience. Task-motivational instructions, on the other hand, tend to affect outward behavior and verbal reports in ways that *mis*represent experience. As such, compliance with task-motivational instructions lies outside the domain of hypnosis (Hilgard, 1973b).

In light of the above research, it is curious that Barber steadfastly maintains the position that hypersuggestibility fully captures all that can be meant by "hypnosis." For example, in a recent publication (Barber & Ham, 1974), the terms hypnosis and trance are exorcised as unscientific, and we are enjoined to use " . . . high responsiveness to test-suggestions [as a term] which is more precise and has much fewer unnecessary connotations and much less surplus meaning" (p. 5). We are asked to support this position because, otherwise, "how do we explain the fact that task-motivated subjects are about as responsive to test-suggestions as subjects who have been exposed to a standardized hypnotic-induction procedure?" (Barber & Ham, 1974, p. 5). In another place, Barber answers his own question as follows:

> both task motivational instructions and a trance induction procedure raise response to test suggestions . . . because they produce more positive attitudes, motivations, and expectancies toward the suggestive situation and a greater willingness to think with and to imagine those things that are suggested [Barber, 1972, p. 128].

This answer conveniently neglects to mention one important fact uncovered by Barber's own research (Spanos & Barber, 1968): no matter how similar the behavioral *outcome* of hypnosis and task motivation, the latter tends to achieve its effect by coercing overt compliance that does not reflect a person's internal experience but, instead, satisfies the external demands to behave and report in a prescribed manner. Consequently, the behavior of task-motivated subjects does not bear relevantly on a consideration of hypnotic phenomena, which is concerned with suggested (and unsuggested) alterations in *experience* as they may be revealed in overt behavior and verbal report.

Waking Suggestibility

If task-motivated behavior can make no legitimate claim to residing within the domain of hypnosis, waking suggestibility (Evans, 1967) most certainly can. Waking suggestibility involves administering suggestions for motoric and sensory alterations to a person who has not previously been hypnotized. Under these waking conditions, there is a surprising degree of responsiveness to suggestion. For example, on the Barber Suggestibility Scale, subjects passed an average of three out of eight suggestions when told they were taking a test of imagination (Barber, 1965). Subjects receiving the same scale under hypnotic conditions scored an average of 5.8. Consequently, the improvement of the hypnotic subjects over the baseline (imagination) condition was only about 2.5 points. It is important to keep this relatively small (but statistically significant) increment in mind, because, as Barber (1965) points out, it is commonly but erroneously assumed that there is *zero* suggestibility without hypnosis and that hypnosis accounts for *all* the person's suggestibility.

Another investigation confirms the importance of waking suggestibility. Weitzenhoffer and Sjoberg (1961) tested two groups of 30 subjects each. Group I received suggestions first under waking and then under hypnotic conditions. On a 17-point scale of suggestibility, the waking mean was 2.67; the mean score under the hypnotic condition was 4.83—a (statistically significant) improvement of 2.15 points. Since the hypnotic condition was always run second, it is conceivable that the improvement was due to practice. This possibility is precluded, however, because Group II in this study received two successive tests of waking suggestibility and showed virtually no improvement from first to second testing ($\bar{X}$ = 2.00 and 2.13, respectively). Indeed, Barber and Glass (1962) showed that suggestibility *decreased* slightly from a first to a second waking-suggestibility session ($\bar{X}$ = 3.13 and 2.58, respectively, out of a possible 8 points). Finally, these authors found that there was a slight increase in suggestibility from waking to hypnotic condition. Other evidence (Hilgard & Tart, 1966) basically confirms this pattern of findings—namely, that waking suggestibility provides a surprisingly high base level of responsiveness to suggestion but that suggestibility in the hypnotic state leads to slight but statistically significant increases over this waking baseline.

The fact that waking suggestibility is as high as it is implies that it may reside within the general domain of hypnosis. The magnitude of the correlations between waking and hypnotic suggestibility both confirms and qualifies this implication. Generally speaking, these correlations hover around .65 (Weitzenhoffer & Sjoberg, 1961; Hilgard & Tart, 1966).[2] This is considerably below the test-retest correlations of hypnotic susceptibility, which, as we saw in the last chapter, go as high as .90+. Nevertheless, the correlations between waking and hypnotic suggestibility are impressive and suggest that, by and large, people who are responsive to hypnotic suggestions are also responsive to waking suggestions and people who are low in one tend to be low in the other.

A very important paper by Hilgard and Tart (1966), however, qualifies the relationship between suggestibility under waking conditions and suggestibility under hypnotic conditions. This study shows that these two forms of suggestibility are related but that they are by no means identical. Figure 6-1 tells the story. This figure consists of a scatter plot showing the scores of 129 subjects seen once under waking or imagination conditions and once after a hypnotic induction. Scores above the diagonal indicate improvement in suggestibility from waking to hypnotic conditions; scores below this diagonal represent a decrement in suggestibility from waking to hypnotic conditions; and scores exactly on the diagonal represent no change from one session to the next. It is plainly evident that most people's suggestibility tends to improve from waking to hypnotic conditions. The improvements are particularly striking for the 34 subjects in the upper left-hand quadrant. These subjects are in the lower half of the suggestibility scale insofar as the waking condition is concerned but in the upper half of the scale in hypnotic suggestibility; a hypnotic, or trance, induction dramatically increases the suggestibility of these 34 subjects. The absence of any subjects in the lower right-hand quadrant is a clear indication that subjects high in waking suggestibility are virtually never low in hypnotic suggestibility.

In sum, these findings imply that, for most people, trance induction is less important than waking suggestibility in determining responsiveness to hypnotic suggestions. This is true because there are many people who are *un*suggestible both before and after receiving a trance induction, but no one high in waking suggestibility is unsuggestible when hypnotized. Nevertheless, there is a large minority of subjects who improve greatly in their suggestibility by virtue of a prior trance induction. This is one kind of evidence for the importance of hypnotic induction. It is also a reason for resisting as premature any conclusion that the induction of hypnosis can be dismissed as unimportant or unnecessary.

Another sort of evidence that something important is contributed by trance induction emerges from a recent report by Ruch, Morgan, and Hilgard (1974). In this investigation, as in the previous one, subjects' suggestibility was assessed under both waking and hypnotic conditions. However, the main question in this investigation, unlike that in the previous one, was not the difference in suggestibility under these two conditions nor the relationship between waking and hypnotic suggestibility. The main question was, rather, how well suggestibility under each of these two conditions would correlate with subjects' performance on a criterion measure of hypnotic susceptibility (the SPS:I, see Table 5-1). All 80 subjects in the investigation were administered this criterion measure while hypnotized, after first taking the BSS and the SHSS either under waking-imaginal conditions ($N = 40$) or after the induction of hypnosis

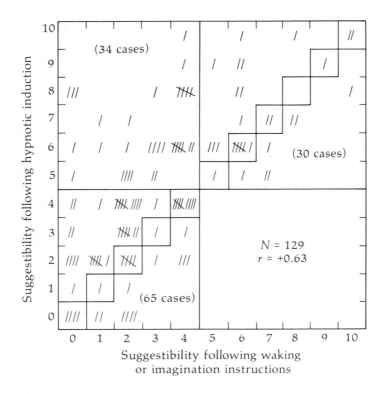

Figure 6-1. Scatterplot of suggestibility scores following waking or imagination instructions. (The scores all fall within three of the four quadrants.) From "Responsiveness to Suggestions Following Waking and Imagination Instructions and Following Induction of Hypnosis," by E. R. Hilgard and C. T. Tart, *Journal of Abnormal Psychology*, 1966, *71*, 196–208. Copyright 1966 by the American Psychological Association. Reprinted by permission.

(N = 40).[3] This arrangement made it possible to see whether waking-imaginal suggestibility or suggestibility under hypnosis correlated higher with the criterion measure of hypnotic susceptibility. Under *waking-imaginal* conditions, an objective measure of the BSS correlated .22 with the criterion measure of hypnotic susceptibility, whereas, under *hypnotic-induction* conditions, the same measure of suggestibility correlated .58 with this criterion measure. Similarly, for the SHSS delivered under waking-imaginal conditions, the resulting correlation of .40 with the criterion measure was much below the analogous correlation of .73 achieved when this same suggestibility scale was delivered after the induction of hypnosis. In other words, on two different measures of suggestibility (BSS and SHSS), the correlation with a criterion measure of hypnotic susceptibility is always considerably higher when the suggestibility scale is administered after hypnotic induction than when it is administered without it.[4]

If we look at the average level of suggestibility instead of the correlational data, we find that the number of items passed is always significantly greater under hypnotic conditions than under waking-imaginal conditions, irrespective of the particular suggestibility scale employed (that is, the BSS or the SHSS). The overall pattern of results thus clearly suggests that, in comparison to a waking-imaginal condition, the hypnotic condition heightens suggestibility and enhances its resemblance to the way people perform on an advanced, criterion measure of hypnotic susceptibility. Evidently, we simply cannot dispense with the induction of hypnosis as an important facilitator of suggestibility, however impressive waking suggestibility itself may be.

Before going any further, it may be wise to discuss an aspect of the previous study that might have bothered the reader. The SHSS and the BSS were considered to be measures of *suggestibility* under hypnotic (as well as waking) conditions. The SPS:I, on the other hand, as a scale tapping the most profound alterations in perception and thinking, has been regarded as a criterion measure of hypnotic *susceptibility*. Just how legitimate is the distinction between suggestibility and hypnotic susceptibility? Earlier in this chapter, I argued for maintaining this distinction on the grounds that not all responsiveness to suggestions falls within the domain of hypnosis. But it is convenient to explore the susceptibility-suggestibility distinction in a somewhat different context.

Basically, the issue boils down to a simple but important distinction between the indicator and what is being indicated—between a thermometer, say, and the temperature it measures. Although we may slip into the habit of identifying temperature with a particular temperature indicator, the fact that they are not synonymous is driven home whenever the thermometer malfunctions and no longer covaries with changes in temperature, or whenever two quite distinct means of measuring temperature are devised, such as a mercury thermometer and a thermocouple. The availability of two such distinct indications of temperature clearly implies that temperature per se is not synonymous with either index of it.

In the context of hypnosis, we have already seen how a person's responsiveness to suggestions may on occasion be an invalid index of his or her hypnotic susceptibility. When this happens, the suggestibility "meter" has in effect malfunctioned. The very fact that this "meter" can break down is a clear reminder that responsiveness to suggestion is not synonymous with the hypnotic susceptibility it ordinarily measures. And as we shall see later on in this chapter, hypnotic susceptibility can be indexed by a measure of "trance depth" as well as by responsiveness to suggestion. As in the case of temperature, the availability of two such separate indicators confirms the distinction between hypnotic suscepti- bility and the various means of measuring it. Evidently, it is not only legitimate but necessary to distinguish between suggestibility and hypnotic susceptibility.

Simulator Paradigm

The legitimacy of this distinction, however, has been jeopardized by a misunderstanding of the simulating paradigm (Orne, 1972b). As we have already seen in previous chapters, low-susceptible subjects simulating hypnosis are often difficult, if not impossible, to distinguish from genuinely hypnotized persons. This has led some people to question whether there is any difference between genuine and simulated hypnosis (Singer, 1971).

From our previous contact with the simulator paradigm, we now know that in *some* experiments simulating and hypnotic subjects *have* behaved differently. Although these studies are not beyond criticism (see Sarbin & Coe, 1972), they at least point out that simulated hypnosis is not inevitably like the genuine article. Moreover, the fact that subjects who try to fake are not always successful suggests that genuine hypnosis cannot be reduced to mere trumpery.

However, instead of simply stating that important differences between genuine and simulated hypnosis exist, it may be worthwhile to investigate the basis of these differences—an examination that may help us arrive at a better understanding of hypnotic phenomena.

To begin with, consider the person who is not sure whether the spidery-looking spot he sees on the wall is really a spider or only a stray shadow. Generally, such a person will test reality by critically scrutinizing the spot—moving his head and body around so as to examine the shadow-spot-spider from different angles. Such bodily displacements virtually "triangulate" the percept under consideration, making what is observed less and less dependent upon any particular point of view. If the spot on the wall looks like a spider irrespective of the angle from which it is observed, then the internal idea, or experience, of a spider is legitimately attributed to a corresponding external reality.

As simple as this *reality testing* strategy seems to be, it can be difficult to maintain under certain circumstances. For example, Morris and Singer (1966) report that sleep-deprived subjects rarely displace their heads and bodies in order to triangulate an ambiguous percept. As we have already seen, sensory deprivation and certain drugs like LSD also seem to disable one's reality testing, and so, to a considerable extent, does the induction of deep hypnosis (Gill & Brenman, 1959). Under each of these conditions, subjects stop "triangulating" reality; that is, they no longer perform multiple and converging behavioral-perceptual acts upon it. Hypnotic subjects, for example, are typified by their behavioral quiescence and "trance stare"—the outward manifestations of a suspended reality-testing orientation. It is precisely this uncritical receptivity, or attentional passivity, that makes it difficult for hypnotic subjects to discriminate the ideas, thoughts, and wishes that are inside their heads from the reality outside them (Bowers & Bowers, 1972). This state of affairs is nicely illustrated by a subject in an experiment on meditation, who was asked to stare at a blue vase in a passive, receptive manner. After a few minutes, the subject reported "At one point it felt . . . as though the vase were in my head rather than out there. . . . I think that I almost felt at that moment as though, you know, the image is really in me, it's not out there" (Deikman, 1963, p. 334).

Evidently, a passively receptive posture makes it increasingly difficult to maintain the inside-outside boundary, with the result that external objects can be experienced as inside one's head and that thoughts, fantasies, and wishes can take on the quality of external reality. It is at this point of suspended reality testing (however achieved) that the idea of a spider, say, can be mistaken for the external presence of one. And if the idea of a spider is aroused by a suggestion administered to a person whose reality testing has been suspended by the induction of hypnosis, the result may be a hypnotic hallucination of a spider.

How different is the state of affairs for the person simulating hypnosis! The simulator actively and critically attends to the so-called demand characteristics of the situation, which continuously tell the person how to appear hypnotized. A major source of demand characteristics is of course represented by the hypnotic suggestions themselves. It is the simulator's implicit reality-testing orientation toward suggestion demands to hallucinate a spider that effectively maintains the distinction between the *idea* of a spider on one hand, and the *perception* of a spider on the other. Hence, the simulator does not hallucinate a spider, but he can purposefully act as if he did.

In sum, the important distinction between hypnotic and simulating subjects rests on the difference between a passive-receptive mode of attention and an active-scanning mode of attention (cf. Silverman, 1968; Deikman, 1971; Bowers & Bowers, 1972). The simulator subject *actively* attends to the hypnotic suggestions, thereby maintaining the distinction between an internally generated idea and the perception of an external reality. The hypnotized subject attends to the hypnotist's suggestions in a *passive*, uncritical fashion. The attentional passivity constitutes the breakdown of a reality-testing orientation toward the suggestions, and it is this breakdown that permits the hypnotic subject to accept an internally generated idea of a (suggested) spider as corresponding to the external presence of one. Similar idea-to-percept transformations can of course take place because of sensory deprivation or with certain psychotomimetic drugs, such as LSD. Some mystical and religious experiences in which an idea of God, say, is experienced as the uncanny perception of a presence (James, 1960) can also be explained in these terms. It is no accident that these experiences frequently take place under conditons of relative sensory isolation and/or extreme fatigue.

Perhaps it is worth stressing that a deeply hypnotized subject can accept an internally generated idea as a convincing perceptual experience even without a specific suggestion to that effect. The idea may "bubble up" from the hypnotized person's past learning or knowledge. For example, a person may in fact "see" a convincing blue afterimage after hallucinating a yellow color patch, yet he may not realize the extent to which his or her previous knowledge of complementary colors determined the afterimage effect (cf. Barber, 1964a). Recall also Pattie's famous case of uniocular blindness, in which the subject, who studied how to appear blind in one eye, evidently did not realize the extent to which later success on the visual test depended upon her prior knowledge and practice. Recall also Orne's demonstration of "spontaneous" dominant arm catalepsy in hypnotized persons who had been erroneously informed, on an earlier occasion, that such behavior was an invariable manifestation of the hypnosis.

There are endless examples of this sort. What should be underlined is that hypnotized subjects' previous knowledge by no means invalidates their behavior as genuinely hypnotic. To argue otherwise implies that responsiveness to suggestion is also an artifactual manifestation of hypnosis, since, after all, suggestions (as well as prior knowledge) simply inform a "hypnotized" person how to behave. This approach completely overlooks how differently suggestions and/or prior knowledge are processed by hypnotized and by simulating persons. In hypnotic subjects, a suggested idea (or one that arises spontaneously) takes on sensory-perceptual qualities; in simulating subjects, it does not.

The Hypnotic Trance

These comments about the suspension of a reality-testing orientation have brought us ever closer to a consideration of the trance aspect of hypnosis. Indeed, Shor (1959) has argued that *"any state in which the generalized reality-orientation has faded into relatively nonfunctional unawareness may be termed a trance state"* (p. 591; emphasis in original). However, as we have mentioned earlier, the whole concept of trance or altered states of consciousness (ASC) has recently been sharply criticized. Consequently, before considering hypnosis as an ASC, we shall briefly review some of these criticisms and point out their inadequacies.

Criticisms of trance. Some critics claim that the view of the hypnotic state or trance as an ASC is based on a circular concept (Barber, 1964c; Sarbin & Coe, 1972), since it is inferred from the same behavior it presumably explains. (How do you know a person is in a hypnotic state or trance? Because of his or her responsiveness to suggestions. Why is the person responsive to suggestions? Because he or she is in a hypnotic trance.)

There is no question that this sort of circularity would be unflattering to the trance concept if it were true. But it need not be. For example, the charge of circularity stands only if it is presupposed that hypnosis causes or explains suggestibility. In fact, however, suggestibility may only be an index of hypnotic depth, and an imperfect one at that. To illustrate this point, Hilgard (1969b) has pointed out that people snore while asleep but that it would be odd to conclude that sleep causes snoring, since people frequently sleep without snoring. Nevertheless, if we know only that a person is snoring, we can reasonably infer that he is also sleeping. In other words, snoring is an imperfect index of sleep. Similarly, suggestibility may be an imperfect index of a hypnotic state— frequently associated with it, but occasionally not.

The distinction between trance as a cause of suggestibility and trance as a concomitant of it is very important to maintain. For, if we presuppose that the connection between trance and suggestibility is a causal one, we have made it unreasonable to investigate the relationship any further. On the other hand, if we simply assume that there is a relationship between trance and suggestibility, then it makes eminently good sense to investigate the nature and magnitude of this relationship. What is clearly needed to cash in on this investigative possibility is a "hypnotic state index" that is independent of suggestibility and that can be correlated with it. As we shall soon see, such an index has been developed in the form of verbal reports of trance depth.

Before examining this evidence, however, it is important to note that any attempt to rely upon a subject's report of trance depth comes equipped with problems of its own—or so critics of the trance state maintain. As these critics have pointed out, verbal reports are influenced by a host of manipulable antecedent variables. For example, if previously hypnotized people are asked "Did you experience the hypnotic state as basically *similar* to the waking state?" 83% respond yes (Barber, Dalal, & Calverley, 1968). If the question format is changed to "Did you experience the hypnotic state as basically *different* from the waking state?" 64% of the sample again report affirmatively. In other words, what a person says about the trance experience seems to change as a function of how the question is phrased (see also Barber & Calverley, 1969).

The general tenor of this argument is that verbal reports of trance are behavioral consequences of the question format and, therefore, *not* of trance per se. However, as Orne (1972b) has cogently argued,

the fact that [biased] wording of questions distorts Ss' responses is well known in the area of public opinion . . . and ought not to be taken as evidence that the manner in which questions are phrased determines the experience that the S is reporting [p. 424].*

Indeed, the appropriate questioning technique involves an unbiased, neutral phraseology that permits the subjects to report what they have experienced, rather than a leading question that elicits obviously distorted answers. "To discover the wording of questions as antecedent variables determining responses is to confuse an artifact with substantive data" (Orne, 1972b, p. 424). As we shall soon see, subjects can in fact report on ASCs in a way that reflects not merely the question format but also their own subjective experiences of trance depth. These reports then become primary sources of data regarding hypnosis as an ASC.

The essential inadequacy of Barber's attack on trance flows from his preferred methodology. For Barber, "the main task of science is to specify quantitatively how variations in one or a combination of antecedent variables affect the dependent variables—the behaviors that are to be explained" (Barber, 1969, p. 14). This ultrabehavioristic, input-output view of science can only attribute observed differences in outcome to observed differences in inputs. Since a trance state is a conditon of the organism—or, if you will, a way of processing information—it is not an observable input; therefore, it cannot, according to Barber's model, explain outputs. In other words, an input-output model in which behavioral outcomes can be explained only by stimulus antecedents is simply blind to ASCs (Bowers, 1973a). This is the real reason why verbal reports of trance depth are not taken seriously by Barber. Since trance is nonexistent within Barber's input-output model, it cannot account for differences in subject's reports of trance depth; as an outcome variable, these reports can be accounted for only by an observable input, such as question format.

In sum, for Barber to deny the existence of trance on the basis of this input-output model of science is a little like denying the existence of four-inch fish after fishing with a net having five-inch holes; everything that is most important about hypnosis simply slips through the methodological net—undetected (Bowers, 1973b). It is important to understand that no conceivable experiment conducted under the auspices of this input-output view of science could ever affirm the existence or usefulness of trance. Since trance is precluded on methodological grounds, it cannot be concluded on empirical grounds that the notion of trance state is unwarranted or silly.

Investigations of hypnosis as an ASC. So much for the objections to

---

*From "On the Simulating Subject as a Quasi-Control Group in Hypnosis Research: What, Why, and How?," by M. T. Orne. In E. Fromm and R. E. Shor (Eds.), *Hypnosis: Research Developments and Perspectives.* Copyright ©1972 by Aldine Publishing Company. This and all other quotes from this source are reprinted by permission.

the trance concept. It is now time to come to grips in a positive way with the idea of trance. The literature on ASCs is growing impressively as a result of a fairly recent "rediscovery" of subjective experience (for example, Gill & Brenman, 1959; Shor, 1959, 1962, 1970; Tart, 1969, 1970b, 1972b; Prince, 1968; Deikman, 1971). Whatever their differences may be, all these accounts agree that trance involves a loss in "generalized reality orientation" (Shor's phrase) such that the subjects become more or less oblivious to everything around them, except perhaps for a very limited range of stimuli in which they can be totally absorbed. Thus, trance can describe the experience of total involvement with a novel, in which the reader so identifies with the story's hero that he experiences the hero's feelings, fights his battles, feels his pain, and so on (Shor, 1970; J. Hilgard, 1970). Alternatively, the person can let himself become so completely absorbed in the words of a hypnotist that the suggestions subjectively create for the person the reality they describe.

But we must be careful here not to identify the simple experiential impact of a hypnotist's (or novelist's) words with an ASC. An ASC, or trance, may permit suggested "realities" to flourish, but it is not synonymous with them. Of several investigators who have focused on the trance aspect of hypnosis, Tart has provided one of the best descriptions of a trance experience (1972b, pp. 469–472). He reports the subjective experiences of a single case, William, who is profoundly hypnotizable. At various states of hypnotic depth, William experiences the following: (a) a marked physical relaxation; (b) an experience of "blackness" that fills itself in as he becomes more deeply hypnotized; (c) a feeling of peacefulness; (d) a diminished awareness of his immediate environment; (e) a diminished sense of identity until, finally, he feels *he* no longer exists and, at the same time, an increased *potentiality* to become anything or anyone; (f) a joke-like feeling that all of these experiences are taking place at the same time; (g) an increased awareness at first of the hypnotist's identity, which then becomes more distant and remote until the hypnotist is just a voice; (h) a sensation that time is passing more slowly until, finally, "his experiences are somehow timeless, they do not have a duration or a place, an order in the scheme of things"; (i) an increased sense of oneness with the universe; (j) a spontaneous diminution of mental activity to an ultimate zero level; (k) a feeling that his own breathing at first grows deeper and then gradually becomes almost imperceptible.

It must of course be remembered that these are the experiences of a single person. There is, however, other evidence that systematically investigates the more qualitative aspects of the hypnotic experience across a number of persons. Arvid As (1967; As & Ostvold, 1968) interviewed 50 female subjects regarding their immediately preceding hypnotic experiences. Each S's interview data were then rated on a 3-

point scale for the (degree of) presence or absence of various experiences
that had previously been selected on empirical and theoretical grounds
for their relevance to hypnosis. The results were then submitted to a
statistical procedure called factor analysis, by which various groupings of
experiences (that is, factors) were identified. As termed Factor I (the first
factor to emerge) the *experience of trance.* Included in this factor were such
experiences as loss of volition, a sense of unreality, a lack of location,
feelings of being totally absorbed in the ongoing experience, and a
lowered conscious awareness. Factor II involved experiences that are
anathema to hypnosis, such as the need to maintain self-control, the
presence of various disturbing thoughts and ideas, an attitude of self-
observation, and the tendency to be distracted by external ideas. As
termed this factor the *experience of ego control.* Finally, Factor III consisted of
feelings of movement, such as sinking or falling, a wish to let go or
surrender, a feeling of trust in the experimenter, and so on. This factor
was called a *desire for regression.*

The next step was to correlate these various experience factors with
hypnotic susceptibility as evaluated on a modified version of the SHSS:A
(see Table 5-1). Factor I (the experience of trance) correlated .69 with
hypnotic susceptibility; Factor II (ego control) correlated −.41. Surprisingly, Factor III (desire for regression) correlated only .07 with hypnotic
susceptibility. Whatever else the pattern of data may show, it clearly
supports the notion that trance experiences are very much a part of the
experience of being hypnotized.

Field and Palmer (1969) adopted a somewhat similar approach but
with a much larger sample of subjects (109 males, 114 females). After
receiving the SHSS:A, subjects were awakened from hypnosis and
administered an inventory of 38 experience-tapping items, each of which
had previously been shown to correlate with hypnotic susceptibility.
Subjects' responses to these 38 items, and to the 12 items of the SHSS:A,
were then submitted to a factor analysis. The first factor that emerged
was termed *hypnotic depth.* All the SHSS:A items were represented on this
factor, together with experiences of absorption, unawareness, compul-
sion, and unusualness. Factor two, *unawareness* by name, was identified by
a lessened awareness, loss of time sense, and obliviousness to and
separateness from external surroundings. These first two factors seem
to reflect trance-like aspects of hypnosis. The third factor, termed
challenge factor, reflected the apparent inability of subjects to behave in
ways proscribed by the hypnotic suggestions (for example, "no matter
how hard you try, you won't be able to bend your arm"). In sum, two
studies have identified experiential groupings, or factors, that clearly
show the trance-like involvement of deep hypnosis.

Unsuggested sequelae of hypnosis. Further support for this trance, or altered state, view derives from the unintended and unsuggested aftereffects of hypnosis. In over a decade of experimental work with hypnosis, I have heard subjects complain of headaches, dizziness, sleepiness, nausea, and once or twice of more serious symptoms while they were being hypnotized or after being aroused from hypnosis. These subjects have always constituted a small but significant minority, and anyone working in the field of hypnosis should be on the lookout for these symptoms of discomfort (while assiduously avoiding any implicit suggestion that such sequelae will occur).

In two studies more than a decade apart, J. Hilgard (1974a; Hilgard, Hilgard, & Newman, 1961) systematically investigated sequelae to hypnosis. In the earlier study, she found that 17 out of 220 subjects (7.7%) reported some unpleasant aftereffects of hypnosis; in the more recent investigation, 37 out of 120 subjects (31%) reported similar sequelae. None of the effects persisted indefinitely, and most of them were over in less than an hour.

The rather striking increase in the frequency of aftereffects revealed by Hilgard's two studies is probably due to differences between the culture of the late 1950s and that of the early 1970s. The use of drugs has of course skyrocketed in the last 15 years and may be a relevant factor in the increase of hypnotic aftereffects. Once in my own research, hypnosis clearly revivified a bad "drug trip" and caused some momentary discomfort to the subject.

Such sequelae support the view that hypnosis is something much more than a simple, straightforward attempt to please the hypnotist and satisfy experimental demand characteristics. Rather, these aftereffects support the view that hypnosis involves a sort of "primitivization," or regression, of psychological functioning (that is, trance) that many subjects enjoy immensely but that others find threatening and distressing. The discomfort is sometimes expressed in terms that have historical significance for the subject—for example, by reliving a bad drug experience. Ironically, there seems to be little or no relationship between the depth of hypnosis and the occurrence of aftereffects, just as there seems to be little relationship between depth of hypnosis and its therapeutic effectiveness (which I shall discuss in Chapter 9).

Studies of trance depth. Yet another sort of evidence supporting the trance view of hypnosis derives from attempts to measure "depth of trance" empirically. We have already discussed how hypnotized subjects show qualitative changes in subjective experience that cluster into various ASC groupings, or factors. Let's now shift our focus from qualitative distinctions to differences in the degree to which trance depth is achieved. This depth can be measured rather easily, because people who are capable of ASC experiences find it quite simple to translate their subjective feelings into a numerical index of trance depth, thus providing a public record of an otherwise very private set of internal and difficult-to-describe experiences. Undoubtedly, such a quantitative index distorts or altogether misses some of the qualitative features of the trance experience. But its advantages far outweigh its disadvantages, since a numerical scale of hypnotic depth allows us to look for patterned relationships of hypnotic depth that can be correlated with other aspects of hypnosis, such as hypersuggestibility.

Although a variety of "depth scales" have been employed (see Tart, 1972b), it may be helpful to describe the instructions for one such scale before reporting the findings of various experiments exploring hypnotic depth. In one investigation, Tart (1970b) employs what he calls the "Long Stanford Scale" of hypnotic depth. The subject is given the following instructions:

> During your experience of hypnosis, I will be interested in knowing just how hypnotized you are. You will be able to tell me this by calling out a number from zero to ten, depending on how hypnotized you feel yourself to be. *Zero* will mean that you are awake and alert, as you normally are. *One* will mean a kind of borderline state, between sleeping and waking. *Two* will mean that you are lightly hypnotized. If you call out the number *five*, it will mean that you feel quite strongly and deeply hypnotized. If you feel really very hypnotized, you would call out an *eight* or *nine*. *Ten* will mean that you are very deeply hypnotized, and you can do just about anything I suggest to you. Naturally, hypnosis can increase and decrease in depth from time to time, and that is the kind of thing I'll be interested in finding out from you [Tart, 1970b, p. 111].*

The instructions go on to tell some subjects (N = 20) to report the first number that pops into their minds (instant report); other subjects (N = 15) are told to think carefully about their psychic condition before reporting a number that represents the trance depth achieved (deliberate condition).

State reports were requested after the induction procedure and following every item on the SHSS:C. At the end of the SHSS:C, a detailed inquiry about the nature of the subject's suggestion-specific hypnotic experiences was carried out.

One major analysis of this study involved correlating the subjects' *mean* depth reports with their objective score on the SHSS:C. In the instant-report condition, the correlation was .85; in the deliberate-report condition, the correlation was .65. Thus, the correlation between hypnotic depth and hypnotic suggestibility was quite high, especially when the subject did not deliberate much on the appropriate number to report.

As the author himself sees, however, the experiment does not avoid a potential difficulty. Since the subject gives state reports after every

*From "Self Report Scales of Hypnotic Depth," by C. T. Tart, *International Journal of Clinical and Experimental Hypnosis*, 1970, *18*, 105-125. Copyrighted by the The Society for Clinical and Experimental Hypnosis, April 1970. Reprinted by permission.

scale item, it is quite possible that these reports are influenced by success or failure on the item just preceding. It is as if the subject said to himself "if I passed that item, I must really be hypnotized" or "since I didn't do well on that item, I must not be very hypnotized." The potential impact of suggestibility on depth reports is problematic, since we are seeking an *independent* measure of hypnosis.

This difficulty can be virtually eliminated by correlating the number of scale items passed with the subjects' *first* state report—that is, the report given after the induction of hypnosis but before any specific hypnotic suggestions are administered. This tactic means that the subjects have to estimate their hypnotic depth totally uninformed as to whether they are responsive to specific suggestions. Under these circumstances, subjects in the instant-report condition showed a correlation of .61 between their initial state report and their overall SHSS:C score; the analogous correlation for the deliberate condition was .58. As one might expect, employing the *initial* instead of the mean state report detracts somewhat from the correlation between state report and suggestibility.

However, in the instant-report condition, if the initial state is correlated with the suggestion-specific *experiential* score (instead of with the number of scale items actually passed), the correlation remains a high .79. In the deliberate-report condition, the comparable correlation is a somewhat lower .63. Generally speaking then, the correlation between initial state reports and suggestions as experienced is higher than the correlation between state reports and suggestions as enacted—especially when the state reports are given instantaneously, without much thought or consideration.

In another investigation, Hilgard and Tart (1966) also demonstrated fairly high correlations (generally about .70) between state reports and suggestibility with several groups of *both* hypnotized and waking-imaginal subjects. Table 6-1 helps us to understand what is going on

Table 6-1. Suggestibility scores (modified SHSS:C; 10 items)

Initial state reports prior to suggestibility tests	Imagination instructions		Hypnotic induction	
	No. of Ss	Mean	No. of Ss	Mean
3—very hypnotized	0	—	5	6.9
2—hypnotized	5	5.0	21	5.7
1—drifting	38	2.5	43	4.0
0—normally awake	38	2.2	12	1.3

From "Responsiveness to Suggestion Following Waking and Imagination Instructions and Following Induction of Hypnosis," by E. R. Hilgard and C. T. Tart, *Journal of Abnormal Psychology*, 1966, *71*, 196–208. Copyright 1966 by the American Psychological Association. Reprinted by permission.

here. Five subjects in the hypnotic-induction condition gave initial state reports indicating they were very hypnotized; no subjects in the waking-imagination group did so. In the hypnotic group, 21 subjects said they were hypnotized, whereas only 5 subjects in the imagination group did so, and so on. In other words, hypnotic induction considerably increased the number of subjects who initially stated they were hypnotized.

The data under the two columns marked "Mean" represent the average number of SHSS:C items passed by subjects at each level of hypnotic depth. Whether or not the subjects were in the imagination or in the hypnotic condition, the suggestibility went up as the reports of hypnotic depth increased. Clearly, however, the distribution of subjects in the two conditions indicates that a higher mean level of suggestibility was achieved in the hypnotic condition than in the waking-imaginal condition. Thus, although the correlations between hypnotic depth and suggestibility were about the same in both the imaginal and the hypnotic conditions, the number of deeply hypnotized individuals was greater in the hypnotic condition, as was the average level of suggestibility.

Nevertheless, it must be acknowledged that some subjects in the waking-imaginal condition became somewhat hypnotized even though they had not received a trance induction. This is probably due to the fact that responding to suggestions may itself help to induce a hypnotic state in some people (Tart, 1970b). Be that as it may, when the authors looked at state reports at various levels of suggestibility, they found "that for an equal amount of suggestibility response there is a lesser state report for the nonhypnotized than for the hypnotized subjects" (Hilgard & Tart, 1966, p. 205).[5] Consequently, state reports are providing additional information not contained in the suggestibility data per se.

The difference between hypnotic depth and suggestibility would surely snap into focus if exceptionally deep hypnosis were accompanied by somewhat *diminished* responsiveness to the hypnotist's suggestions. This possibility has not been systematically explored, but it has been hinted at by a variety of investigators (Hilgard & Tart, 1966; White, 1937; Shor, 1962; Burgess, 1965). As it is, the distinction between suggestibility and hypnotic depth is clear enough if we keep in mind that the *experience* of hypnosis is simply not the same as the overt enactment of suggested behavior. Separate measurements of experiential and behavioral aspects of hypnosis empirically confirm the warrant of this intuitively plausible claim.

Trance logic. One aspect of hypnosis that deserves special attention is the so-called *trance logic* of the deeply hypnotized subject (Orne, 1959). This notion is best introduced by an example. If a profoundly hypnotized subject is given suggestions to negatively hallucinate a chair that is in the middle of the room, he will not see it. Nevertheless, as we noted earlier in this book, if the subject is given further suggestions to remain hypnotized and to walk around the room with his eyes open, *he will not bump into the chair* (Orne, 1962a). Clearly, such a person is effectively registering the presence of the chair at one level, even though he does not appreciate the chair's presence at another, more conscious level of experience. The situation is somewhat analogous to that of a sleep walker who can negotiate a complex environment without serious injury, even though by ordinary waking standards he remains oblivious to his surroundings (Kales, Paulson, Jacobson, & Kales, 1966).

Interestingly enough, a simulating subject given instructions to negatively hallucinate a chair will generally make a point of bumping into it. He does so under the mistaken idea that this would inevitably happen to a genuinely hypnotized subject who was negatively hallucinating the chair. What the simulator does not realize is that it is possible to register reality at one level while remaining unaware of it at other levels of experience. By ordinary logic, it makes no sense to simultaneously see and not see a chair; by trance logic, this paradoxical possibility is realized without difficulty.

Trance logic is exemplified in a variety of ways. A hypnotized subject given suggestions to hallucinate a person sitting in a chair will often acknowledge seeing the back of the chair right through its hallucinated occupant. This "illogical" state of affairs is quite readily accepted as reasonable by the deeply hypnotized person. Equally acceptable is the simultaneous presence of an actual person and his or her hallucinated double. The hypnotized subject viewing both the real person and the person's hallucinated counterpart will simply resign himself to this unusual "doubling" of reality, whereas the simulator, who knows that such things are impossible, will ordinarily deny the existence of one or the other image.

A dramatic example of trance logic involves a curious incident with an age-regressed subject. As reported by Orne (1972b):

> Another S who spoke only German at age six and who was age regressed to that time answered ["Nein"] when asked whether he [understood] English. ... When this question was rephrased to him 10 times in English, he indicated each time in German that he was unable to comprehend English, explaining in childlike German such details as that his parents speak English in order that he not understand. While professing his inability to comprehend English, he continued responding appropriately in German to the hypnotist's complex English questions [p. 427].

Orne goes on to indicate that simulators, bound by ordinary rules of logic, recognize the incongruity of such a conversation and consequently do not perpetrate such nonsense.

Finally, recall the deeply hypnotized subjects given suggestions for hypnotic analgesia, who suffered ischemic pain at one level that they did not feel at all at another level of experience (see Chapter 2). Here too we have an incongruous set of events that appears illogical by ordinary standards, but which nevertheless seems to characterize the behavior and experience of deeply hypnotized subjects.

The position taken by some investigators that trance logic does not characterize hypnosis (Johnson, Maher, & Barber, 1972) is a difficult one to maintain (Hilgard, 1972). In my judgment, the notion of trance logic does point to an important aspect of hypnosis, since it is simple enough to demonstrate in deeply hypnotized subjects and is absent in ordinary, alert subjects. What's more, trance logic embodies the important and fertile idea that a person can register information at one level of functioning that remains unappreciated at other levels (cf. Hilgard, 1973a, 1974). A number of "hard-nosed" experimental investigations support such a multilevel state of affairs (for example, Dixon, 1971; Kahneman, 1973), and some forms of psychopathology seem to presuppose the existence of multiple, quasi-independent levels of informational processing (cf. Ellenberger, 1970).

The human possibilities for multilevel functioning, demonstrated so nicely by trance logic, must be kept in mind when evaluating experiments that might otherwise cast doubt upon the genuineness of hypnosis. For example, admissions of pain by the "hidden observer" in studies of hypnotic analgesia (see Chapter 2) do not invalidate or disqualify the subject's honest denials of pain under "open report" conditions. Similarly, hypnotically induced deafness is not undone by the subject's muscle potential response to a loud tone (see, for example, Malmo et al., 1954) nor by the subject's apparently paradoxical ability to respond appropriately to verbal suggestions that he or she supposedly cannot hear. Such anomalies simply point to complexities in nature that go beyond the simple minded idea that you either have pain or you don't, that you either hear something or you don't, and so on. This sort of simplistic account of perception is false, but a mistaken allegiance to it has raised doubts about the validity of various hypnotic phenomena by encouraging acceptance of organic deafness, say, as *the* standard of what it means not to hear anything. Consequently, any difference *at any level* between organic and hypnotic deafness is sometimes taken as evidence that the latter is not genuine. Clearly, hypnotic deafness is not the same in all particulars as organic deafness. Indeed, it is the difference between them that makes hypnotic deafness so interesting, pointing as it does to some of the subtleties of what it means to hear (or not to hear). Hilgard (1973a, 1974) has begun to develop a neodissociation theory of hypnosis that more adequately and forthrightly comes to terms with some of these genuine complexities. I will say more about this issue in Chapter 8.

An experimental demonstration of trance. I have been maintaining throughout this chapter that hypnosis cannot be reduced to suggestibili-ty. Specifically, I have emphasized that deep hypnosis also involves an altered state of consciousness. Evidence for this trance aspect of hypnosis derives from (a) empirically identifiable experience clusters that correlate with susceptibility, (b) some hypnotic sequelae, (c) the direct reports of trance depth that correlate in reasonable ways with measures of suggestibility, and (d) the trance logic exemplified in deep hypnosis. A final sort of evidence regarding the importance of trance to an understanding of hypnosis is more experimental in nature. In particular, two studies by Evans and Orne (Orne & Evans, 1966; Evans & Orne, 1971) deserve special consideration because they illuminate the altered-state view of deep hypnosis.

These investigators assumed that a hypnotic state has a sort of psychic inertia, such that an abrupt interruption in the hypnotic proceedings would not immediately terminate hypnosis. To legitimize such an interruption required a certain amount of ingenuity. The problem was finessed by hypnotizing well-trained subjects with a tape recording that was suddenly interrupted by a rigged power failure. The interruption occurred after the subjects were given suggestions to (a) keep their eyes tightly shut, (b) keep their right arm stuck fast to their chair, and (c) tap out the rhythm of hallucinated music with their foot. Just as this last suggestion was given, the power failure occurred, affecting not only the tape recorder but room lights and various other equipment as well. The experimenter then jumped up and ran out of the room, audibly muttering "the damn fuse" as he left. Of course the experimenter did not check the fuse but, instead, went into the adjacent room to observe the subject's behavior. As expected, subjects took about 10 to 20 minutes to emerge from hypnosis, a process later described by them as "difficult."[6]

What makes this experiment particularly informative is the behavior of the subjects who simulated hypnosis. The reader will recall that simulators are under instruction to fake hypnosis with a hypnotist who does not know which subjects are genuinely hypnotized, and which are not. The first time Orne and Evans (1966) conducted the "disappearing hypnotist" experiment, five out of six simulators behaved as if they were hypnotized for the entire duration of the experimenter's absence from the room (about 30 minutes). In other words, the simulators apparently "out-hypnotized" the genuinely hypnotic subjects—an outcome properly regarded by the authors as problematic.

The problem was that the investigators had paid insufficient attention to subtle but important demand characteristics that simulators viewed with suspicion. For example, the presence of a one-way mirror may have suggested to them that their behavior was in fact being monitored, even though the experimenter was no longer in the room. This possibility in turn implied that the power failure was not genuine but was instead part of the experiment. As we have noted earlier, simulators tend to persist in their "hypnotic" performance when they think their behavior is being experimentally evaluated.

The second experiment in this series (Evans & Orne, 1971) took care to remove all basis for suspicion regarding the genuineness of the power failure. For example, the one-way mirror was covered, and the subjects were instead viewed through a hole in the wall covered by a silk-screen painting. This little-used but effective means of observation was unsuspected by the simulators, as indicated by their relatively prompt termination of hypnotic-like behavior. Table 6-2 provides the data for both experiments. It will be noted that the hypnotic subjects' behavior changed very little from the first to the second experiment, whereas the simulators' behavior altered rather dramatically. Incidentally, although the simulators in the second experiment ceased their charade soon after the experimenter left to check the errant fuse, they resumed their hypnotic act when they heard his returning footfalls 40 minutes later. The genuinely hypnotic subjects did not behave in this manner but, instead, remained alert and expressed curiosity about the power failure.

Table 6-2. Performance of hypnotic and simulating subjects following a power failure perceived as a part of the experiment or as an accident

	Time (in minutes)			
	Power failure perceived as part of experiment		Power failure perceived as an accident	
	N = 6	N = 6	N = 6	N = 6
Response	Simulating	Hypnosis	Simulating	Hypnosis
Eyes opened	25	11	2	17
Foot stopped tapping	17	2	4	11
Arm lifted	22	15	12	19
No. of Ss who did not open eyes by 30 minutes	5	1	0	0
No. of Ss who opened eyes immediately after E left	0	0	5	0

From "The Disappearing Hypnotist: The Use of Simulating Subjects to Evaluate How Subjects Perceive Experimental Procedures," by F. J. Evans and M. T. Orne, *International Journal of Clinical and Experimental Hypnosis*, 1971, *19*, 277–296. Copyright © 1971 by the Society for Clinical and Experimental Hypnosis. Reprinted by permission.

The results of these two experiments are revealing in several ways. First of all, they confirm in a particularly illuminating fashion our earlier discussion regarding the importance of experimental demand characteristics; subtle and easily overlooked factors in the experimental situation can have a profound impact upon an investigation's outcome. More important from our current perspective, the hypnotic subjects, in contrast to simulators, were virtually unaffected by differences in experimental demands. This stability of genuine hypnotic behavior over

two importantly different experimental setups "suggests that hypnotized Ss were not responding maximally to the cues inherent in the
situation, but rather were responding to those cues derived from their
ongoing subjective experience" (Evans & Orne, 1971, p. 290).

It is of course just this experiential aspect of hypnosis that I have
continually emphasized in this chapter. Hypnotic subjects are not
actively trying, in any ordinary sense, to behave purposefully in
accordance with role requirements (Sarbin, 1950), demand characteristics, or hypnotic suggestions. Instead, suggested events are experienced
as *happening to them* in ways that would require active effort to resist.
Somehow, an altered state of consciousness helps to create this effortless
involvement in the suggested state of affairs.

Weitzenhoffer and Sjoberg (1961) are especially clear about this
issue. They point out that subjects seen under conditions of waking
suggestibility tend to experience *themselves* as working to produce the
suggested effects. They do so by actively concentrating on the
suggestions, repeating them over and over, and so on. However, when
these same subjects were hypnotized, they experienced the *hypnotist* as
doing all the work while they themselves did nothing. Indeed, one subject
commented that it was the hypnotist who concentrated for her
(Weitzenhoffer & Sjoberg, 1961, p. 218). Evidently, hypnosis is adding
something important to the way in which suggested behavior is
experienced, even though a particular person's suggestibility may change
very little from waking to hypnotic conditions. It is this experiential
quality of hypnosis that is so easy to neglect while emphasizing the
behavioral manifestations of hypnotically suggested behavior.

Footnotes

[1]The demands for simple compliance are even stronger in other experiments.
For example, in Barber and Calverley (1963), subjects are told "Everyone
passed these tests when they tried. . . . I want you to score as high as you can
because we're trying to measure the maximum ability of people to imagine. If
you don't try to the best of your ability, the experiment will be worthless and
I'll tend to feel silly" (p. 108).

[2]Barber and Glass (1962) found a correlation of waking to hypnosis
suggestibility of .85.

[3]Although there is an element of arbitrariness in selecting any particular
hypnotic susceptibility scale over another as a criterion measure, the SPS:I is
particularly suited for this purpose. It taps a broad range of perceptual-
cognitive distortions and has relatively few items in common with the BSS
and SHSS scales, which are more similar to each other than either is to the
SPS:I. As a demanding and difficult scale that emphasizes alterations in
perception and experience, the SPS:I comes closer to directly tapping the
experiential character of hypnosis than the other two scales.

[4]The fact that the correlations of the SHSS with the criterion measure of

hypnotic susceptibility are higher than those of the BSS is interesting for other reasons, having to do with the relatively greater amount of social compliance invited by the BSS.

[5]This fact is not apparent in Table 6-1, since the table looks at suggestibility as a function of state report instead of the other way around.

[6]In effect, this outcome answers the oft-asked question about the fate of a hypnotized person who is, one way or another, abandoned by the hypnotist. In effect, such a person eventually terminates his or her own involvement with hypnosis.

7.
The Correlates of Hypnotic Susceptibility

The last two chapters have shown that hypnotic susceptibility is a personal characteristic of considerable stability, identified as much (or more) by a quality of experiencing as by overt responsiveness to suggestion. The last chapter in particular has brought us closer to some sort of understanding of the hypnotic experience.

The full understanding of a phenomenon, however, is possible only if the phenomenon becomes conceptually and empirically embedded in a wider frame of reference. For example, it is not obvious that falling water and a lump of coal have something in common until it is understood that they are both sources of energy. It is the *concept* of energy, which connects various and diverse empirical entities or events, that allows us to understand each of them better by virtue of appreciating what they have in common.

The Trait Approach

The search for commonalities in psychology is typically the province of correlational research. Thus, an investigator simply assesses two or more variables for each of many persons. The magnitude of the relationship between the variables (how variation in one is accompanied by variation in the other) can then be expressed in a correlation coefficient. However, even when they are very high, correlation coefficients are not self-explanatory; they need to be conceptualized and understood in ways that make the empirical connection psychologically (and not just statistically) significant.

Investigators have long attempted to better understand hypnotic susceptibility by seeking out its correlates. Only fairly recently has this effort been rewarded by some curious but fascinating results. It has been discovered, in fact, that hypnotic susceptibility correlates with such diverse things as the direction of a person's gaze when asked a question, a certain pattern of brain waves, imaginativeness, and a history of unrealistic experience in the person's daily life. The conceptual basis for these and other connections is not immediately apparent, and it is probably not singular. Nevertheless, these correlational findings do embed hypnotic susceptibility in a context of relationships that deepens our understanding of it.

But we have gotten ahead of ourselves. The hunt for correlates of hypnotic susceptibility was initially quite unrewarding. The early investigations employed various personality inventories in an attempt to establish a relationship between hypnotic susceptibility and various personality traits, such as acquiescence, neuroticism, and hysteria. Although it was reasonable to expect such relationships, they did not emerge (Deckert & West, 1963; Barber, 1964d; Dana & Cooper, 1964; Hilgard, 1965). It is not that susceptibility never correlated with any trait; it simply did not do so reliably. Sometimes a moderately high correlation would be reported in one study, but another investigation would not replicate the finding and would sometimes even reverse the direction of correlation from plus to minus. As one team of authors concluded, "There may indeed be personality traits which distinguish persons of relatively different degrees of hypnotic susceptibility, and these traits may be well worth discovering; but it seems quite clear that they are not going to be discovered by any of our existing gross personality inventories. . . . It is time to stop doing studies [of this sort] and to seek a fresh approach" (Schulman & London, 1963, p. 159).

The largely negative findings of this approach means that there is no simple answer to the oft-asked question "What kind of person can be hypnotized?" Indeed, the fact that hypnotic susceptibility does not correlate with enduring personality traits suggests to some workers that hypnosis is more accurately viewed as the outcome of more transient attitudinal and motivational characteristics of the person (Barber, 1964d).

A subject's attitude and motivation regarding hypnosis are undoubtedly important; after all, an ordinarily susceptible subject can, for a variety of reasons, be uncooperative and resist becoming hypnotized. And systematic attempts to relate persons' attitudes toward hypnosis with hypnotic susceptibility do yield moderate correlates (Shor, Orne, & O'Connell, 1966), especially in women (Melei & Hilgard, 1964). As we have seen, however, hypnotic susceptibility is a stable characteristic of a person, and it is unlikely that this stability derives from patterns of attitude and motivation that are readily modifiable. Nor, for that matter, is it necessary for this stability to derive from an association with some other personality trait; hypnotic susceptibility seems to be stable in its own right.

Still, the negligible correlations between hypnotic susceptibility and other stable personality characteristics are surprising. Perhaps our understanding of hypnosis would be advanced by exploring some possible reasons for these unexpectedly low correlations.

The Trait Approach Reconsidered

(1) A common assumption regarding personality traits is that they should express themselves across a wide spectrum of behavior. Thus, a person with a high trait of aggression would be aggressive in all circumstances; an acquiescent person would be forever yielding; and so on. In fact, traits do not have the degree of cross-situational influence that they were expected to have (Mischel, 1968; Peterson, 1968; Bowers, 1973b). An acquiescent person who frequently yields to another's influence may rise up in rebellion when pushed too far, and an aggressive person may be very tender and forbearing when making love. Finally, a person who is highly susceptible to hypnosis displays this characteristic clearly under a very limited set of circumstances; indeed, there is only one way to tell for sure how susceptible a person is, and that is to hypnotize him!

In sum, the low correlations between hypnotic susceptibility and various personality traits may derive from the fact that such traits are more limited and specific in their impact than was initially suspected. Consequently, traits such as deference and acquiescence may simply have little to do with becoming hypnotized.

(2) It may be that hypnotic susceptibility does correlate with other personality characteristics but only in people preselected for certain *other* qualities. Rosenhan (1969), for example, found that an index of warmth correlated with susceptibility in low-anxious people (r = .60) but not in high-anxious people (r = -.18) and only marginally across people of both temperaments (r = .25). This so-called moderator analysis may indeed boost correlates of susceptibility, but its limitations become obvious if too many moderator variables are necessary for respectable correlations to emerge. If hypnotic susceptibility correlated with acquiescence only in low-anxious, aggressive, but self-effacing middle-aged females, the theoretical and practical value of the finding would be limited indeed (Wallach & Leggett, 1972). There is, however, very good reason to employ sex as a moderator variable in every attempt to find correlates of hypnotic susceptibility (Bowers, 1971b). As we shall see later, the pattern of susceptibility correlates is very different in men and women.

(3) A third reason why hypnotic susceptibility may not correlate highly with personality traits rests more in the nature of hypnosis per se and less in the limitations of the trait view of personality. As we have already seen in Chapter 5, a particular hypnotic susceptibility *score* may be a relatively invalid index of hypnotic suscept-*ability*. In other words, a particular hypnotic performance may reflect less a person's hypnotic

susceptibility than his or her apprehension, concern for autonomy, lack of familiarity with hypnosis, and so on. These attitudinal and motivational variables may ordinarily be more significant for a beginner at hypnosis than for a seasoned veteran. Consequently, one might expect the pattern of correlates with susceptibility *scores* to change as a function of experience. Early on, it may be that attitudinal and motivational variables are well represented in susceptibility scores, and, consequently, variables tapping this attitudinal domain should correlate with performance on a hypnotic scale. When and if these attitudinal factors begin to fade as important influences on hypnotic performance, the associated pattern of correlations should also change: attitudinal correlates of susceptibility should diminish, and variables tapping the ability and experiential domain should show a stronger relationship with hypnotic performance.

Although this scenario may well be erroneous in its particulars, there is some evidence supporting the likelihood that correlates of susceptibility shift with experience (Melei & Hilgard, 1964; Evans, 1972). This may be one important reason why personality correlates of susceptibility lack reliability across different investigations. If different investigators use subjects of varying hypnotic experience, the pattern of susceptibility correlates may well change from one study to the other.

(4) Still another, and perhaps more fundamental reason for the low correlations between hypnotic susceptibility and various personality traits may be due to subtle complexities inherent in hypnosis itself. This possibility has been articulated by several investigators, and it will be informative to consider briefly a few of these formulations.

White (1937) suggested that there are two forms of hypnosis—active and passive. The active subject "acts as if his dominant need in the experiment were to be controlled by the hypnotist, to yield initiative, and be his willing instrument" (p. 283). The passive subject, on the other hand, seems unconcerned by the hypnotist and his wishes and instead "behaves as if his dominant need were to enter a sleep-like state, free from the necessity of expending energy" (p. 283). White proceeds to marshal some evidence suggesting that these two different kinds of hypnosis have very different patterns of correlates—a possibility that is obscured when the active-passive distinction is not made. He notes, for example, that the need for affiliation is very high in subjects demonstrating active hypnosis and very low in their passive counterparts.

Shor (1959, 1962, 1970) has extended White's position by arguing for three dimensions of hypnotic depth—hypnotic role-taking involvement, trance, and archaic involvement. According to Shor, *hypnotic role-taking involvement* concerns the subject's ability to act upon the hypnotist's suggestions in a nonvolitional manner. In consequence of the subject's role-taking involvement, "the ongoing hypnotic experiences and behaviors become executed by the subject without the experience of conscious intention and often in defiance of it" (Shor, 1962, p. 29).

Trance depth, as I have previously noted, involves the fading of a generalized reality orientation into a nonfunctional unawareness. The generalized reality orientation maintains the boundary between external reality and the inner world of thoughts and fantasies, so the progressive loss of this orientation (that is, the increasing trance depth) "makes the distinction between reality and imagination progressively less relevant" (Shor, 1962, p. 30). The reader can perhaps intuit this condition by remembering the experience of "coming to," after having been totally and obliviously absorbed in a narrow range of activities. This transition period of "coming to" marks the interface between a trance state and a fully reinstituted reality orientation.

The *depth of archaic involvement* concerns the irrationally heightened importance of the hypnotist to the person being hypnotized. The hypnotist is invested with psychomagical powers that satisfy the subject's archaic, infantile wish fantasies. (A political demagogue, such as Hitler, plays upon these same infantile needs that reside within all of us, but he does so for his own, instead of for his victim's, benefit.) In the clinical use of hypnosis, the profound archaic involvement sometimes experienced by the patient is called transference, and it can be wisely employed by the therapist for his or her client's benefit.

Shor thinks that these three separate dimensions of hypnosis can be represented in equal measure in some subjects but that frequently one or more dimensions can be over- or under-represented in the final hypnotic composite. Shor gives various examples of how a subject having an uneven profile behaves and experiences when hypnotized. For example, if archaic involvement and trance are deep but role-taking involvement is superficial, the subject may be phenomenologically and interpersonally immersed in the hypnotic episode, even though he or she remains disinclined to follow the specific suggestions.

Although Shor does not present empirical evidence to document his three-dimensional view of hypnosis, his theorizing makes uncommonly good sense to me. And if indeed these three dimensions of hypnosis exist, and in different proportions in different subjects, then it is eminently reasonable that correlations of various personality traits with any single index of hypnotic susceptibility are bound to be both low and unreliable.

I have been arguing that the multidimensional character of hypnosis tends to undermine any simple pattern of correlates with hypnotic susceptibility. White's and Shor's theories, as we have seen, support this multidimensional view of hypnosis, and so does some empirical evidence of the multidimensional nature of hypnotic susceptibility, which we are now going to review.

Hilgard and his colleagues (1961) provide strong evidence that hypnotic susceptibility has a bimodal distribution. We can look at this distribution as a two-humped camel, with one "hump," or mode, peaking at a fairly low level and the other, less prominent, occurring at a quite high level of hypnotic susceptibility. That each of these humps defines a qualitatively different dimension of hypnotic susceptibility is a genuine possibility. If this is in fact the case, the correlates of hypnotic susceptibility should change as one shifts from subjects in the lower hump of the distribution to subjects in the higher hump. There is indeed some evidence confirming this possibility (Shor, Orne, & O'Connell, 1962; Bowers, 1971b), but we will forestall consideration of these findings until later. Suffice it to say at this point that, if correlational analyses are performed without regard to genuine dimensional distinctions, the results will be generally unsatisfactory.

In addition to the evidence for the bimodal distribution of hypnotic susceptibility, there are also some other investigations suggesting that hypnotic susceptibility is "factorially complex" (Hilgard, 1965, pp. 270–282). What this means in detail goes beyond the scope of this book. In a very general sense, factorial complexity implies, among other things, that hypnotic susceptibility is not a one-dimensional characteristic. Instead, it seems to be a composite of several factors, or dimensions, that can be differentially represented in various persons. Again, this complexity would work against high-magnitude correlations of other variables with a single index of hypnotic susceptibility.

Summary of Trait View

We have reviewed several reasons why hypnotic susceptibility cannot be reliably correlated with any standard measures of personality. The first two reasons concern limitations of personality traits that work against such correlations. The last two reasons are more specific to hypnosis per se—the shifting proportion of ability and nonability factors as a person becomes more experienced with hypnosis and the multidimensional, or bimodal, nature of hypnotic susceptibility. These last two reasons should have an impact on any and all correlates of susceptibility. Consequently, as we turn to an examination of nontrait correlates of susceptibility, it will be useful to keep in mind the subjects' experience with hypnosis, their level of hypnotic ability, and so on. In general, we should not expect extremely high correlates of hypnotic susceptibility whenever the entire range of any single index of hypnosis is employed; such attempts ignore, among other things, the multidimensional character of hypnotic susceptibility.

Experiential Correlates of Hypnotic Susceptibility

In retrospect, there seems to have been an implicit assumption behind the quest for trait correlates of hypnotic susceptibility: since hypnotized subjects apparently submit so completely to the authority of the hypnotist, they must be very acquiescent sorts of people. As it turns out, acquiescence, deference, and gullibility refer to traits that bear only a very superficial resemblance to what goes on in hypnosis. It should also be noted that the association between submissive-type traits and hypnotic susceptibility was itself an implicit extension of two other tenacious but erroneous notions: (1) subjects who submit to the influence of hypnosis are relatively weak-willed and helpless in the face of a stronger person; and (2) the central feature of hypnosis is the subject's behavioral acquiescence to the hypnotist's suggestions.

This conceptual cul-de-sac was escaped in part because the experiential aspects of hypnosis gradually came into their own. In fact, the hypnotic *experience* is not characteristically submissive in nature, even though hypnotic behavior may appear to be. Submissiveness implies a yielding to external pressure out of some combination of duty, fear, and habit. Although occasioned by outside forces, submissive behavior is experienced by people as something they have done and for which they may feel pride or shame. By contrast, the typical reaction of people enacting hypnotic suggestions for the first time is one of surprise at their own behavior. They are surprised because they do not experience themselves as making the behavior happen; instead, they experience the behavior as happening to them. For example, when suggestions are given to hypnotized persons that their arms levitate, they do not experience themselves as raising their arms; rather, they experience their arms as rising by themselves. Frequently, a subject new to hypnosis will smile in wonderment as the arm goes higher and higher without apparent aid or effort.

Being "visited" in this fashion by various unusual experiences is a central characteristic of hypnosis, although by no means unique to it. As we have seen in Chapter 6, psychotomimetic drugs and sensory deprivation can also engender various "experiential visitations." What is more, some people tend to have uncanny experiences thrust upon them spontaneously in their ordinary waking life. Sometimes these experiences have religious or mystical overtones, but often they are secular episodes that can be terrifying, deeply satisfying, or simply noteworthy. In any event, such episodes are far more frequent than is commonly acknowledged, although their occurrence is often swept under the rug, since they don't "fit" the model of rationality so valued by Western man.

Both Ronald Shor and Arvid As, working independently, recognized that the spontaneous occurrence of these experiential visitations resembled the subjective events reported by hypnotized subjects. It occurred to them that people who had more frequent or intense hypnotic-like experiences in their ordinary waking life might also be more susceptible to hypnosis. In order to test this hypothesis, they developed various so-called experience inventories, which tapped the domain of unusual and uncanny experiences that occasionally thrust themselves upon humankind. Some questions selected from Shor's (1960) inventory follow: (a) Have you ever experienced a part of your body move and had the feeling that it was moving without your volition? (b) Have you ever been unsure whether you did something or just thought about having to do it? (c) Have you ever had the mystical experience of oneness with the universe, a melting into the universe, or a sinking into eternity?

A surprisingly high percentage of students acknowledged having had these sorts of experiences (see also As, O'Hara, & Munger, 1962). Moreover, when advanced statistical techniques were applied to subjects' experiential reports, two main "experience clusters" emerged (As, 1962b; 1963; As et al., 1962). One such cluster reflected an ability to become totally absorbed in something, whether it be nature, art, or a particular role. The second major cluster involved a tolerance for unusual trance-like experiences, in which the persons felt somehow separated or dissociated from their ordinary ways of experiencing things, and in which logical considerations were in abeyance. Both of these response clusters, based on reports of unusual *waking* experience, seem to have a great deal in common with the experience of hypnosis. For example, we have already seen how dissociation and absorption were also quite prominently represented in subjects' reports of *hypnotic* experience (As, 1967; As & Ostvold, 1968).

Direct attempts to relate the unusual experiences of waking life to hypnotic susceptibility have yielded a fairly reliable, albeit modest, correlation, usually between .25 and .50 (As, 1962b, 1963; Shor et al., 1962, 1966; Lee Teng, 1965; Van Nuys, 1973). As promising as these results are, they either have not been replicated by other investigators (Barber & Calverley, 1965; London, Cooper, & Johnson, 1962) or have been replicated only for one sex (Bowers, 1971b). Moreover, even the successful studies contained bothersome inconsistencies. For example, the study by Shor and his associates (1962) found no correlation of hypnotic susceptibility with the *frequency* of hypnotic-like experiences in waking life—only with their intensity. Still, the many successes with the experience inventories are something to savor after so many disappointing attempts to find correlates of susceptibility.

Some interesting patterns emerge if the correlations between experience inventories and hypnosis scores are computed only for subjects who are in the higher "hump" of hypnotic susceptibility. On strictly statistical grounds, such a restriction of range should diminish the size of the resulting correlations. But, in fact, the limited evidence on this question suggests that the correlations increase. For example, Shor and his co-workers (1962) found that in their eight most susceptible subjects the intensity of personal experiences correlated .84 with hypnotic susceptibility. Bowers (1971b) found that in 12 highly susceptible women a similar index of experiential intensity correlated .68

with hypnotic susceptibility. (High-susceptible men, on the other hand, showed a near-zero correlation between these two indices.) Thus, we have some indication (albeit based on small samples) that the correlates of susceptibility increase as we focus on high-susceptible subjects, especially women. This outcome supports our previous contention that subjects in the higher hump of hypnotic susceptibility are qualitatively and not just quantitatively different from subjects low in susceptibility. Moreover, the possibility of sex differences in the correlates of susceptibility is beginning to emerge. On his experience inventory, for example, As found that hypnotizable women were inclined to mystical and illogical experiences and to changes in mental states because of social influences or reading, whereas hypnotizable men reported more unusual experiences of an impulsive, aggressive sort. In general, women's unusual experiences tended to be linked more to external stimuli, whereas men's were triggered more by internal, drive-related conditions.

Disregarding for a moment the sex-related nature of these findings, a tendency for absorptive and dissociative experiences stimulated by external (rather than by internal) events seems closer to the interpersonal character of hypnosis. Indeed, in her elegant research on hypnosis as imaginative involvement (see below), J. R. Hilgard (1970) comes to a similar conclusion. She states that "the distinction between stimulus-incited and . . . impulse-incited imagination appears to be an important one in relation to hypnotic susceptibility, with such evidence as we have pointing to greater hypnotizability on the part of those capable of stimulus incitation" (p. 103). Thus, the external *source* of waking hypnotic-like experiences may be as important as their occurrence in understanding the relationship between hypnotic susceptibility and various experience inventories.

Now, if it is true that women are more responsive than men to external excitations of hypnotic-like episodes in their ordinary, waking life, perhaps they are also more susceptible to hypnosis. The evidence on this issue is somewhat mixed, but denials of woman's superiority in this regard may be based in part upon limitations of the susceptibility scales employed. If the scale items are not sufficiently difficult, they may not be able to discriminate genuine sex-related differences in the upper range of hypnotic susceptibility. In two studies where such scale limitations were not a problem, women did indeed prove to be more hypnotizable than men (Shor, Orne, & O'Connell, 1966; Bowers, 1971b).

Hypnosis and Absorptive Experiences

In reviewing the experiential aspects of hypnosis and related waking phenomena, allusions to the subjective sense of complete absorption in the ongoing experience seem to occur over and over again. Although such absorption is often identified with a trance view of hypnosis, this is not always the case. For instance, Sarbin and his colleagues totally eschew the trance concept of hypnosis, but nevertheless refer to the "organismic involvement" of subjects who are deeply hypnotized, "bewitched" or otherwise immersed in what they are doing and experiencing (Sarbin & Coe, 1972, pp. 71–76). Whether such absorption is called "trance" or "organismic involvement" is of course less relevant than recognizing the importance of this experiential component to an understanding of hypnosis. Several lines of research dramatize this absorption experience quite nicely.

Van Nuys (1973) asked 47 male undergraduates to focus attention on their own breathing for 15 minutes. The attention requested of the subject was the passive sort depicted in the last chapter. The subject was instructed as follows:

> . . . I am going to ask you to close your eyes and focus your attention on your breathing. I don't want you to try to change your breathing. Nor do I want you to think about your breathing or try to analyze it. I just want you to watch yourself breathing . . . to focus on the in-and-out of your belly [p. 64].

The subject was further instructed to press a button whenever he got caught up in a distracting thought that interfered with his concentration. It was hypothesized that the number of button presses would be *negatively* related to the effectiveness of subjects' attention (absorption, for our purposes). In addition, all the subjects were administered, among other things, the Harvard Group Scale of Hypnotic Susceptibility.

The results showed a correlation of –.42 between the number of button presses and hypnotic susceptibility. According to the author, "good hypnotic *S*s, on the average, tended to experience 35 fewer intrusions during meditation than did the poor hypnotic *S*s. Thus, reasonably good concentration seems to be a necessary condition for hypnotizability" (p. 66). It is unfortunate that this study employed only men and did not use a measure of susceptibility that was more advanced and demanding than the group scale. It is possible that rectifying either or both of these limitations would provide even better evidence for the relationship of attention (absorption) and susceptibility to hypnosis.

Tellegen and Atkinson (1974) proceeded in a very different fashion to demonstrate essentially the same point. They developed a questionnaire based in part on items culled from various experience inventories. Other items assessed various personality traits, such as ego resiliency and ego control. This questionnaire was administered to several samples of women (total $N = 471$), and the results were submitted to factor analysis. Three major factors emerged, but only one of them—absorption—was consistently related to indices of hypnosis, with correlations ranging from .27 to .43. Two examples of items that help to define this absorption factor are (1) "The sound of a voice can be so fascinating to me that I can just go on listening to it"; and (2) "If I wish, I can imagine (or daydream) some things so vividly that they hold my attention in the way a good movie or story does" (p. 270).

The authors state that the absorptive attention defined by these and similar items involves a *"full commitment of available perceptual, motoric, imaginative, and ideational resources to a unified representation of the attentional object"* (Tellegen & Atkinson, 1974, p. 274). They further argue that such absorption precludes thoughts *about* the primary representation, such as "this is only my imagination." Moreover, absorbed individuals seem impervious to external stimuli that would ordinarily be distracting.

Parenthetically, this experience of total involvement can have an ineffable quality that refreshes and revitalizes the perceiver (Schachtel, 1959) and may serve as one basis for both peak experiences (Maslow, 1968) and creativity (Bowers & Bowers, 1972). Indeed, the available data reflect a correlation between hypnotic susceptibility and performance on tests of creativity (Bowers & van der Meulen, 1970). The relationship is manifested more in women than in men (Perry, Wilder, & Appignanesi, 1973), and it is especially evident in high-susceptible women (Bowers, 1971b). The relationship between creativity test performance and the intensity of unusual *waking* experiences is also greatest in high-susceptible women (Bowers, 1971b). Thus, we have further evidence that correlates of hypnotic susceptibility are moderated both by sex and by susceptibility itself.

Perhaps the most compelling case for the importance of absorption to an understanding of hypnosis has been made by J. R. Hilgard (1970) in her book *Personality and Hypnosis: A Study of Imaginative Involvement*. In this fascinating and eminently readable account, the author reports the evidence of carefully conducted clinical interviews with subjects of varying hypnotic ability. She found that

> the hypnotizable person was capable of a deep involvement in one or more imaginative-feeling areas of experience—reading a novel, listening to music, having an aesthetic experience of nature, or engaging in absorbing adventures of body or mind [pp. 4–5].*

Hilgard reviews in considerable detail the sort of involvement reported by hypnotizable subjects across a spectrum of activities, such as reading, drama, religion, sports, and so on. I shall limit consideration here to the relationship between hypnosis and reading.

One highly susceptible subject related her experiences of hypnosis and involvement with reading in the following way:

> Hypnosis was like reading a book. . . . It's stronger in a way than reading. When I get really involved in reading, I'm not aware of what is going on

*From *Personality and Hypnosis*, by J. R. Hilgard. Copyright 1970 the University of Chicago Press. This and all other quotes from this source are reprinted by permission.

around me. I concentrate on the people in the book or the movie and react the way they react. The intense concentration is the same in a book or a movie or in imagination as it is in hypnosis. Reading a book can hypnotize you [p. 24].

The intensity of reading involvement that some people can experience is brought home by another subject, who became engrossed by the novel *Lord of the Flies*. Hilgard paraphrases the subject's account as follows:

Toward the end when Ralph was being chased by the rest of the boys and they meet a naval officer, [the subject] was suddenly aware that she had been the height of a young boy, that she had been running with the boys, and that "all of a sudden, when the young naval officer appeared, I felt I grew a couple of feet" [p. 28].

As it happens, there are many people who read frequently and with considerable enjoyment, but who nevertheless do not become totally absorbed in the material in the manner described above, and it is precisely subjects' rating of emotional involvement in reading that correlates with hypnotic susceptibility. Table 7-1 shows this relationship. Clearly, high-involved readers are much more likely to be susceptible to hypnosis than low-involved readers.

Table 7-1. The relationship between reading involvement and hypnotic susceptibility

Reading involvement	Susceptibility (SHSS-C)		
	Low	Medium	High
High	2	6	5
Medium	8	8	13
Low	18	16	6
	$X^2 = 9.61; p < .05$		

From *Personality and Hypnosis*, by J. R. Hilgard. Copyright 1970 by the University of Chicago Press. Reprinted by permission.

The capacity for this depth of involvement seems to develop early in life—before the onset of adolescence. Indeed, on the basis of her interview data, Hilgard suggests that there might be a critical period for the emergence of absorptive skills. Moreover, she notes that "if such a capacity has been absent for any length of time it cannot be recaptured" (p. 32). If these conjectures are correct and applicable to involvement with hypnosis as well as with reading, they may account at least in part for the increasing stability of hypnotic susceptibility with age.

One possible basis for the development of absorptive skills that emerged from Hilgard's study was a complete surprise: there seems to be a relationship between hypnotic susceptibility and the (remembered) severity of punishment received as a child. Thus, "of those most severely punished, 41 of 63 subjects, or about two-thirds, fell in the upper half of hypnotic susceptibility scores. Of those least severely punished, only 21 of 58, or about one-third, had high hypnotic susceptibility scores" (J. Hilgard, 1972, p. 396). In a later report on a new sample (Hilgard, 1974b), 21 of 42 high-susceptible subjects reported receiving moderate to severe punishment in their childhood, whereas only 2 of 15 low-susceptible subjects received even moderate punishment.

The reason for the relationship between punishment received in childhood and hypnotic susceptibility is perhaps not obvious. However, Hilgard (1974b) has recently found that a majority of high-susceptible subjects psychologically "escaped" moderate to severe childhood punishment by involving themselves completely in fantasy. Since low-susceptible subjects were evidently not punished as severely as high-susceptible subjects, the availability of such fantasy "escape routes" was presumably less important to them. What we may have here is an unexpected embellishment of an old adage: Spare the rod and spoil the child's (later) hypnotic ability. For, if punishment helps to develop in children the fantasy resources necessary for deep hypnosis, unpunished children may not realize their potential for imaginative involvement. On the other hand, alternative "natural hazards," such as boredom, isolation, lack of playmates, and prolonged childhood sicknesses, may also serve to develop in childhood the fantasy skills necessary for adult susceptibility to hypnosis. Moreover, as we have already seen, there seem to be relatively "hazard-free" routes into the development of absorptive skills. So, although punishment may serve as one basis for high hypnotic susceptibility, it is probably not necessary for its development.

We have reviewed evidence suggesting that the capacity for complete subjective involvement (absorption) in an ongoing activity is an important basis for hypnotic susceptibility. And if becoming hypnotized involves both ability and attitudinal components, as I suggested earlier, then surely this capacity for absorption is one important aspect of hypnotic suscept-*ability*. We have also seen that this absorptive skill seems to have a developmental basis and may not be readily subject to significant modification after adulthood. Thus, the capacity for absorption seems to share some important characteristics with hypnotic susceptibility and, indeed, may partially account for some of them.

Hypnotic Susceptibility and Mental Imagery

Since so many absorptive experiences both in and out of hypnosis seem to involve mental imagery of some sort, it seems to make a good deal of sense to ask whether people with better imagery are also more susceptible to hypnosis. The question as phrased is difficult to answer, since the term "mental imagery" does not refer to a singular phenomenon (cf. Richardson, 1969). For example, eidetic, or "photographic," imagery is by no means the same thing as a vivid night dream, yet both qualify as instances of mental imagery. A study by a team of Australian investigators is an especially good example of how various forms of imagery relate differently to hypnotic susceptibility (Sutcliffe, Perry, & Sheehan, 1970).

In the first part of their study, these investigators correlated hypnotic susceptibility with the results of a questionnaire regarding subjects' ability to image in a variety of sensory modalities. For example, subjects were asked to think of the "sun sinking below the horizon" or "the whistle of a locomotive" and to rate the vividness of the resulting image. For men, the correlation between vividness of imagery and hypnotic susceptibility was .58; for women it was .20. Upon closer examination of their data, however, the investigators found that poor imagers tended to be unsusceptible to hypnosis, whereas vivid imagers tended to be both high and low in susceptibility. When the extremes of susceptibility were examined, the "highs" had achieved significantly more vivid imagery than the "lows." All in all, the results suggest that if a person is highly susceptible to hypnosis, he or she is probably a vivid imager; but being a vivid imager reveals little about the person's susceptibility. On the other hand, being low in hypnotic susceptibility implies poor imagery, *and* poor imagery implies poor susceptibility.

In a second part of the study, these same investigators explored the relationship between fantasy and hypnotic susceptibility. The measure of fantasy was a "distortion index" based on subjects' reports of night dreams. This index was based on judgments regarding the "possibleness" and "realityhood" of the dream as reported. The more impossible or unreal the dream, the greater the distortion index. Unlike the previous study, the findings of this investigation showed *no* significant relationship between hypnotic susceptibility and fantasy. On the basis of these and other findings (for example, Palmer & Field, 1968), Sheehan (1972) concludes that, "to the extent that imagery and fantasy are different cognitive functions, hypnosis may be more related to the former than to the latter" (p. 311). On the other hand, Shor (1970) and Bowers and Bowers (1972) have argued, more on theoretical than on empirical grounds, that there *is* a close connection between fantasy and hypnosis. So there seem to be some differences of opinion that need to be resolved. Perhaps an illustration can help provide a resolution.

Suppose that a person were interrupted in a flight of "unbidden" fantasy (Horowitz, 1970) and offered a penny for his thoughts. And suppose that he were able to retrieve the content of the fantasy and report honestly and accurately to the effect that he was picturing himself as Hannibal crossing the Alps on an elephant. If the matter were pursued, the subject would be apt to verify that the fantasy had the qualities of novelty, substantiality, vividness, and coloration that Richardson (1969) says characterize imagination imagery. If you were then to take this fantasy output and ask other people to imagine themselves as Hannibal crossing the Alps on an elephant, many of them would be unable to experience the image in the same experiential genre as the first subject. Instead of experiencing the Hannibal-Alps image as effortless and unbidden, they would experience it as effortful and directed; in other words, they would be making the image happen instead of experiencing it as happening to them. On the other hand, there do seem to be people who can accomplish the apparently paradoxical feat of translating an injunction to imagine themselves as Hannibal crossing the Alps into the experience of an effortless, spontaneous-seeming *fantasy*. People who can do this kind of thing readily are apt, I think, to be highly susceptible to hypnosis.

It is important to note that the person who originally imagined himself as Hannibal may not be highly susceptible despite his vivid fantasy life; for, as we have noted previously, it is not simply imaginative involvement that is an important basis of hypnosis but *its ability to be incited by external stimulus conditions*. (Hilgard, 1970). Suppose, for example, that our hero's fantasy of Hannibal were organized around power and aggressive drives and represented a need to maintain control and autonomy. Such an internal dynamic might make our hero suspicious of hypnosis and actually render him *less* susceptible to external suasions than he might otherwise be.

Now, the trouble with a good deal of the negative evidence regarding the role of *fantasy* in hypnosis is that assessments of it do not involve asking the subject to fantasize something; rather, they involve subjects' recall of prior unbidden flights of fancy. In other words, measures of fantasy typically ignore the source of imaginative excitation. For example, in the study by Sutcliffe and his colleagues (1970), the dream distortion index is completely indifferent to this distinction. People who have "distorted" dreams may or may not be susceptible to external excitation of their imaginative involvement—we simply don't know. On the whole, however, we can safely assume that night dreams generally organize themselves around highly idiosyncratic drives and personal concerns, and, consequently, measures of fantasy based on such material are not apt to correlate with hypnotic susceptibility.

On the other hand, *imagery*, which evidently does correlate with susceptibility, is generally assessed by asking subjects to imagine something. Thus, imagery, by the very way it is identified, has an interpersonal character that is fairly close to that of hypnosis. And, as Coe, Allen, Krug, and Wurzman (1974) have argued, "as imagination measures become more like the tasks that are required in hypnotic suggestions, the more predictive they seem to be of hypnotic responsiveness" (p. 159). We can only add that certain sorts of requested or instructed imagery are more apt to have the spontaneous-seeming, unbidden quality characteristic of fantasy.

This last proviso may account for Sutcliffe's (1970) curious finding that vivid imagers were both high and low in hypnotic susceptibility. The vivid imagers who were highly susceptible may have shifted from an image that was bidden (that is, instructed) to one that was *experienced* as effortless and unbidden; their low-susceptible counterparts, on the other hand, may simply have been unable to make this transition and continuously worked instead to maintain the vivid "picture" in their mind. Unfortunately, the authors present no data that bear on this potentially important point. But if this surmise holds up, there is no particular contradiction between Sheehan's (1972) contention that hypnotic susceptibility is related to imagery and the contention by others that it is related to fantasy (Shor, 1970; Bowers & Bowers, 1972); for it is *externally initiated, fantasy-like imagery* that may be most closely associated with hypnosis.

Another related series of studies supports this general view and, indeed, extends it. In work initiated by Spanos (1971), it has been argued that *goal-directed fantasy* is not only a concomitant of hypnotic responsiveness but, at least in some persons, a probable cause of it. By goal-directed fantasy, Spanos means any image that, *if true*, would result in the suggested state of affairs; for example, a person's hand would in fact rise up into the air if it were attached to balloons full of helium; imagining an arm so attached is thus a fantasy directed toward the goal of having one's arm levitate. According to Spanos (1971; Barber et al., 1974) and others (Coe et al., 1974), suggestions that are successfully carried out are generally accompanied by such goal-directed fantasies. However, the data do not clearly support a causal role of goal-directed fantasy vis-a-vis hypnotic responsiveness (for example, Spanos & Barber, 1972).

To summarize this section, it seems clear that there is a modest relationship between hypnotic susceptibility and imagery of a certain kind. Specifically, it has been argued that imagery evoked by an external agency and experienced as effortless and unbidden is most apt to be associated with hypnosis.

Susceptibility and Brain Organization[1]

The question to be considered in this section is whether hypnotic susceptibility and some of its correlates, such as imaginative involvement, absorption, and imagery, have a biological basis. The answer that is beginning to emerge is yes.

It all started with a simple but clinically astute observation by M. Day (1964): when people are asked a question requiring some reflection, they tend to break eye contact and swing their eyes consistently either to the left or to the right. Duke (1968) soon lent experimental support to Day's clinical observation: in response to reflective questions (but not to simple questions of fact), subjects were indeed quite self-consistent in the direction of their lateral eye movements. On the average, 86% of eye movements made by a subject were in the same direction. Bakan and Svorad (1969) reported similar findings.

Personality-related differences between consistent "right-movers" and consistent "left-movers" were noted from the very outset, but Bakan (1969) was the first to investigate whether or not these consistencies were related to hypnotic susceptibility. Dividing his subjects according to susceptibility level, he found that "13 of the 18 right-movers fell in the low hypnotizability group, and 16 of the 24 left-movers fell in the high hypnotizability group" (Bakan, 1969, p. 929)—a statistically significant relationship that has since been replicated (Morgan, McDonald, & Macdonald, 1971; Gur & Gur, 1974). Moreover, Bakan found a tendency for left-movers to have clearer imagery than right-movers. Indeed, all five subjects who rated an (instructed) image as very clear (just like real) were left-movers. Given our previous discussion relating imagery and susceptibility, such a finding cannot fail to pique considerable interest. Just what in the world is going on here?

It has been known for a long time that the brain's left hemisphere controls the right side of the body and the right hemisphere controls the left side. More recently, it has been determined that conjugate eye movement to the left is activated by the right hemisphere and that eye movement to the right is activated by the left hemisphere. And now there is a growing body of literature demonstrating even more profound hemispheric specialization. For most people, the left hemisphere serves verbal, logical, and analytic functions, whereas the right hemisphere serves spatial, imaginative, and synthetic functions (see Galin, 1974, and Ornstein, 1972, Chapter 3, for readable summaries of some of this research).

This evidence for hemispheric specialization converges tantalizingly with some of the findings regarding hypnotic susceptibility. For example, the tendency for high-susceptible subjects to look leftward may reflect a pervasive dominance of the right hemisphere in their every-day functioning. It is, of course, precisely the right hemisphere that specializes in imagery and imaginative functions so important to an understanding of hypnosis. In light of these and similar considerations, it has been proposed that hypnosis is predominantly a right-hemisphere function (Bakan, 1969, 1971).

Data supporting this claim are only just beginning to emerge. I have already indicated in a previous chapter that the alpha EEG range of 7–13 cps is ordinarily accompanied by pleasant, relaxed feelings similar to the subjective experiences of hypnotized subjects. These sorts of experiences seem more congenial to the more passively receptive right hemisphere than to the actively analytic left one. Moreover, we reviewed evidence indicating that susceptibility and alpha production are correlated

(London et al., 1968, 1974; Nowlis & Rhead, 1968). Bakan and Svorad (1969) replicated and extended these findings. First, they found a correlation of .60 between hypnotic susceptibility and percentage of alpha and a *negative* correlation between susceptibility and percentage of eye movements to the *right* ($r = -.77$). Both these results confirm past findings previously reported. In addition, however, they found that the tendency to move the eyes to the *right* (when asked a reflective question) was correlated *negatively* with the percentage of alpha in the EEG of resting subjects ($r =$ about $-.60$). Thus, the more the eye movements to the right, the less the amount of alpha EEG. By implication, of course, eye movement to the left is positively associated with the percentage of resting alpha. This pattern of findings suggests a close interdependence of lateral eye movement, brain wave activity, and hypnotic susceptibility. Evidently, dominance of right-hemisphere functioning in high-susceptible subjects (as indicated by their left-looking tendencies) is associated with considerable alpha production in the resting state.

As it happens, Bakan and Svorad (1969) recorded alpha in the right hemisphere. However, each of the two hemispheres generates its own alpha rhythm, and it is possible to measure the alpha activity in both hemispheres separately but simultaneously. When this is done, the right hemisphere practically always generates more alpha EEG than the left hemisphere, regardless of whether persons are high or low in susceptibility (Morgan et al., 1971; Morgan, Macdonald, & Hilgard, 1974). This finding suggests that the right hemisphere is more "relaxed" and less alert than the more analytic left hemisphere—a possibility that somehow rings true if the right hemisphere is especially important for hypnosis. It seems to follow that, if the right side of the brain is of such central importance to hypnosis, the *proportion* of right-hemisphere alpha to the total amount recorded from both sides should be larger in high- than in low-susceptible subjects. This, however, is *not* the case (Morgan et al., 1971, 1974). Only the *total* amount of alpha is greater in high-susceptible than in low-susceptible subjects.

The qualification above regarding the relationship of susceptibility and brain functioning is only the opening salvo announcing a host of further complexities. For example, Gur and Gur (1974) report that only for males is the direction of eye movement associated with susceptibility. Moreover, this relationship seems to hold primarily for right-handed individuals. In Figure 7-1, we have depicted the varying degrees of association between susceptibility and eye movement when both sex and handedness are taken into account. As the table shows, the direction and magnitude of the relationship is reversed for left-handed females and right-handed males. So what started out as a simple relationship between conjugate lateral eye movement and hypnotic susceptibility has suddenly become much more complex, thereby illustrating a "natural law" of scientific investigation: anything gets more complicated the more closely you look at it.

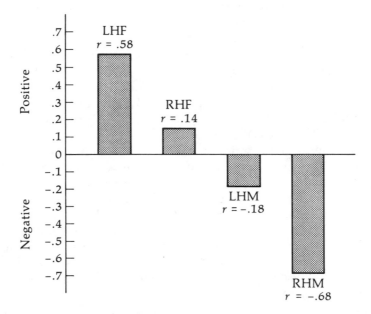

Figure 7-1. Magnitude and direction of correlations between number of eye movements to the right and hypnotic susceptibility for right-handed males (RHM), left-handed males (LHM), right-handed females (RHF), and left-handed females (LHF). From "Handedness, Sex, and Eyedness as Moderating Variables in the Relationship between Hypnotic Susceptibility and Functional Brain Asymmetry," by R. C. Gur and R. E. Gur, *Journal of Abnormal Psychology,* 1974, *83,* 635–643. Copyright 1974 by the American Psychological Association. Reprinted by permission.

A generality does emerge from the Gurs' investigation, however: "the ability to become hypnotized is subserved in the nonverbal, holistic, synthetic, or 'appositional' hemisphere" (Gur & Gur, 1974, p. 640). The complication here is that such functions are often located in different hemispheres for people of different sex and handedness, and in some individuals the lateralization of brain functioning is partial and incomplete. Nevertheless, it is becoming increasingly clear that hypnotic susceptibility and its correlates are deeply embedded in a person's biological organization. This is undoubtedly one reason for the relative stability of hypnotic susceptibility in mature people.

Footnotes

[1]I would like to thank Dr. Arlene Morgan for her helpful comments on this section.

8.
Hypnosis and Dissociation

In examining the correlates of hypnotic susceptibility, the capacity for absorption in externally initiated imaginings emerges as an especially promising variable. Indeed, investigators of quite different persuasion seem to be converging on this conclusion (Spanos & Barber, 1974). Nevertheless, I wish to argue that this "absorptive" account of hypnosis and hypnotic susceptibility is insufficient in important ways that I hope to clarify in this chapter.

Let us begin by recalling a finding presented earlier. In the review of hypnotic analgesia, we found that certain virtuoso subjects were able to block pain from conscious awareness that they could nevertheless detect and communicate through the so-called "hidden observer." In effect, this hidden observer had access to information that was *dissociated,* or split off, from conscious experience (Hilgard, 1973a, 1974). Although such a dissociative process seems extraordinary, let me recount some fairly familiar observations that "normalize" the concept somewhat.

Consider first of all the person who is sound asleep. Ordinarily, we think of such a person as oblivious to his or her surroundings, but a little reflection clearly shows that this is far from the truth. Everyone has had the experience of being awakened by an alarm clock or a baby's cry that must have been "heard" while asleep in order to disturb slumber effectively. Less common, perhaps, are people who talk in their sleep, and who can even respond appropriately to questions put to them by an amused roommate or spouse. Such dialogues are not consciously experienced by the "sleep talker." Then there is the undeniable fact that most adults do not fall out of bed at night. It is my (somewhat hazy) impression that our success in this regard results from unconsciously reconnoitering the bed's boundary by an extension of the arms and legs; when the edge of the bed is thus located, the next major body movement is directed away from it. The ability of the sleeping subject to negotiate the hazards of the bed's edge is of course a mere shadow of the sleepwalker's successful avoidance of reality hazards in his path (Kales et al., 1966).

The point of these examples is to remind the reader that the sleeping subject, although "unconscious" by ordinary waking standards, is very much in touch with some aspects of reality. Or, to put my point somewhat more forcefully, these examples establish the fact that various reality features can be effectively registered in the nervous system without being consciously perceived. (Although it would constitute too much of a digression to review the findings in any detail here, I wish to point out that there is now a fairly extensive literature *not* dealing with hypnosis that establishes this same point with considerable authority— for example, Dixon, 1971; Smith and Groen, 1974; MacKay, 1973; Lewis, 1970.) As we have already seen, the possibility for "registration without perception" seems to be of fundamental importance for trance logic, which permits a deeply hypnotized subject to successfully avoid the negatively hallucinated chair that he does not consciously see. In a similar fashion, hypnotic analgesia can easily be viewed as a negative hallucination of an (ordinarily) painful stimulus, which is not consciously perceived, but which is certainly registered well enough to be detected under specially contrived conditions.

Now, the point I wish to make is that there is growing reason to believe that high-susceptible subjects are especially responsive to information that is somehow "dissociated," or split off, from conscious awareness. Moreover, this ability is manifested not only in hypnosis but in other states as well. In particular, the evidence suggests that, even when asleep, high-susceptible subjects process external information more effectively than low-susceptible subjects.

Before presenting this evidence, however, it is important to mention that hypnosis and normal sleep are quite distinct, despite the fact that the word "hypnosis" derives from the Greek word *hypnos* (sleep), and despite the hypnotist's frequent invocation of the chant "go to sleep." Such sleep suggestions are by no means essential to the induction process; indeed, subjects can be intimidated into something like hypnosis by suggestions inducing a tense "hyperalert state" rather than a pleasant relaxed one (Ludwig & Lyle, 1964). And a very famous hypnotherapist, Milton Erickson, employs a variety of induction techniques that make no reference at all to sleep (see Haley, 1967). However, the final argument for the distinctiveness of sleep and hypnosis is based on their very different patterns of brain waves. Hypnotized subjects typically display an EEG pattern much more like a waking than a sleeping state (Evans, 1972). The fact that sleep and hypnosis are in fact quite different psychological states implies that the evidence that follows points to a *general* mode of functioning by high-susceptible subjects—one not limited to hypnosis per se.

Sleep Learning and Suggestibility

Let us begin with some accounts of sleep learning that were initially recorded by Russian investigators (Hoskovek, 1966, reviews these studies). In one such investigation, 20 out of 25 subjects were able to perceive and remember spoken material presented during natural sleep (Svyadoshch, 1962; reported in Hoskovec, 1966). In all these cases, "the actual process of perception of the texts by [subjects] was not a conscious one: they slept and did not realize that during this period they were hearing and remembering speech" (Hoskovec, 1966, p. 310).

Cooper and Hoskovec (1972) have tried to replicate these Russian investigations of sleep learning. The subjects were first hypnotized and given a set (that is, "primed") to perceive and remember material that would subsequently be presented in their sleep. Then, when the subjects were in a light stage of sleep (Stage 1 REM),[1] they were administered a list of ten Russian words, each with its paired English translation. Immediately after the list of paired words was presented, subjects were awakened and tested for their learning. Under these conditions, about 30% of the material was retained. However, in a waking control condition, 90% of the Russian-English word pairs were mastered. Thus, although the evidence for sleep learning is theoretically exciting, learning while asleep is nowhere near as efficient as learning while awake.

In conducting their study, Cooper and Hoskovec employed subjects highly susceptible to hypnosis. They did so for a reason that is of particular importance to my current discussion. According to the Russian reports, sleep learning is most evident in highly hypnotizable, or suggestible, subjects (Cooper & Hoskovec, 1972, p. 102). What we have here is the strong possibility that effective processing of information while asleep is correlated with hypnotic susceptibility. This conjecture has been confirmed in a series of fascinating investigations recently summarized by Evans (1972).

The general strategy of these studies involved administering simple suggestions to sleeping subjects and monitoring their subsequent behavior for signs of suggestion-specific responsiveness. In the first such study (Cobb et al., 1965), four high- and four low-susceptible subjects were given the following suggestions: "Whenever I say the word 'pillow,' your pillow will begin to feel uncomfortable, and you will want to move it with your hand" and "Whenever I say the word 'itch,' your nose will itch until you scratch it." One of these suggestions was administered during the first emergent Stage-1 sleep, and the other suggestion was administered during sleep Stage 2, 3, or 4. Each of these suggestions was given three or four times before the cue word ("pillow" or "itch") was presented. After the cue word was presented, about 30 seconds were allowed for the suggested behavior to take place.

The results of this first study were quite clear-cut. All four high-susceptible subjects responded behaviorally to the sleep-administered verbal suggestions, but *only* when these suggestions were administered in Stage-1 sleep. The suggested response was successfully cued during the particular period of Stage-1 sleep in which the suggestion had been administered and also in another Stage 1-sleep that occurred later on the same night. By way of contrast, none of the four low-susceptible subjects responded to sleep-administered suggestions. Thus, we have some impressive initial evidence that suggestibility in Stage-1 sleep is associated with hypnotic susceptibility.

For a variety of cogent reasons, the investigators interpreted these results very cautiously and proceeded to conduct another similar experiment of improved design (Evans et al., 1969, 1970). For example, the Stage-1 sleep during which the suggestions and subsequent cue words were always delivered was alpha-free. Since the presence of alpha waves in the sleeping subject often indicates arousal, a requirement that there be no alpha in the pertinent Stage-1 sleep is a conservative estimate of physiological sleep. Another improvement in the experiment involved a reordering of the procedure. Instead of being preselected for their hypnotizability, subjects were first tested in the sleep phase of the study, and then, about a month later, their hypnotic susceptibility was assessed. This safeguard eliminated any possibility that subjects' knowledge of their own susceptibility could subtly affect their responsiveness to sleep-administered suggestions. Moreover, it guaranteed that the experimenters were "blind" regarding the subjects' susceptibility while they were conducting the sleep phase of the experiment. This naivete prevented the investigators from unintentionally biasing the subjects' sleeping suggestibility in a direction favorable to the hypothesis under investigation (Rosenthal, 1966). (The person assessing the subjects' susceptibility was also ignorant of their prior sleep behavior.) Finally, subjects' responsiveness to the pertinent cue words was assessed not only on the same night that the suggestion was administered but during a subsequent night's sleep as well.

During the two nights in which subjects slept at the laboratory, 416 cue words were delivered, and 89 correct responses were observed (21.1%). Sixteen out of the 19 subjects gave clearly defined responses to the appropriate cue words, and the average response rate per subject was 18.2%. A subsequent investigation (Perry et al., reported in Evans, 1972, p. 69) demonstrated that such sleep responses were in fact specific to the combination of suggestions and cues the sleeping subjects had received. For example, a dummy cue word, unrelated to prior sleep-administered suggestions, was ineffective in eliciting the behavior so suggested. And a genuine cue word was effective in triggering off specific behavior only after its related suggestion had been administered; before that time, the cue word fell on deaf ears, so to speak. Thus, we have additional clear evidence that suggestions administered in Stage-1 sleep can have considerable and quite specific impact on the behavior of a sleeping subject.

In the studies by Evans and his associates, the outcome was somewhat complicated by the fact that low-susceptible subjects tended to wake up more often than their high-susceptible counterparts when suggestions or cue words were administered. As a result, low-susceptible subjects were administered fewer total cue words than high-susceptible subjects. It was therefore necessary to employ a percentage score comprised of the proportion of actual cued responses to the total number of cue words delivered. The correlation between this percentage response rate and hypnotic susceptibility was about .40, which was not quite significant by conventional statistical standards. However, this relationship is considerably strengthened when susceptibility is correlated with sleep-cued behavior enacted during the subjects' *second* night of participation in the investigation. The correlation of second-night (percentage) responsiveness and susceptibility varied from .60 to .64, depending upon the particular susceptibility scale employed. This relationship is statistically significant.

Since suggestions were administered only during the first night's sleep, the fact that subjects responded at all to cue words administered during their second night's sleep is somewhat surprising. What is even more remarkable is the behavior of five subjects who returned to the sleep laboratory for a third time. They responded to sleep-administered cues delivered about *five months* after the initial suggestions had been given. This was true even though the suggestion had not been repeated during the interim period and despite the fact that the subjects had no waking memory of the suggestion, of the cue word, or of the behavior elicited by them (Evans et al., 1966).

Another somewhat surprising finding was that suggestibility during sleep correlated more highly with the more difficult and demanding hypnotic suggestions—namely, suggestions for hallucinations and posthypnotic amnesia. Thus, responsiveness to simple motor suggestions in sleep is most closely associated with the profound cognitive distortions characteristic of deep hypnosis. This association is especially evident when suggestibility scores based on the second night's sleep are employed. Apparently, introducing a temporal discontinuity between the initial sleep-administered suggestion and the relevant cue word considerably augments the relationship between sleep suggestibility and the ability to experience deep hypnosis.

All in all, the results of the sleep studies convincingly establish an important point made at the beginning of this chapter: *a person can register and be affected by information he or she does not consciously perceive* (at least by any conventional standard of "conscious perception"). For it is clear that most (high-susceptible) subjects registered fairly complex suggestions while remaining physiologically asleep, maintained this information in operational form over extended periods of time, and acted upon it when confronted with an appropriate cue word that was also administered during sleep. Moreover, all this was accomplished with subjects who, for the most part, had no waking memory of any of the above events.

Perhaps it is becoming clear why the absorptive account of hypnosis and hypnotic susceptibility, although illuminating, is not entirely satisfactory. The capacity for such absorptive involvement does not easily account for the fact that highly susceptible subjects are so much more responsive to sleep-administered suggestions than the low-susceptible ones. It simply presses credibility too far to assume that sleeping subjects, even highly susceptible ones, become imaginatively absorbed in suggestions administered to them while they are asleep. Something else is necessary to account for this phenomenon, and this "something" seems to involve the subject's ability to register and process information that is not fully represented in ordinary waking consciousness.

General Anesthesia and Unconscious Hearing

A particularly dramatic illustration of this ability is demonstrated by surgical patients under general anesthesia. David Cheek (1959, 1966) and others (for example, Erickson, 1963) have for many years been alerting a generally skeptical medical community that anesthetized patients undergoing surgery were able to hear the ongoing conversation of the operating team. To quote Cheek (1959) directly,

> The anesthetized patient may lose all motor reflexes, lose all ability to communicate with the outside world, lose all sense of pain, but the anesthetized patient is able to hear and remember important events at a deep level of subconscious thought. This level can be uncovered and the events recalled by hypnotic techniques [p. 101].

A number of clinical accounts establish the authority of this claim (for example, Brunn, 1963; Cheek, 1959) but a report by Levinson (1967) seems to clinch the issue rather dramatically. Levinson's report begins with a description of a chemically anesthetized patient undergoing plastic surgery. During the course of the operation the surgeon put his finger in the patient's mouth, felt a lump there, and said "Good gracious! . . . It may not be a cyst at all; it may be cancer! . . . "

Back in the ward the next day, the patient was totally oblivious to these comments. Nevertheless, she was depressed and weepy. After several abortive attempts to ameliorate her discomfort hypnotically,

Levinson finally succeeded in "reaching" her. Under hypnosis, the patient was told that if something was disturbing her, her right hand would lift. It did. Soon, amidst a flood of tears, the patient blurted out the surgeon's "Good gracious!" followed by the rending words "He is saying—this may be malignant." After being reassured, the patient was aroused from hypnosis. Her depression had lifted.

As a result of this dramatic episode, Levinson decided to explore more thoroughly the extent to which anesthetized patients registered complex information. He selected the first ten hypnotizable patients over 21 years of age who were willing to participate in some research on anesthesia and brain waves. Each subject was anesthetized with pentothal and his EEG was continuously monitored throughout the course of the operation. When the patient's EEG indicated he was profoundly anesthetized, a signal was given, and the entire operating theater became suddenly quiet. Then the anesthetist, in his most urgent tone of voice, made the following standardized statement: "Just a moment. I don't like the patient's colour! The lips are too blue, very blue! More oxygen please!" (Levinson, 1967, p. 206). After a suitable pause, the anesthetist expressed satisfaction with the patient's condition and the operation proceeded.

Each subject was subsequently seen by the author to assess his recall of the above events. After first hypnotizing the subjects, Levinson age-regressed them back to the time of the operation. Under these circumstances, four out of the ten subjects

> were able to repeat practically verbatim the traumatic words used by the anaesthetist. A further 4 patients displayed a severe degree of anxiety while reliving the operation. At a crucial moment they woke from the hypnosis and refused to participate further. The remaining 2 patients, though seemingly capable of reliving the operation under hypnosis, denied hearing anything [Levinson, p. 202].

To be sure, Levinson's study does not tell us some things we would like to know. For example, we don't know whether hypnosis was absolutely essential for the retrieval of the traumatic information acquired under anesthesia. Nor do we know whether anesthetized subjects low in susceptibility could register and/or recall this information as well as the high-susceptible subjects employed in the investigation. Still, it seems unequivocally clear that at least some chemically anesthetized patients who are hypnotizable do in fact register and retain meaningful and complex information; yet, the information processed in an anesthetized condition is evidently retained in a form that is dissociated from ordinary conscious awareness and is retrievable only with special effort and techniques.

Despite its unavailability to ordinary awareness and memory, information acquired under anesthesia can have a dramatic impact upon a person's functioning (recall, for example, the first patient's weepy depression after "hearing" under anesthesia that she might have cancer). As Cheek (1966) notes, "unconscious people are terribly vulnerable to pessimistic thoughts ... " (p. 275). Consequently, he admonishes surgical teams to be very careful about what they say while operating on anesthetized patients. In fact, he goes further and proposes that they make optimistic and hopeful comments during the course of surgery. Once again, there is evidence that supports his advice. Anesthetized subjects exposed to benign suggestions showed a significant reduction in the need for pain-relieving medication during the postoperative period (Hutchings, 1961). In another study (Pearson, 1961), 43 anesthetized subjects receiving tape-recorded suggestions for a quick recovery were released from the hospital an average of 8.63 days after surgery; 38 subjects receiving tape-recorded music and/or silence were released an average of 11.05 days after surgery. The 2.42 days' difference in the length of time spent in the hospital by these two patient groups is statistically significant. These findings are especially persuasive since the investigation was run double-blind: none of the attending surgeons knew which tape recording their patient was hearing (since the patient wore earphones), and the discharging physician was also ignorant in this regard. Consequently, the decision about when to release a patient could not be influenced by a knowledge of which tape recording the patient had received.[2] As we shall see in the next chapter, therapeutic suggestions administered to hypnotized, instead of anesthesized, subjects can also have a pronounced and positive effect on the course of various maladies.

For now, however, I shall confine myself to a summary of the implications of the anesthesia studies in order to see how they advance our understanding of hypnosis. Clearly, these studies support the contention that people can register information and be profoundly affected by it even though they have no conscious perception of the information in question. A demonstration of this process with anesthetized patients perhaps makes it easier to accept the possibility that a similar dissociation of input from conscious perception may occur in hypnosis, especially deep hypnosis. We have already seen how severe pain can be registered at one level while remaining unappreciated at other, more conscious levels of experience. And we can now see more clearly how hypnotically deaf subjects can honestly deny hearing a verbal suggestion or a loud noise and yet respond to them; for it now makes very good sense to say that such persons do not consciously *realize* they hear the auditory input. To claim that the subjects' responsiveness to such an input proves they were not deaf is certainly true, but it misses the crucial point. One might as well argue that the anesthetized subject "really heard" the surgeon's remark or "really felt" the pain of the surgeon's knife. To be sure, anesthetized subjects evidently do discern sound (and perhaps pain) *at some level;* but it is equally clear that they do not consciously hear or hurt in the same exquisite way that they would without the anesthesia. From the patient's point of view, the difference is decisively important. Similarly, the fact that deeply hypnotized subjects respond to sound when they are "deaf" and show some evidence of pain when they are analgesic does not mean they experience sound and pain at the same level or in the same fashion as they would in an ordinary waking state. And, again, the difference is decisive.

Dissociation and Absorption

I have been maintaining that highly hypnotizable subjects can dissociate better than their low-susceptible counterparts. By dissociation I have meant the ability to register (and sometimes respond to) information that is not consciously perceived. This superior capacity for dissociation in highly hypnotizable subjects not only is revealed in hypnosis—where it seems basic to trance logic—analgesia, and other classic hypnotic phenomena but is also manifested in responsiveness to sleep-administered suggestions and to helpful or hurtful comments made while the subject is anesthetized.

This superior capacity for dissociation is doubtless operative in waking life too, as suggested by the experience inventories reviewed in the last chapter. A particularly striking example of such waking dissociation was brought to my attention by an extraordinarily hypnotizable young lady who was also a very talented singer. She acknowledged nearly panicking on several occasions during operatic performances because she had no clear memory of having sung an aria that, according to ongoing music, she must have just completed. It is as if the young lady had been so absorbed in singing that even the sound of her own voice was somehow dissociated; that is, it was not fully integrated into a conscious awareness of herself singing. In effect, there had been very little of "her" left over to notice that "she" was singing.

Perhaps this illustration provides a clue regarding how dissociative and absorptive aspects of hypnosis are related. Specifically, I would like to argue that the capacity for dissociation of a highly susceptible subject facilitates his or her absorptive involvement in reading, drama, hypnosis, and so forth. The rationale for this position is briefly presented in the following paragraphs.

There is clearly adaptive value in processing information without having to do so consciously. If we were forced to attend consciously to every facet of our environment, we could never concentrate on any one thing for very long. We would be, to understate the case, highly distractible. On the other hand, there is considerable advantage in processing peripheral information outside of awareness—in other words, preattentively (Neisser, 1967). For if we were *totally* unresponsive to anything except what occupied consciousness, our cave-dwelling ancestors, for example, would have been easy prey indeed for various stealthy creatures looking for dinner. It is crucial that we be able to register background sounds at a relatively low level of analysis without having to continuously focus conscious attention on them. In this way, when something that may be significant does happen (a twig snapping on the ancient veldt; our name paged at a modern airport), we can quickly attend to the input consciously and take appropriate action.

What I am suggesting is that highly susceptible people are better able than low-susceptible ones to process and appraise information preattentively—that is, without being distracted from their primary involvement. Recall, for example, that high-susceptible subjects were seldom disturbed by suggestions administered to them while they slept, whereas low-susceptible subjects were frequently awakened by the presentation of the suggestions. Thus, low-susceptible persons may need to awaken somewhat in order to determine whether the noise they registered while asleep constitutes a significant input; high-susceptible persons, on the other hand, may be able to make this "decision" at a lower level of analysis that does not disturb their sleep. Similarly, deeply hypnotized high-susceptible subjects may process and appraise peripheral information preattentively, thereby preserving their effortless absorption in the hypnotist's ongoing suggestions. By contrast, low-susceptible subjects may find themselves constantly "peeking" at various internal and external stimuli in order to appraise them, thus preventing the total and uninterrupted concentration necessary for deep hypnosis (cf. Evans et al., 1969, p. 475). Certainly the study by Van Nuys (1973) reviewed earlier suggests that low-susceptible subjects are more distractible than the high-susceptible ones.

It may be, of course, that low-susceptible subjects can also concentrate uninterruptedly on hypnotic suggestions, but only with extraordinary effort. But this effortful, actively directed attention seems to be precisely what the high-susceptible subjects do *not* engage in. Rather, they typically experience their attention as effortless, almost as if the hypnotist were doing their concentration for them (Weitzenhoffer & Sjoberg, 1961). It is this effortless concentration, which we earlier called *passive attention*, that seems characteristic of deeply hypnotized individuals. Perhaps, then, it is the seemingly effortless attention to the task at hand (hypnotic suggestions, reading of a novel, and so on) that is permitted and preserved by the highly susceptible subjects' talent for dissociation; conversely, the relative lack of such talent on the part of the low-susceptible subjects may be the reason why they often experience themselves as working hard to concentrate—the better to overcome various internal and external distractions by "brute force."

These comments relating dissociative and absorptive aspects of hypnosis are frankly speculative and in many ways unsatisfactory. They are, however, rendered with the hope of encouraging research more organized around the subtleties of attention, perception, and information processing than has been true in the past.

Even now, however, it seems evident that hypnosis reflects in especially illuminating fashion some of the subtle complexities of thinking and perceiving that ordinarily escape our notice. In particular, hypnosis involves absorptive and dissociative experiences that are less visible than hypnotic suggestibility per se but that are perhaps even more important in determining the domain of hypnosis (Hilgard, 1973b). Many of the objections lodged against the genuineness of hypnotic phenomena simply evaporate when they are considered in light of these absorptive and dissociative possibilities: hypnotic amnesia may not be like never having known something, but the subjects' temporary unawareness of what they know is nevertheless genuine; hypnotic analgesia to the cold pressor may not duplicate exactly the reaction of an arm placed in lukewarm water, but the subject's lack of experienced pain is no less genuine for that. Only when the multilevel quality of human perception, thinking, and experience is acknowledged, can we begin to make sense of these apparent paradoxes. Only then can we recognize that hypnotic phenomena are indeed genuine.

Footnotes

[1]As it happens, there are four different stages of sleep, each with distinctive EEG patterns. REM is the acronym for rapid eye movement that appears in Stage-1 sleep. Night dreams are most often associated with Stage-1 REM sleep (see Evans, 1972).

[2]It is too bad that the investigator was unable to assess the participating patients' hypnotic susceptibility. According to the notions developed in this chapter, highly hypnotizable subjects under anesthesia should be more affected by benign suggestions than low-hypnotizable subjects.

9.
Clinical Implications and Applications of Hypnosis

In this last chapter, I will review some of the evidence regarding the clinical effectiveness of hypnosis. The range of human problems to which hypnosis has been applied with at least presumptive success is truly extraordinary, so that it would be impossible to review adequately all the relevant clinical uses of hypnosis in an entire book, let alone in a single chapter. Consequently, I will again be highly selective in my presentation. For those readers interested in broader and/or more esoteric accounts of clinical hypnosis, the following sources may be of help: Schneck, 1963; Haley, 1967; Wolberg, 1948; Kroger, 1963; Brenman and Gill, 1947; Rosen, 1953.

A Case Study

When I first heard about her problem, I was not optimistic that I could be of any help. The patient, a 40-year-old woman, had literally dozens of open sores the size of silver dollars all over her body. They were extremely tender and sensitive when touched—and it was impossible for all of them to remain untouched at the same time. The disorder had been diagnosed by skin specialists as an extreme case of hidradenitis suppurative, a sort of colossal acne caused by a tendency for the sweat glands to become infected and form huge, festering pimples. Some of the worst ones had been surgically removed, especially those on the face and arms that would have made her socially repugnant.

The patient had suffered this malady for more than 20 years and had received the attention of some of the most competent medical authorities on the continent. They had virtually guaranteed the patient that a very expensive operation to remove all the sores would not prevent their return and that eruptions would continue until she ran out of sweat glands. The patient was desperate, but she had also become convinced that hypnosis could be of help.

As a clinical psychologist who had worked with hypnosis both in treatment and in research contexts, I was willing to try to help her; a previously reported success with a similar case (Jabush, 1969) suggested that hypnotic treatment might well be of real benefit to the patient. As it happens, the patient was an excellent hypnotic subject, who readily behaved and experienced in accordance with suggestions. We met more or less regularly for about three months, with one prolonged inter-ruption necessitated by the patient's hospitalization.

During the course of treatment, I administered repeated suggestions for the patient to imagine herself being sprayed by or swimming in shimmering, sunlit liquids that would purify and cleanse her skin. I also told her to become aware of her skin and to experience it as warm and cold, as prickly and smooth, and so on—suggestions that constituted lessons in skin awareness and control, so to speak. She was instructed to practice these exercises by herself and, especially, to imagine her skin as smooth and unblemished.

At the end of treatment, the patient was virtually free of sores. The tendency for pustules to form remained, but, instead of progressing to monstrous open wounds, they retreated promptly and soon disappeared. Her dermatologist was amazed, and, frankly, so was I. A recent two-year follow-up revealed that the problem was still under control.

Just exactly what "ingredient" or combination of ingredients was responsible for the dramatic remission of symptoms is not clear; whether hypnosis was essential to the cure, or the vivid imagery, or simply the patient's conviction that I could cure her remains unknown. What is virtually certain, however, is that the effective remedy was psychologi-cally induced. Just as psychological problems can precipitate psychoso-matic disorders, such as ulcers and migraine headaches, so can psychological factors engender "psychosomatic cures."

Partly because the patient in this case study had suffered such a disfiguring and painful malady for so long and partly because the disorder had not succumbed to more conventional remedies, the successful treatment of the patient's condition by hypnosis seems especially dramatic. However, there is considerable evidence in the clinical literature that hypnotic treatment of skin problems is not at all uncommon.

Hypnosis and the Cure of Warts

Perhaps the skin disorder most frequently treated by hypnotic suggestions is warts (Allington, 1952; Ullman, 1959). Warts are classified as epidermal tumors, and they seem to be caused by a virus. Their appearance and disappearance, however, seem to be occasioned by psychological factors that alter the biochemical balance of the skin. For example, on the knuckle of the forefinger of my right hand, there is a small, nearly invisible layer of skin that used to be a wart and may become one again under certain biological conditions obscurely related to my psychological state. This particular wart has appeared and disappeared at least three times that I can remember, and its eruption is generally accompanied by several other warts in the same general area.

The fact that warts come and go "spontaneously" is of course a problem whenever it is claimed that the warts of a particular patient have been successfully removed by hypnosis; for it is always possible that the treatment accidentally coincided with a natural remission that would have occurred even without treatment. By the same token, however, the fact that warts often disappear spontaneously strongly suggests that they can thrive only in a relatively narrow range of biological environments that is frequently exceeded in the ordinary course of events. It is but a small step to suggest that a biological environment outside this critical (that is, wart-viable) range can be artificially induced by various psychological treatment regimens. In sum, it may be true that the spontaneous remission of warts creates hazards for a definitive claim of treatment success in any particular cure of warts by hypnosis; such natural remissions, however, render plausible the general claim that warts are susceptible to psychological treatment. Let us review a few pertinent investigations.

Ewin (1974) reported on all four patients he had treated for condyloma acuminatum—a condition in which warts appear on the genitalia or around the anus. Although his strategy differed somewhat for each patient, Ewin typically gave hypnotic or waking suggestions for the patient to experience the affected areas as warm, producing dilation of the blood vessels and enhancing the supply of white blood cells to fight the infection. The warmth was to be maintained

> until the warts are healed and your skin becomes normal in every way. You can forget about the warts and turn your conscious thoughts to other things, because your natural healing processes will cure the warts without your having any further concern about them [pp. 74–75].

In addition to these suggestions, Ewin rather neatly dealt with some difficult psychological problems in each patient that no doubt had a significant role in causing the warts to appear in the first place. In all four cases, the patient made a complete recovery. In two cases, the cure was effected in less than a month after treatment began.

Clawson and Swade (1975) reported a case of an 18-year-old girl who had received five years' treatment by a dermatologist for a particularly bad case of warts. "Her face and body were literally covered with pinhead-size warts. There were hundreds of them, including five large ones on her arms" (p. 163). The therapist hypnotized the patient and informed her that "your subconscious mind has the ability to control the blood supply to any part of the body. Now I want you to stop the blood supply to each wart on your body" (p. 163). The patient returned for several such treatments, and in two months all the warts were gone, with no recurrence in three and a half years.

Both of the above articles are essentially case-history accounts, which are persuasive in their own way, but more systematic evidence is also available.

In one of the most impressive studies (Sinclair-Gieben & Chalmers, 1959), 14 patients were given hypnotic suggestions that warts *on one side* of the body would disappear. Of the ten subjects judged to be adequately hypnotized, nine were either completely free of warts, or almost so, between five weeks and three months after treatment began. However, the cure was limited to the treated side of the body; there was virtually no improvement on the untreated half of the body. None of the four inadequately hypnotized subjects showed any improvement at all. Subsequent attempts to replicate this "one-sided cure" of warts have not been as successful. In one such investigation (Surman, Gottlieb, Hackett, & Silverberg, 1973), 17 patients were treated hypnotically once a week for five weeks. Nine of the patients (53%) showed partial or complete remission of their warts, but in only one case was the effectiveness confined to the treated side of the body. None of the seven nontreated control subjects showed any improvement in the condition of their warts. However, four of these control subjects subsequently received hypnotic treatment for their warts, and two of them showed significant improvement. (Of the remaining two subjects, one showed spontaneous remission of his warts by the first hypnotic treatment.)

It is not at all clear in the above accounts that hypnosis per se is essential to the treatment of warts. Ewin, for example, did not use hypnosis at all in one of his four successful cases of wart removal. In another study (Hellier, 1951), 74 patients placed both their wart-afflicted hands under an X-ray tube, but in fact received a fractional dose of radiation in only one hand. Nevertheless, of the 29 patients who were cured completely of warts in one hand, 27 showed clearing of both hands. For most subjects, the *implicit* suggestion that both hands received treatment was evidently as effective as actually receiving the X-ray treatment.

We have already indicated that waking suggestibility is highly correlated with hypnotic suggestibility; therefore, if hypnotic suggestions are helpful in removing warts, it should not be entirely surprising that waking suggestions (either explicit or implicit) are similarly beneficial, at least for some persons. On the other hand, the article by Sinclair-Gieben and Chalmers (1959) does indicate that the effectiveness of suggestion in the cure of warts may be most pronounced in people of reasonably high hypnotizability. In that study, nine of the ten subjects who were hypnotizable to at least a moderate degree were cured of warts on one side of their bodies, whereas none of the four low-hypnotizable subjects was helped at all. The 90% cure rate of warts by suggestion in persons selected for their susceptibility to hypnosis is much higher than the 25 to 50% effectiveness more often reported for subjects unselected in this regard. Thus, as far as the hypnotic treatment of warts is concerned, the person receiving suggestions may turn out to be as important as the suggestions the person receives.

The Hypnotic Control of Blood Flow

Assuming that suggestion is an effective treatment of warts for at least some people (especially those who are at least moderately hypnotizable), just what is the mechanism by which suggestion—mere words—can have such a curative impact? According to Ullman (1959), it was proposed as early as 1913 that "suggestive influences mediating through the sympathetic nervous system altered the blood supply and thus effected a cure" (p. 475). And in a clinical article already cited (Clawson & Swade, 1975), the authors suggest that warts can be starved of blood supply through capillary constriction. For example, in the case of the 18-year-old girl successfully treated for hundreds of pinhead warts, the patient was told to "stop the blood supply to each wart on your body" (p. 163). The authors go so far as to suggest that malignant tumors may also be "starved" by terminating their supply of blood by hypnotic suggestion.

However effective this "blood-starvation" rationale may have been for wart-afflicted patients, it has limited value as a scientific explanation of why the warts disappeared. We have already seen, for example, how another clinician (Ewin, 1974) utilized precisely the opposite sort of suggestion in his treatment of warts; that is, he gave suggestions for the local warming of tissues and a concomitant *increasing* supply of blood and, therefore, of infection-fighting white corpuscles. Although these two clinical reports seem contradictory in important respects, they *both* suggest an interesting possibility—namely, that blood flow can be effectively altered by suggestion. Evidence of a different sort confirms this possibility.

Clawson and Swade (1975) themselves report on a 16-year-old boy who severely lacerated his hand and was bleeding profusely. After hypnotizing the boy, Clawson said

> "Scott, your subconscious mind has the ability to stop pain and control bleeding. Now I want you to stop your pain and stop this bleeding." . . . I then removed the blood-soaked towel and bandage, and there was not even any oozing of blood from the lacerated palm [p. 161].

Subsequent suggestions permitted a surgeon to repair the injured hand "without even a local anesthetic" (p. 161).

In another case study cited in the same article, Clawson was called upon to stop the bleeding of his own grandson undergoing emergency surgery. While the patient was under a deep general anesthesia, Clawson said "'Jac, your subconscious mind has the ability to stop bleeding. Now I want you to stop this bleeding.' The bleeding stopped immediately, and the operation was completed" (p. 162). Incidentally, this last case study is yet another illustration of how suggestions administered to a patient under general anesthesia can be effective even though they are not consciously perceived.

Perhaps an even more dramatic illustration of the suggestive control over blood flow was reported by Dubin and Shapiro (1974). A patient suffering a particularly severe form of hemophilia needed a left upper molar removed. There was considerable concern about postoperative hemorrhaging, and, as a consequence, a decision was made to employ hypnosis as a way of minimizing the patient's blood loss. Training and preparation before the surgery included repeated hypnotizing of the patient, suggestions for pain anesthesia, and suggestions that he would not hemorrhage before or after surgery. The patient was told to accomplish this last suggestion by visualizing blood as water coming from a faucet that he could turn off, willfully constricting his blood vessels, or mentally suturing the sides of his wounds. According to the authors, "the extraction was accomplished without incident and with minimal bleeding" (p. 82). The "patient was discharged on the eighth postoperative day, having required no blood or plasma replacement" (p. 82).

Newman (1971) reports similar success in inhibiting blood flow in a dental patient with hypnotic suggestions. After the last tooth extraction, the patient had bled for eight hours "even though sutures and medication were employed" (p. 126). In order to avoid a similar incident in her next extraction, hypnosis was utilized. After the tooth was removed, the patient was told while hypnotized that the bleeding would stop. Further,

> She was . . . told that when she awoke from hypnosis, she would feel very comfortable and wonderful, so much so that in a day she would feel very normal in the front areas of her mouth, just as though nothing were done in these areas. It required about one minute for the bleeding to stop. The patient was then awakened and any questions were answered. She reported that she felt so good that she wished to return to work. She was allowed to do so. The entire procedure had taken about fifteen minutes [Newman, 1971, p. 127].

There is also evidence of a more experimental kind that blood flow (and, consequently, skin temperature as well) is affected by hypnotic suggestions. In one study (Roberts, Kewman, & Macdonald, 1973), a subject was able to produce a temperature difference of 9.2°C from one hand to the other as a result of pertinent hypnotic suggestions. A follow-up of this subject indicated that decreased hand temperature was accompanied by "blood flow [that] was almost completely cut off except during the suppressed arterial pulse. When the subject increased temperature in the hand, an accelerated pulse and blood flow was detected" (p. 168).

In a considerably more ambitious study, Grabowska (1971) studied 38 subjects including 23 diabetics and 3 people suffering from Raynaud's disease (a condition in which blood supply to the extremities is severely curtailed, with a concomitant drop in hand temperature). Skin temperature and blood flow were carefully monitored throughout the course of individual hypnotic sessions conducted two or three times a week for an average of four weeks. In addition, subjects were asked to engage in daily autosuggestions to induce both relaxation and changes in blood flow. According to Grabowska (1971), the mean velocity of blood flow spontaneously decreased to 70% of its initial level under deep hypnosis; a further decrease to 62% of the initial level took place following suggestions of cold. After the suggestion of warmth, the velocity of blood flow increased to 163% of its initial value. "The velocity of capillary blood flow following the suggestion of warmth was 2.6 times higher than after the suggestion of cold" (p. 1047).

Pulse-rate data showed similar responsiveness to hypnotic intervention. From an average resting rate of 67 beats per minute, the pulse fell to 56 bpm after hypnotic suggestions of cold and rose to 75 bpm after suggestions of warmth. Increases and decreases in skin temperature corresponding to heightened and lowered blood flow and pulse rate were also noted.

Of considerable interest is the clinical effect of such blood and thermal responsiveness to hypnotic suggestions. Diabetics frequently have circulatory problems, and their extremities tend to be cold and painful, often causing the sufferer to limp. In the Grabowska study, these symptoms were totally eliminated for a while in at least 2 of the 23 diabetics originally suffering from such problems; in 13 other diabetics, much improvement was registered. Of the three people suffering from Raynaud's disease, one patient showed a complete alleviation of symptoms, and two others showed "considerable" alleviation of symptoms five weeks after the beginning of treatment. Recurrences of the symptoms were easily treated by five minutes of hypnotic suggestions of warmth.

We have seen how suggestions of warmth and dilation of blood vessels proved to be effective in the case of warts (Ewin, 1974). Hypnotic suggestions of warmth and cold may be effective in treating other skin disorders as well. In the patient I treated for hidradenitis suppurative, various suggestions for skin "control," including suggestions of warmth and coolness, were part and parcel of the therapeutic regimen. In another case study presented by Frankel and Misch (1973), a man who had been suffering from a particularly severe case of psoriasis for 20 years was successfully treated by hypnosis.

In the trance state he was asked to imagine himself basking in the sun with the warmth of the sun on his shoulders and upper back. He was encouraged to picture the sunlight reflected directly on those parts of his body, creating a feeling of pleasurable comfort in that whole area [p. 125].

After treatment was well advanced, a local increase in skin temperature from 85.4°F to 87.5°F was recorded from the commencement of trance to a time just before its termination. While the psoriasis was never completely eliminated, it was well under control by the end of treatment, thus permitting the patient to behave socially and vocationally with greater effectiveness and less self-consciousness.

The Hypnotic Treatment of Migraine Headaches

Skin disorders are not the only problem responsive to hypnotic suggestions for vascular changes; migraine headaches appear to be similarly affected. It seems clear that the onset of migraine headaches is due to the dilation of cerebral blood vessels (Bakal, 1975), and medical attempts to control the disorder generally involve administration of vasoconstrictors. A recent article (Anderson, Basker, & Dalton, 1975), however, presents strong evidence that hypnotherapy may be very effective in the control of migraine. Of 47 migraine sufferers, 23 were randomly assigned to hypnotic therapy and 24 to drug therapy. Those in hypnotherapy were seen at least six times at intervals of 10 to 14 days. The other 24 subjects were administered prophylactic medication four times a day for the first month and two times a day for the remaining 11 months.

All four participating therapists were experienced in hypnosis and confident in its ability to help treat migraine patients. They were permitted some leeway in their use of suggestions, and each informed his patients that migraine headaches have a vascular basis. The patients were told to visualize the arteries in their heads becoming smaller and smaller as they, the patients, became more and more relaxed. The patients were also instructed in autohypnosis with the hope that they could immediately ward off an impending headache with helpful self-suggestions.

The results clearly indicated the superiority of the hypnotic treatment versus the drug treatment. The median number of migraine headaches per month for patients under hypnotic therapy went from 4.5 in the six months before treatment started to 0.5 during the second six months of treatment; the corresponding figures for the drug group were 3.3 and 2.9, respectively. In the six months prior to treatment, 13 patients in the hypnotic group had suffered attacks of the most severe "blinding" migraines; in the second six months of treatment, only five patients suffered such severe attacks. In the drug therapy, 10 patients had blinding headaches in the six months prior to treatment, whereas 14 patients had such attacks during the second six months of treatment.

Finally, 10 of the original 23 patients in hypnotherapy (43.5%) had a complete remission of symptoms during the last three months of therapy, whereas only 3 out of 24 patients (12.5%) in drug therapy showed similar complete remission. Clearly, the use of hypnosis seems to have a positive impact on migraine sufferers.

This conclusion essentially confirms the previous report by Harding (1967). This investigator used hypnosis to treat 90 migraine patients who were refractory to more conventional medical treatment. Seventy-four of these subjects (80%) responded to an inquiry regarding treatment effectiveness. "Of the respondents 34 patients or 38 percent . . . reported complete relief for periods up to 8 years" (p. 131). In addition, 16 patients reported 75% relief, 9 reported 50% relief, and 4 reported 25% relief. So, 62 patients out of the 74 who responded indicated at least partial relief of their migraine condition, and the majority of the respondents showed complete remission of their migraine headaches for an extended period of time.

Now, the vascular system, which seems to be implicated in migraine headaches and in at least some skin disorders, is of course governed largely by the autonomic nervous system (ANS). Even though the ANS is vegetative and largely involuntary in its functioning, it is clearly (and to some considerable extent) responsive to suggestive influences more closely associated with the central nervous system (CNS). The fact that some people often blush with embarrassment or shame is an illustration of how vegetative functions are reactive to interpersonal events processed by the CNS (Platonov, 1959).

Perhaps the most dramatic demonstration in the literature of how pervasive and forceful such CNS-mediated influences can be on ANS functioning is one reported by Raginsky (1959). In this article, the author reports the results of an experiment he had conducted almost two decades earlier on a man who had been suffering from a heart disorder diagnosed as Stokes-Adams disease. The disorder was clinically manifested by fainting spells of two- to three-minutes duration, accompanied by heart pain. It was also discovered that cardiac arrest of five to ten seconds could be precipitated by artificially stimulating the patient's carotid sinus. As a result of these findings, the presumed neural basis for the disorder was surgically eliminated; in fact, postoperative stimulation of the carotid sinus was ineffective in producing cardiac arrest. Moreover, there were no recurrences of the fainting spells for the one and a half years between the operation and the time when Raginsky first saw the patient.

During the course of their meetings, the patient consented to participate in an experiment involving hypnosis. While hypnotized, the man "was asked to visualize with all clarity possible his worst attack of faintness" (Raginsky, 1959, p. 56). At first such suggestions led to a good deal of restlessness and agitation but no fainting. A second and third trial, however, led to sudden limpness, paleness, and heart stoppages of four and a half and five seconds, respectively (as measured on an electrocardiogram). When awakened from hypnosis, the man seemed unconcerned and somewhat forgetful regarding what had happened; he lived another 16 years to a ripe old age of 81, with no further cardiac problems. This happy ending notwithstanding, it is clear that the impact of hypnotic suggestions on the man's life was potentially catastrophic, and the author of the experiment reflectively acknowledges both the ethical hazard entailed by the performance of the experiment and his good fortune that nothing untoward happened. Experiments of this kind serve to remind us that hypnosis' dramatic benefits exist in equilibrium with its potential for harm. Hypnosis is by and large far less dangerous than aspirin, but it is not a psychological toy. Thus, it should not be used nor submitted to lightly or improvidently.

Hypnosis, Asthma, and Smoking

In the account above, the temporary cardiac arrest was an extreme ANS reaction to an explicit verbal communication processed by the CNS. However, CNS-mediated information need not be so explicit in order to wreak havoc with various autonomic functions. For example, one influential view of psychosomatic illness sees particular disorders, such as ulcers and asthma, as extreme ANS reactions to *specific attitudes* processed by the CNS (Grace & Graham, 1952; Graham, 1954, 1955). For instance, the Graham (1955) investigation found that all four persons suffering from Raynaud's disease "reported essentially the same attitude toward disturbing events. This was the wish to take some direct *hostile* action against a person who was behaving in an unacceptable way" (p. 201). Asthma, on the other hand, seems to be characterized by an attitude of apathy toward a noxious situation (Grace & Graham, 1952). Other psychosomatic disorders also seem to be accompanied by a distinct and specific attitude toward the source of distress. Just how suggestions disrupt the somatic expression of underlying psychic distress is not clear, but they certainly seem effective in this respect.

Yet another example of how a serious psychosomatic disorder is treatable through hypnotic techniques was reported by Maher-Loughnam (1970). In this article, he presented three studies involving a total of more than 400 patients suffering from asthma. In one of the studies, a random half of moderate or severe asthmatics were assigned to a hypnosis group; the remaining subjects were assigned to a control group. The subjects in the hypnotic group were given suggestions for deep relaxation and confidence in their recovery. They were also trained in autohypnosis so that they would be able to effect the same internal sense of relaxation on their own and on a regular basis. The control subjects were administered progressive relaxation followed by breathing exercises "aimed at teaching respiration with a minimum of expiratory or inspiratory effort" (p. 6). During the year of treatment, only 7 of the 127 subjects in hypnotherapy had to withdraw from the program, whereas 17 of the 125 controls were forced to do so. Remaining subjects in both groups showed some improvement. However, "independent clinical assessors considered the asthma to be much improved in 59% of the hypnosis group and in 43% of the control group, the difference being statistically significant" (Maher-Loughnan, 1970, p. 7). In another study by the same author, 141 out of 173 asthma sufferers (82%) responded "convincingly" to hypnotic treatment (also involving autohypnosis).

Parenthetically, the author claims that "with the introduction of autohypnosis there seemed to be no correlation between trance depth and clinical responses . . . " (p. 13). This finding supports the emphatic assertion of two psychoanalytic writers on hypnosis that *there is no correlation between the depth of hypnosis obtainable in a patient and the therapeutic result*" (Gill & Brenman, 1959, p. 333). Whether this is true across all disorders treatable by hypnosis is not yet proved, and it is almost certainly false regarding the induction of hypnotic analgesia to protect a person from surgical-level pain. Yet, to the extent that hypnotic depth is more or less irrelevant to the clinical effectiveness of hypnotic interventions, there is some real hope that a variety of persons—not just those who are highly hypnotizable—can be helped by the therapeutic use of hypnosis.

In this chapter on the clinical uses of hypnosis, we have so far concentrated on the therapeutic impact of suggestions on disorders rooted in a person's biological function and structure. However, hypnosis has also been used extensively to alter maladaptive behavior patterns, such as cigarette smoking. In one of the most impressive investigations of this sort, Kline (1970) saw 60 habitual smokers in groups of 10 for one 12-hour hypnotherapy session. The patients were told to refrain from smoking for a period of 24 hours prior to the session, thereby guaranteeing a high deprivation level for all participants. Also, the patients brought an unopened pack of their favorite brand of cigarettes with which they would later tantalize themselves.

First, the subjects were individually hypnotized, until the entire group was in a state of hypnosis. Then they were instructed to recognize and acknowledge the onset of any tension as it occurred during the entire course of the therapy session. After a brief period of relaxation, discussion was initiated regarding the participants' reactions to their period of smoking deprivation. The experience of deprivation, which most participants acknowledged, was then singled out by the therapist "as the most important consideration in the treatment of smoking habituation" (Kline, 1970, p. 276). Then followed a period of relaxation, itself followed by a "series of procedures designed to intensify feelings of smoking deprivation" (p. 276). Aided by hypnosis, subjects were told to recall times and places where smoking was most gratifying. While engaged in this reverie, participants were told to touch, hold, and smell the cigarettes—and to visualize actually smoking them. At no time, however, were they to place the cigarettes in their mouths. When the tension aroused by such "torture" was at a high pitch,

> hypnosis was used in a systematic manner to produce complete relaxation. Hypnotically induced gratification similar to that which had been reported following smoking was induced first by the therapist and then by each patient using self-hypnosis [p. 277].

Repeated practice at this tension-relaxation cycle was given during the 12-hour therapy session.

At a one-year follow-up of patients participating in this investigation, 43 out of 50 males and all 10 females reported that they were still not smoking. This 88% cure rate compares quite favorably with the 20 to 30% success more generally reported by investigators in one-year follow-ups of their treatment regimens (Hunt, Barnett, & Branch, 1971). Moreover, Kline reports that the respiratory irregularities characteristic of deprivation tension were eliminated through hypnotic relaxation—an accomplishment that took less and less time for most subjects to achieve as they became more experienced in relaxing themselves. As in the study of asthma previously reviewed, the impact of relaxation on respiration seems to have special significance for effective treatment. (Readers curious about other hypnotic approaches to smoking should consult the October 1970 special issue of the *International Journal of Clinical and Experimental Hypnosis*.)

Some Final Remarks

To anyone even slightly aware of the clinical uses to which hypnosis has been put, the coverage of this final chapter must seem slim indeed. But it is time for our odyssey to end. I trust that enough has been said to convey some of the potential benefits that hypnosis has to offer sick and suffering human beings. Even for those unfortunate individuals wracked by painful terminal illness, the skillful use of hypnosis can have remarkably benign effects that provide both relief from pain and enhanced effectiveness right up to the moment of death (see, for example, Clawson & Swade, 1975; Crasilneck & Hall, 1973; Erickson, 1959, 1966).

No claim is made here that hypnosis per se is absolutely necessary to effect these dramatic nonmedical reversals in human illnesses. Some combination of placebo effect and nonhypnotic suggestion has long been known to exert a formidable impact on the human body and its functioning (Frank, 1973; Shapiro, 1971; Evans, 1974a, b). And, more recently, biofeedback therapy has been forwarded as a remedy for a variety of human maladies (Blanchard & Young, 1974). To cite a single example, one group of investigators (Sargent, Green, & Walters, 1973) has reported some modest success in the treatment of migraine headaches with a combination of biofeedback and autogenic training (Shutz & Luthe, 1969).

Despite the undeniable impact of placebo, nonhypnotic suggestion, and biofeedback on human suffering, anyone who has worked clinically with hypnosis finds it difficult to resist the conviction that as a treatment modality it offers special advantages for some people some of the time. And in fact there is at least one experimental investigation that shows quite conclusively that in high-susceptible subjects the hypnotic alleviation of pain is separate and distinct from the relief brought about by placebo alone (McGlashan, Evans, & Orne, 1969). It would be somewhat surprising if this extra margin of effectiveness due specifically to *hypnotic* suggestions were limited to the alleviation of pain. In any case, human suffering responds to the spoken word rendered by compassionate persons cast in the role of healer. Even though men have known this for a long, long time, it is still very good news.

References

Allington, H. V. Review of the psychotherapy of warts. *Archives of Dermatology and Syphiology*, 1952, *66*, 316–326.

Anderson, J. A. D., Basker, M. A., & Dalton, R. Migraine and hypnotherapy. *International Journal of Clinical and Experimental Hypnosis*, 1975, *13*, 48–58.

Anderson, W. L., & Sachs, L. B. Modification of hypnotic susceptibility. *International Journal of Clinical and Experimental Hypnosis*, 1967, *15*, 172–180.

As, A. A note on distractibility and hypnosis. *American Journal of Clinical Hypnosis*, 1962, *5*, 135–137.(a)

As, A. Non-hypnotic experiences related to hypnotizability in male and female college students. *Scandinavian Journal of Psychology*, 1962, *3*, 112–121.(b)

As, A. Hypnotizability as a function of non-hypnotic experiences. *Journal of Abnormal and Social Psychology*, 1963, *66*, 142–150.

As, A. Hypnosis as subjective experience. In J. Lassner (Ed.). *Hypnosis and psychosomatic medicine*. New York: Springer-Verlag, 1967, pp. 1–6.

As, A., Hilgard, E. R., & Weitzenhoffer, A. M. An attempt at experimental modification of hypnotizability through repeated individualized hypnotic experience. *Scandinavian Journal of Psychology*, 1963, *4*, 81–89.

As, A., & Lauer, L. W. A factor-analytic study of hypnotizability and related personal experiences. *International Journal of Clinical and Experimental Hypnosis*, 1962, *10*, 169–181.

As, A., O'Hara, R., & Munger, M. P. The measurement of subjective experiences presumably related to hypnotic susceptibility. *Scandinavian Journal of Psychology*, 1962, *3*, 47–64.

As, A., & Ostvold, S. Hypnosis as subjective experience. *Scandinavian Journal of Psychology*, 1968, *9*, 33–38.

Bakal, D. A. Headache: A biopsychological perspective. *Psychological Bulletin*, 1975, *82*, 369–382.

Bakan, P. Hypnotizability, laterality of eye movement and functional brain asymmetry. *Perceptual and Motor Skills*, 1969, *28*, 927–932.

Bakan, P. The eyes have it. *Psychology Today*, 1971, *4*, 64.

Bakan, P., & Svorad, D. Resting EEG Alpha and asymmetry of reflective lateral eye movements. *Nature*, 1969, *223*, 975–976.

Barber, T. X. Antisocial and criminal acts induced by "hypnosis": A review of experimental and clinical findings. *Archives of General Psychiatry*, 1961, *5*, 301–312.

Barber, T. X. The effects of "hypnosis" on pain. *Psychosomatic Medicine,* 1963, *25,* 303–333.

Barber, T. X. Toward a theory of "hypnotic" behavior: Positive visual and auditory hallucinations. *Psychological Record,* 1964, *14,* 197–210.(a)

Barber, T. X. Hypnotic "colorblindness," "blindness," and "deafness." *Diseases of the Nervous System,* 1964, *25,* 529–537.(b)

Barber, T. X. "Hypnosis" as a causal variable in present day psychology: A critical analysis. *Psychological Reports,* 1964, *14,* 839–842.(c)

Barber, T. X. Hypnotizability, suggestibility and personality: V. A critical review of research findings. *Psychological Reports,* 1964, *14,* 299–320.(d)

Barber, T. X. Measuring "hypnotic-like" suggestibility with and without "hypnotic induction"; psychometric properties, norms, and variables influencing responses to the Barber Suggestibility Scale (BSS). *Psychological Reports,* 1965, *16,* 809–844.

Barber, T. X. *Hypnosis: A scientific approach.* New York: Van Nostrand, 1969.

Barber, T. X. *LSD, marihuana, yoga, and hypnosis.* Chicago: Aldine-Atherton, 1970.

Barber, T. X. Suggested ("Hypnotic") behavior: The trance paradigm versus an alternative paradigm. In E. Fromm & R. E. Shor (Eds.), *Hypnosis: Research developments and perspectives.* Chicago: Aldine-Atherton, 1972, pp. 115–182.

Barber, T. X., & Calverley, D. S. The relative effectiveness of task motivating instructions and trance induction procedure in the production of "hypnotic-like" behaviors. *Journal of Nervous and Mental Disease,* 1963, *137,* 107–116.

Barber, T. X., & Calverley, D. S. Experimental studies in "hypnotic" behaviour: Suggested deafness evaluated by delayed auditory feedback. *British Journal of Psychology,* 1964, *55,* 439–446.(a)

Barber, T. X., & Calverley, D. S. An experimental study of "hypnotic" (auditory and visual) hallucinations. *Journal of Abnormal and Social Psychology,* 1964, *68,* 13–20.(b)

Barber, T. X., & Calverley, D. S. Hypnotizability, suggestibility, and personality: II. Assessment of previous imaginative-fantasy experiences by the As, Barber, Glass, and Shor questionnaires. *Journal of Clinical Psychology,* 1965, *21,* 57–58.

Barber, T. X., & Calverley, D. S. Toward a theory of "hypnotic" behavior: Experimental analyses of suggested amnesia. *Journal of Abnormal Psychology,* 1966, *71,* 95–107.

Barber, T. X., & Calverley, D. S. Multi-dimensional analysis of "hypnotic" behavior. *Journal of Abnormal Psychology,* 1969, *74,* 209–220.

Barber, T. X., Dalal, A. S., & Calverley, D. S. The subjective reports of hypnotic subjects. *American Journal of Clinical Hypnosis,* 1968, *11,* 74–88.

Barber, T. X., & Glass, L. B. Significant factors in hypnotic behavior. *Journal of Abnormal Psychology,* 1962, *64,* 222–228.

Barber, T. X., & Hahn, K. W. Physiological and subjective responses to pain producing stimulation under hypnotically-suggested and waking-imagined "analgesia." *Journal of Abnormal Psychology,* 1962, *65,* 411–418.

Barber, T. X., & Ham, M. W. *Hypnotic Phenomena.* Morristown, N. J.: General Learning Press, 1974.

Barber, T. X., Spanos, N. P., & Chaves, J. F. *Hypnotism, imagination, and human potentialities.* New York: Pergamon, 1974.

Beecher, H. K. *Measurement of subjective responses: Quantitative effects of drugs.* New York: Oxford University Press, 1959.

Bentler, P. M., & Hilgard, E. R. A comparison of group and individual induction of hypnosis with self-scoring and observer-scoring. *International Journal of Clinical and Experimental Hypnosis,* 1963, *11,* 49–54.

Bernheim, H. *Hypnosis and suggestion in psychotherapy: The nature and uses of hypnotism.*

New York: University Books, 1964. Originally published in English in 1888 under the title *Suggestive Therapeutics*.

Bexton, W. H., Heron, W., & Scott, T. H. Effects of decreased variation in the sensory environment *Canadian Journal of Psychology*, 1954, *8*, 70–76.

Blanchard, E. B., & Young, L. D. Clinical applications of biofeedback training. *Archives of General Psychiatry*, 1974, *30*, 573–592.

Bowers, K. S. Hypnotic behavior: The differentiation of trance and demand characteristic variables. *Journal of Abnormal Psychology*, 1966, *71*, 42–51.

Bowers, K. S. The effect of demands for honesty on reports of visual and auditory hallucinations. *International Journal of Clinical and Experimental Hypnosis*, 1967, *15*, 31–36.

Bowers, K. S. The effects of UCS temporal uncertainty on heart rate and pain. *Psychophysiology*, 1971, *8*, 382–389.(a)

Bowers, K. S. Sex and susceptibility as moderator variables in the relationship of creativity and hypnotic susceptibility. *Journal of Abnormal Psychology*, 1971, *78*, 93–100.(b)

Bowers, K. S. Hypnosis, attribution and demand characteristics. *International Journal of Clinical and Experimental Hypnosis*, 1973, *21*, 226–238.(a)

Bowers, K. S. Situationism in psychology: An analysis and a critique. *Psychological Review*, 1973, *80*, 307–336.(b)

Bowers, K. S. The psychology of subtle control: An attributional analysis of behavioral persistence. *Candian Journal of Behavioral Science*, 1975, *7*, 78–95.

Bowers, K. S., & Bowers, P. G. Hypnosis and creativity: A theoretical and empirical rapprochement. In E. Fromm & R. E. Shor (Eds.), *Hypnosis: Research developments and perspectives*. Chicago: Aldine-Atherton, 1972, pp. 255–291.

Bowers, K. S., & Gilmore, J. B. Subjective report and credibility: An inquiry involving hypnotic hallucinations. *Journal of Abnormal Psychology*, 1969, *74*, 443–451.

Bowers, K. S., & van der Meulen, S. J. Effect of hypnotic susceptibility on creativity test performance. *Journal of Personality and Social Psychology*, 1970, *14*, 247–256.

Bowers, K. S., & van der Meulen, S. A comparison of psychological and chemical techniques in the control of dental pain. Paper delivered at the Society for Clinical and Experimental Hypnosis Convention, Boston, Fall, 1972.

Brenman, M., & Gill, M. M. *Hypnotherapy: A survey of the literature*. New York: John Wiley & Sons, 1947.

Brunn, J. T. The capacity to hear, understand, and remember experiences during chemoanesthesia: A personal experience. *American Journal of Clinical Hypnosis*, 1963, *6*, 27–30.

Burgess, T. O. Hypnosis in dentistry. In L. M. LeCron (Ed.), *Experimental Hypnosis*. New York: Citadel, 1965, pp. 322–351.

Cheek, D. B. Unconscious perception of meaningful sounds during surgical anesthesia as revealed under hypnosis. *American Journal of Clinical Hypnosis*, 1959, *1*, 101–113.

Cheek, D. B. The meaning of continued hearing sense under general chemoanesthesia: A progress report and a report case. *American Journal of Clinical Hypnosis*, 1966, *8*, 275–280.

Clawson, T. A., & Swade, R. H. The hypnotic control of blood flow and pain: The cure of warts and the potential for the use of hypnosis in the treatment of cancer. *American Journal of Clinical Hypnosis*, 1975, *17*, 160–169.

Cobb, J. C., Evans, F. J., Gustafson, L. A., O'Connell, D. N., Orne, M. T., & Shor, R. E. Specific motor response during sleep to sleep-administered suggestion: An exploratory investigation. *Perceptual and Motor Skills*, 1965, *20*, 629–636.

Coe, W. C., Allen, J. L., Krug, W. M., & Wurzman, A. G. Goal-directed fantasy in hypnotic responsiveness: Skill, item wording, or both? *International Journal of Clinical and Experimental Hypnosis,* 1974, *22,* 157–166.

Cooper, L. M. Hypnotic amnesia. In E. Fromm & R. E. Shor (Eds.), *Hypnosis: Research developments and perspectives.* Chicago: Aldine-Atherton, 1972, pp. 217–252.

Cooper, L. M., Banford, S. A., Shubot, E., & Tart, C. T. A further attempt to modify hypnotic susceptibility through repeated individualized experience. *International Journal of Clinical and Experimental Hypnosis,* 1967, *15,* 118–124.

Cooper, L. M., & Hoskovec, J. Hypnotic suggestions for learning during Stage I REM sleep. *American Journal of Clinical Hypnosis,* 1972, *15,* 102–111.

Cooper, L. M., & London, P. The development of hypnotic susceptibility: A longitudinal (convergence) study. *Child Development,* 1971, *42,* 487–503.

Crasilneck, H. B., & Hall, J. A. Clinical hypnosis in problems of pain. *American Journal of Clinical Hypnosis,* 1973, *15,* 153–161.

Dana, R. H., & Cooper, G. W. Jr. Prediction of susceptibility to hypnosis. *Psychological Reports,* 1964, *14,* 251–265.

Darnton, R. *Mesmerism and the end of enlightenment in France.* New York: Schocken, 1970.

Day, M. E. An eye movement phenomenon relating to attention, thought, and anxiety. *Perceptual and Motor Skills,* 1964, *19,* 443–446.

Deckert, G. H., & West, L. J. The problem of hypnotizability: A review. *International Journal of Experimental Hypnosis,* 1963, *11,* 205–235.

Deikman, A. J. Experimental meditation. *Journal of Nervous and Mental Disease,* 1963, *136,* 329–343.

Deikman, A. J. Bimodal consciousness. *Archives of General Psychiatry,* 1971, *25,* 481–489.

Dermen, D., & London, P. Correlates of hypnotic susceptibility. *Journal of Consulting Psychology,* 1965, *29,* 537–545.

Diamond, M. J. Modification of hypnotizability: A review. *Psychological Bulletin,* 1974, *81,* 180–198.

Dixon, N. F. *Subliminal perception: The nature of a controversy.* London: McGraw-Hill, 1971.

Dubin, L. L., & Shapiro, S. S. Use of hypnosis to facilitate dental extraction and hemostasis in a classic hemophiliac with a high antibody titer to Factor VIII. *American Journal of Clinical Hypnosis,* 1974, *17,* 79–83.

Duke, J. Lateral eye-movement behavior. *Journal of General Psychology,* 1968, *78,* 189–195.

Edmonston, W. E., & Grotevant, W. R. Hypnosis and alpha density. *American Journal of Clinical Hypnosis,* 1975, *17,* 221–232.

Ellenberger, H. F. *Discovery of the unconscious: The history and evaluation of dynamic psychiatry.* New York: Basic Books, 1970.

Engstrom, D. R., London, P., & Hart, J. T. EEG alpha feedback training and hypnotic susceptibility. *Proceedings of the 78th Annual Convention of the American Psychological Association,* 1970, *5,* 837–838.

Erickson, M. H. Hypnosis in painful terminal illness. *American Journal of Clinical Hypnosis,* 1959, *1,* 117–121.

Erickson, M. H. Chemo-anesthesia in relation to learning and memory. *American Journal of Clinical Hypnosis,* 1963, *6,* 31–36.

Erickson, M. H. Deep hypnosis and its induction. In L. M. LeCron (Ed.), *Experimental Hypnosis.* New York: Citadel Press, 1965, pp. 70–112.

Erickson, M. H. The interpersonal hypnotic technique for symptom correction and pain control. *American Journal of Clinical Hypnosis,* 1966, *8,* 198–209.

Esdaile, J. *Hypnosis in medicine and surgery.* New York: Julian Press, 1957. Originally published in 1850 under the title *Mesmerism in India.*

Evans, F. J. Suggestibility in the normal waking state. *Psychological Bulletin,* 1967, *67,* 114–129.

Evans, F. J. Hypnosis and sleep: Techniques for exploring cognitive activity during sleep. In E. Fromm & R. E. Shor (Eds.), *Hypnosis: Research developments and perspectives.* Chicago: Aldine-Atherton, 1972, pp. 43–83.

Evans, F. J. The placebo response in pain reduction. In J. J. Bonica (Ed.), *Pain.* New York: Raven Press, 1974, pp. 289–296.(a)

Evans, F. J. The power of the sugar pill. *Psychology Today,* 1974, *7,* 55–59.(b)

Evans, F. J. Gustafson, L. A., O'Connell, D. N., Orne, M. T., & Shor, R. E. Response during sleep with intervening waking amnesia. *Science,* 1966, *152,* 666–667.

Evans, F. J., Gustafson, L. A., O'Connell, D. N., Orne, M. T., & Shor, R. E. Sleep-induced behavioral response: Relationship to susceptibility to hypnosis and laboratory sleep patterns. *Journal of Nervous and Mental Disease,* 1969, *148,* 467–476.

Evans, F. J., Gustafson, L. A., O'Connell, D. N. Orne, M. T., & Shor, R. E. Verbally induced behavioral responses during sleep. *Journal of Nervous and Mental Disease,* 1970, *150,* 171–187.

Evans, F. J., & Kihlstrom, J. F. Posthypnotic amnesia as disrupted retrieval. *Journal of Abnormal Psychology,* 1973, *82,* 319–323.

Evans, F. J., & Orne, M. T. The disappearing hypnotist: The use of simulating subjects to evaluate how subjects perceive experimental procedures. *International Journal of Clinical and Experimental Hypnosis,* 1971, *19,* 277–296.

Evans, F. J., & Schmeidler, D. Relationship between the Harvard Group Scale of Hypnotic Susceptibility and the Stanford Hypnotic Susceptibility Scale: Form C. *International Journal of Clinical and Experimental Hypnosis,* 1966, *14,* 333–343.

Evans, M. B., & Paul, G. L. Effects of hypnotically suggested analgesia on physiological and subjective responses to cold stress. *Journal of Consulting and Clinical Psychology,* 1970, *35,* 362–371.

Ewin, D. M. Condyloma acuminatum: Successful treatment of four cases by hypnosis. *American Journal of Clinical Hypnosis,* 1974, *17,* 73–78.

Faw, V., & Wilcox, W. W. Personality characteristics of susceptible and unsusceptible hypnotic subjects. *Journal of Clinical and Experimental Hypnosis,* 1958, *6,* 83–94.

Field, P. B. An inventory scale of hypnotic depth. *International Journal of Clinical and Experimental Hypnosis,* 1965, *13,* 238–249.

Field, P. B., & Palmer, R. D. Factor analysis: Hypnosis inventory. *International Journal of Clinical and Experimental Hypnosis,* 1969, *17,* 50–61.

Fisher, S. The role of expectancy in the performance of posthypnotic behavior. *Journal of Abnormal and Social Psychology,* 1954, *49,* 503–507.

Fogel, S., & Hoffer, A. The use of hypnosis to interrupt and to reproduce an LSD-25 experience. *Journal of Clinical and Experimental Psychopathology,* 1962, *23,* 11–16.

Frank, J. D. *Persuasion and healing: A comparative study of psychotherapy.* Baltimore: Johns Hopkins Press, 1973.

Frankel, F. H., & Misch, R. C. Hypnosis in a case of long-standing psoriasis in a person with character problems. *International Journal of Clinical and Experimental Hypnosis,* 1973, *21,* 121–130.

Fromm, E., & Shor, R. E. *Hypnosis: Research developments and perspectives.* Chicago: Aldine-Atherton, 1972.

Galin, D. Implications for psychiatry of left and right cerebral specialization. *Archives of General Psychiatry,* 1974, *31,* 572–583.

Gill, M. M., & Brenman, M. *Hypnosis and related states: Psychoanalytic studies in regression.*

New York:International Universities Press, 1959.

Goldstein, M. S., & Sipprelle, C. N. Hypnotically induced amnesia versus ablation of memory. *International Journal of Clinical and Experimental Hypnosis,* 1970, *18,* 211–216.

Gordon, J. E. *Handbook of clinical and experimental hypnosis.* New York: Macmillan, 1967.

Gordon, M. C. Age and performance differences of male patients on modified Stanford hypnotic susceptibility scales. *International Journal of Clinical and Experimental Hypnosis,* 1972, *20,* 152–155.

Grabowska, M. J. The effect of hypnosis and hypnotic suggestion on the blood flow in the extremities. *Polish Medical Journal,* 1971, *10,* 1044–1051.

Grace, W. J. & Graham, D. T. Relationship of specific attitudes and emotions to certain bodily diseases. *Psychosomatic Medicine,* 1952, *14,* 243–251.

Graham, C., & Leibowitz, H. W. The effect of suggestion on visual acuity. *International Journal of Clinical and Experimental Hypnosis,* 1972, *20,* 169–186.

Graham, D. T. The relation of psoriasis to attitude and to vascular reactions of the human skin. *Journal of Investigative Dermatology,* 1954, *22,* 379–388.

Graham, D. T. Cutaneous vascular reactions in Raynaud's disease and in states of hostility, anxiety and depression. *Psychosomatic Medicine,* 1955, *17,* 200–207.

Graham, D. T., Stern, J. A., & Winokur, G. Experimental investigation of the specificity of attitude hypothesis in psychosomatic disease. *Psychosomatic Medicine,* 1958, *20,* 446–457.

Gray, A. L., Bowers, K. S., & Fenz, W. D. Heart rate in anticipation of and during a negative visual hallucination. *International Journal of Clinical and Experimental Hypnosis,* 1970, *18,* 41–51.

Gur, R. C., & Gur, R. E. Handedness, sex, and eyedness as moderating variables in the relation between hypnotic susceptibility and functional brain asymmetry. *Journal of Abnormal Psychology,* 1974, *83,* 635–643.

Gur, R., & Reyher, J. Relationship between style of hypnotic induction and direction of lateral eye movements. *Journal of Abnormal Psychology,* 1973, *82,* 499–505.

Hackett, T. P. The surgeon and the difficult pain problem. In H. S. Abram (Ed.), *Psychological aspects of surgery.* Boston: Little Brown & Co., 1967, pp. 171–188.

Haley, J. *Advanced techniques of hypnosis and therapy: Selected papers of Milton H. Erickson, M.D.* New York: Grune & Stratton, 1967.

Harding, C. H. Hypnosis in treatment of migraine. In J. Lassner (Ed.), *Hypnosis and psychosomatic medicine.* New York: Springer-Verlag, 1967, pp. 131–134.

Hellier, F. F. The treatment of warts with X-rays. Is their action physical or psychological? *British Journal of Dermatology,* 1951, *63,* 193–194.

Heron, W. The pathology of boredom. *Scientific American,* 1957, *196,* 52–56.

Hilgard, E. R. *Hypnotic susceptibility.* New York: Harcourt Brace & World, 1965.

Hilgard, E. R. A quantitative study of pain and its reduction through hypnotic suggestion. *Proceedings of the National Academy of Sciences,* 1967, *57,* 1581–1586.

Hilgard, E. R. Pain as a puzzle for psychology and physiology. *American Psychologist,* 1969, *24,* 103–113.(a)

Hilgard, E. R. Altered states of awareness. *Journal of Nervous and Mental Disease,* 1969, *149,* 68–79.(b)

Hilgard, E. R. Hypnotic phenomena: The struggle for scientific acceptance. *American Scientist,* 1971, *59,* 567–577.(a)

Hilgard, E. R. Pain: Its reduction and production under hypnosis. *Proceedings of the American Philosophical Society,* 1971, *115,* 470–476.(b)

Hilgard, E. R. A critique of Johnson, Maher, & Barber's "Artifact in the 'essence of hypnosis': An evaluation of trance logic" with a reconceptualization of their findings. *Journal of Abnormal Psychology*, 1972, *79*, 221-233.

Hilgard, E. R. A neo-dissociation theory of pain reduction in hypnosis. *Psychological Review*, 1973, *80*, 396-411.(a)

Hilgard, E. R. The domain of hypnosis. *American Psychologist*, 1973, *28*, 972-982.(b)

Hilgard, E. R. Toward a neo-dissociation theory: multiple cognitive controls in human functioning. *Perspectives in Biology and Medicine*, 1974, *17*, 301-316.

Hilgard, E. R. Hypnosis. *Annual Review of Psychology*, 1975, *26*, 19-44.

Hilgard, E. R., Morgan, A. H., Lange, A. F., Lenox, J. R., Macdonald, H., Marshall, G., & Sachs, L. B. Heart rate changes in pain and hypnosis. *Psychophysiology*, 1974, *11*, 692-702.

Hilgard, E. R., Ruch, J. C., Lange, A. F., Lenox, J. R., Morgan, A. H., & Sachs, L. B. The psychophysics of cold pressor pain and its modification through hypnotic suggestion. *American Journal of Psychology*, 1974, *87*, 17-31.

Hilgard, E. R., & Tart, C. T. Responsiveness to suggestions following waking and imagination instructions and following induction of hypnosis. *Journal of Abnormal Psychology*, 1966, *71*, 196-208.

Hilgard, E. R., Weitzenhoffer, A. M., Landes, J., & Moore, R. K. *Psychological Monographs*, 1961, *75*, whole No. 8.

Hilgard, J. R. *Personality and hypnosis: A study of imaginative involvement.* Chicago: U. of Chicago Press, 1970.

Hilgard, J. R. Evidence for a developmental-interactive theory of hypnotic susceptibility. In E. Fromm & R. E. Shor (Eds.), *Hypnosis: Research developments and perspectives.* Chicago: Aldine-Atherton, 1972, pp. 387-397.

Hilgard, J. R. Sequelae to hypnosis. *International Journal of Clinical and Experimental Hypnosis*, 1974, *22*, 281-298.(a)

Hilgard, J. R. Imaginative involvement: Some characteristics of the highly hypnotizable and the non-hypnotizable. *International Journal of Clinical and Experimental Hypnosis*, 1974, *22*, 138-156.(b)

Hilgard, J. R., Hilgard, E. R., & Newman, M. Sequelae to hypnotic induction with special reference to earlier chemical anesthesia. *Journal of Nervous and Mental Disease*, 1961, *133*, 461-478.

Horowitz, M. J. *Image formation and cognition.* New York: Appleton-Century-Crofts, 1970.

Hoskovec, J. Hypnopedia in the Soviet Union: A critical review of recent major experiments. *International Journal of Clinical and Experimental Hypnosis*, 1966, *14*, 308-315.

Hull, C. L. *Hypnosis and suggestibility: An experimental approach.* New York: Appleton-Century-Crofts, 1933.

Hunt, W. A., Barnett, L. W., & Branch, L. G. Relapse rate in addiction programs. *Journal of Clinical Psychology*, 1971, *27*, 455-456.

Hutchings, D. The value of suggestion given under anesthesia. *American Journal of Clinical Hypnosis*, 1961, *4*, 26-29.

Jabush, M. A case of chronic recurring multiple boils treated with hypnotherapy. *Psychiatric Quarterly*, 1969, *43*, 448-455.

James, W. *The varieties of religious experience.* London: Fontana Library, 1960.

Johnson, R. F. Q., Maher, B. A., & Barber, T. X. Artifact in the "Essence of Hypnosis": An evaluation of trance logic. *Journal of Abnormal Psychology*, 1972, *79*, 212-220.

Kahneman, D. *Attention and effort.* Englewood Cliffs, N. J.: Prentice-Hall, 1973.

Kales, A., Paulson, M. J., Jacobson, A., & Kales, J. D. Somnambulism: Psychophysiological correlates: II. Psychiatric interviews, psychological testing and discussion. *Archives of General Psychiatry*, 1966, *14*, 595–604.

Kamiya, J. Operant control of the EEG alpha rhythm and some of its reported effects on consciousness. In C. T. Tart (Ed.), *Altered states of consciousness*. New York: John Wiley & Sons, 1969, pp. 507–517.

Kaplan, E. A. Hypnosis and pain. *Archives of General Psychiatry*, 1960, *2*, 567–568.

Kidder, L. H. On becoming hypnotized: How skeptics become convinced: A case study of attitude change? *Journal of Abnormal Psychology*, 1972, *80*, 317–322.

Kihlstrom, J. F., & Evans, F. J. Posthypnotic amnesia in disorganized retrieval. *Proceedings of the 79th Annual Convention of the American Psychological Association*, 1971, *6*, 775–776.

Kinney, J. M., & Sachs, L. B. Increasing hypnotic susceptibility. *Journal of Abnormal Psychology*, 1974, *83*, 145–150.

Kline, M. V. The use of extended group hypnotherapy sessions in controlling cigarette habituation. *International Journal of Clinical and Experimental Hypnosis*, 1970, *18*, 270–282.

Kline, M. V. The production of antisocial behavior through hypnosis: New clinical data. *International Journal of Clinical and Experimental Hypnosis*, 1972, *20*, 80–94.

Kline, M. V., Guze, H., & Haggerty, A. D. An experimental study of the nature of hypnotic deafness: Effects of delayed auditory feedback. *Journal of Clinical and Experimental Hypnosis*, 1954, *2*, 145–156.

Knox, V. J., Morgan, A. H., & Hilgard, E. R. Pain and suffering in ischemia. *Archives of General Psychiatry*, 1974, *30*, 840–847.

Kramer, E., & Tucker, G. R. Hypnotically suggested deafness and delayed auditory feedback. *International Journal of Clinical and Experimental Hypnosis*, 1967, *15*, 37–43.

Kroger, W. S. *Clinical and experimental hypnosis*. Philadelphia: Lippincott, 1963.

Kuhn, T. S. *The structure of scientific revolutions*. Chicago: U. of Chicago Press, 1962.

Lacey, J. I. Somatic response patterning and stress: Some revisions of activation theory. In M. H. Appley & R. Trumbell (Eds.), *Psychological Stress*. New York: Appleton-Century-Crofts, 1967, pp. 14–37.

Lacey, J. I., Kagan, J., Lacey, B., & Moss, H. A. The visual level: Situational determinants and behavioral correlates of autonomic response patterns. In P. H. Knapp (Ed.), *Expressions of motion in man*. New York: International University Press, 1963, pp. 161–196.

Lassner, J. *Hypnosis and psychosomatic medicine*. New York: Springer-Verlag, 1967.

Lee Teng., E. Trance-susceptibility, induction susceptibility, and acquiescence as factors in hypnotic performance. *Journal of Abnormal Psychology*, 1965, *70*, 383–389.

Lenox, J. Effect of hypnotic analgesia on verbal report and cardiovascular responses to ischemic pain. *Journal of Abnormal Psychology*, 1970, *75*, 199–206.

Levine, J., & Ludwig, A. M. Alterations in consciousness produced by combinations of LSD, hypnosis, and psychotherapy. *Psychopharmacologia*, 1965, *7*, 123–137.

Levinson, B. W. States of awareness during general anesthesia. In J. Lassner (Ed.), *Hypnosis and psychosomatic medicine*. New York: Springer-Verlag, 1967, pp. 200–207.

Lewis, J. L. Semantic processing of unattended messages using dichotic procedures. *Journal of Experimental Psychology*, 1970, *85*, 225–228.

London, P., & Cooper, L. M. Norms of hypnotic susceptibility in children. *Developmental Psychology*, 1969, *1*, 113–124.

London, P., Cooper, L. M., & Engstrom, D. R. Increasing hypnotic susceptibility by brain wave feedback. *Journal of Abnormal Psychology*, 1974, *83*, 554–560.

London, P., Cooper, L. M., & Johnson, H. J. Subject characteristics in hypnosis

research. *International Journal of Clinical and Experimental Hypnosis,* 1962, *10,*
13-21.

London, P., Hart, J., & Leibovitz, M. EEG alpha rhythms and hypnotic
susceptibility. *Nature,* 1968, *219,* 71-72.

Ludwig, A. M., & Lyle, W. H. Tension induction and the hyperalert trance. *Journal
of Abnormal and Social Psychology,* 1964, *69,* 70-76.

Lynch, J. J., Paskewitz, D. A., & Orne, M. T. Some factors in the feedback control
of human alpha rhythm. *Psychosomatic Medicine,* 1974, *36,* 399-410.

MacKay, D. G. Aspects of the theory of comprehension, memory and attention.
Quarterly Journal of Experimental Psychology, 1973, *25,* 22-40.

Maher-Loughnan, G. P. Hypnosis and autohypnosis for the treatment of asthma.
International Journal of Clinical and Experimental Hypnosis, 1970, *18,* 1-14.

Malmo, B., Boag, T. J., & Raginsky, B. B. Electromyographic study of hypnotic
deafness. *Journal of Clinical and Experimental Hypnosis,* 1954, *2,* 305-317.

Maslow, A. H. *Toward a psychology of being.* New York: Van Nostrand, 1968.

McGlashan, T. H., Evans, F. J., & Orne, M. T. The nature of hypnotic analgesia
and placebo response to experimental pain. *Psychosomatic Medicine,* 1969, *31,*
227-246.

Meeker, W. B. & Barber, T. X. Toward an explanation of stage hypnosis. *Journal of
Abnormal Psychology,* 1971, *77,* 61-70.

Melei, J., & Hilgard, E. R. Attitudes toward hypnosis, self predictions and
hypnotic susceptibility. *International Journal of Clinical and Experimental Hypnosis,*
1964, *12,* 99-108.

Melzack, R. *The puzzle of pain.* Harmondsworth, England: Penguin, 1973.

Melzack, R., & Wall, P. D. Pain mechanisms: A new theory. *Science,* 1965, *150,*
971-979.

Miller, R. J., Lundy, R. N., & Galbraith, G. G. Effects of hypnotically induced
hallucination of a color filter. *Journal of Abnormal Psychology,* 1970, *76,* 316-319.

Mischel, W. *Personality and assessment.* New York: John Wiley and Sons, 1968.

Mitchell, M. B. Hypnotizability and distractibility. *American Journal of Clinical
Hypnosis,* 1970, *13,* 35-45.

Moore, R. K. Susceptibility to hypnosis and susceptibility to social influence.
Journal of Abnormal and Social Psychology, 1964, *68,* 282-294.

Morgan, A. H. The heritability of hypnotic susceptibility in twins. *Journal of
Abnormal Psychology,* 1973, *82,* 55-61.

Morgan, A. H., & Hilgard, E. R. Age differences in susceptibility to hypnosis.
International Journal of Clinical and Experimental Hypnosis, 1973, *21,* 78-85.

Morgan, A. H., Hilgard, E. R., & Davert, E. C. The heritability of hypnotic
susceptibility of twins: A preliminary report. *Behavior Genetics,* 1970, *1,*
213-224.

Morgan, A. H., Johnson, D. L., & Hilgard, E. R. The stability of hypnotic
susceptibility: A longitudinal study. *International Journal of Clinical and
Experimental Hypnosis,* 1974, *22,* 249-257.

Morgan, A. H., Macdonald, H., & Hilgard, E. R. EEG alpha: Lateral asymmetry
related to task and hypnotizability. *Psychophysiology,* 1974, *11,* 275-282.

Morgan, A. H., McDonald, P. J., & Macdonald, H. Differences in bilateral alpha
activity as a function of experimental task, with a note on lateral eye
movements and hypnotizability. *Neuropsychologia,* 1971, *9,* 451-469.

Morris, G. O., & Singer, M. T. Sleep deprivation: The context of consciousness.
Journal of Nervous and Mental Disease, 1966, *143,* 291-304.

Moss, C. S. *Hypnosis in perspective.* New York: Macmillan, 1965.

Nace, E. P., Orne, M. T., & Hammer, G. Posthypnotic amnesia as an active
process. *Archives of General Psychiatry,* 1974, *31,* 257-260.

Neider, C. (Ed.). *The autobiography of Mark Twain.* New York: Harper, 1959.

Neisser, U. *Cognitive psychology.* New York: Appleton-Century-Crofts, 1967.

Nelson, R. A. *A complete course in stage hypnotism.* Columbus, Ohio: Nelson Enterprises, 1965.

Newman, M. Hypnotic handling of the chronic bleeder in extraction: A case report. *American Journal of Clinical Hypnosis,* 1971, *14,* 126–127.

Nowlis, D. P., & Rhead, J. C. Relation of eyes-closed resting EEG alpha activity to hypnotic susceptibility. *Perceptual and Motor Skills,* 1968, *27,* 1047–1050.

Orne, M. T. Hypnosis: Artifact and essence. *Journal of Abnormal Psychology,* 1959, *58,* 277–299.

Orne, M. T. Hypnotically induced hallucinations. In L. J. West (Ed.), *Hallucinations.* New York: Grune & Stratton, 1962, pp. 211–219.(a)

Orne, M. T. On the social psychology of the psychological experiment: With particular reference to demand characteristics and their implications. *American Psychologist,* 1962, *17,* 776–783.(b)

Orne, M. T. Hypnosis, motivation and compliance. *American Journal of Psychiatry,* 1966, *122,* 721–726.

Orne, M. T. Demand characteristics and the concept of quasi-controls. In R. Rosenthal and R. L. Rosnow (Eds.), *Artifact in behavioral research.* New York: Academic Press, 1969, pp. 143–179.

Orne, M. T. Hypnosis, motivation, and the ecological validity of the psychological experiment. In W. J. Arnold & M. M. Page (Eds.), *Nebraska Symposium on Motivation.* Lincoln, Nebraska: University of Nebraska Press, 1970, pp. 187–265.

Orne, M. T. The simulation of hypnosis: Why, how and what it means. *International Journal of Clinical and Experimental Hypnosis,* 1971, *19,* 183–210.

Orne, M. T. Can a hypnotized subject be compelled to carry out otherwise unacceptable behavior? *International Journal of Clinical and Experimental Psychology,* 1972, *20,* 101–117.(a)

Orne, M. T. On the simulating subject as a quasi-control group in hypnosis research: What, why, and how? In E. Fromm & R. E. Shor (Eds.), *Hypnosis: Research developments and perspectives.* Chicago: Aldine-Atherton, 1972, pp. 399–443.(b)

Orne, M. T., & Evans, F. J. Social control in the psychological experiments: Anti-social behavior and hypnosis. *Journal of Personality and Social Psychology,* 1965, *1,* 189–200.

Orne, M. T., & Evans, F. J. Inadvertent termination of hypnotized and simulating subjects. *International Journal of Clinical and Experimental Hypnosis,* 1966, *14,* 61–78.

Orne, M. T., & Scheibe, K. E. The contribution of nondeprivation factors in the production of sensory deprivation effects: The psychology of the "panic button." *Journal of Abnormal and Social Psychology,* 1964, *68,* 3–12.

Orne, M. T., Sheehan, P. W., & Evans, F. J. Occurrence of posthypnotic behavior outside the experimental setting. *Journal of Personality and Social Psychology,* 1968, *9,* 189–196.

Ornstein, R. E. *The psychology of consciousness.* San Francisco: W. H. Freeman, 1972.

Palmer, R. D., & Field, P. B. Visual imagery and susceptibility to hypnosis. *Journal of Consulting and Clinical Psychology,* 1968, *32,* 456–461.

Paneth, F. A. Science and miracle. *Durham University Journal,* 1948-9, *10,* 45–54.

Pascal, C. R., & Salzberg, H. C. A systematic approach to inducing hypnotic behavior. *International Journal of Clinical and Experimental Hypnosis,* 1959, *7,* 161–167.

Paskewitz, D. A., & Orne, M. T. Visual effects on alpha feedback training. *Science,* 1973, *181,* 360–363.

Pattie, F. A. A report of attempts to produce uniocular blindness by hypnotic suggestion. *British Journal of Medical Psychology*, 1935, *15*, 230-241.

Pattie, F. A. *A brief history of hypnotism.* In J. E. Gordon (Ed.), *Handbook of clinical and experimental hypnosis.* New York: Macmillan, 1967, pp. 10-43.

Pearson, R. E. Response to suggestions given under general anesthesia. *American Journal of Clinical Hypnosis*, 1961, *4*, 106-114.

Perry, C., Wilder, S., & Appignanesi, A. Hypnotic susceptibility and performance on a battery of creativity measures. *American Journal of Clinical Hypnosis*, 1973, *15*, 170-180.

Peterson, D. R. *The clinical study of social behavior.* New York: Appleton-Century-Crofts, 1968.

Platonov, K. *The word as a physiological and therapeutic factor.* Moscow: Foreign Language Publishing House, 1959.

Polanyi, M. *Personal knowledge: Towards a post-critical philosophy.* New York: Harper, 1958.

Prince, R. *Trance and possession states.* Montreal: Bucke, 1968.

Raginsky, B. B. Temporary cardiac arrest induced under hypnosis. *International Journal of Clinical and Experimental Hypnosis*, 1959, *7*, 53-68.

Reyher, J. Brain mechanisms, intrapsychic processes and behavior: A theory of hypnosis and psychopathology. *American Journal of Clinical Hypnosis*, 1964, *7*, 107-119.

Richardson, A. *Mental imagery.* New York: Springer, 1969.

Roberts, A. H., Kewman, D. G., & Macdonald, H. Voluntary control of skin temperature: Unilateral changes using hypnosis and feedback. *Journal of Abnormal Psychology*, 1973, *82*, 163-168.

Roberts, A. H., & Tellegen, A. Ratings of "trust" and hypnotic suceptibility. *International Journal of Clinical and Experimental Hypnosis*, 1973, *21*, 289-297.

Rosen, G. Mesmerism and surgery: A strange chapter in the history of anesthesia. *Journal of the History of Medicine*, 1946, 527-550.

Rosen, H. *Hypnotherapy in clinical psychiatry.* New York: Julian Press, 1953.

Rosenhan, D. Hypnosis and personality: A moderator variable analysis. In L. Chertok (Ed.), *Psychophysiological mechanisms of hypnosis.* New York: Springer-Verlag, 1969.

Rosenthal, R. *Experimenter effects in behavioral research.* New York: Appleton-Century-Crofts, 1966.

Rowland, L. W. Will hypnotized persons try to harm themselves or others? *Journal of Abnormal and Social Psychology*, 1939, *34*, 114-117.

Ruch, J. C., Morgan, A. H., & Hilgard, E. R. Behavioral predictions from hypnotic responsiveness scores when obtained with and without prior induction procedures. *Journal of Abnormal Psychology*, 1973, *82*, 543-546.

Ruch, J. C., Morgan, A. H., & Hilgard, E. R. Measuring hypnotic responsiveness: A comparison of the Barber Suggestibility Scale and the Stanford Hypnotic Susceptibility Scale, Form A. *International Journal of Clinical and Experimental Hypnosis*, 1974, *22*, 365-376.

Sachs, L. B. Comparison of hypnotic analgesia and hypnotic relaxation during stimulation by a continuous pain source. *Journal of Abnormal Psychology*, 1970, *76*, 206-210.

Sachs, L. B. Construing hypnosis as modifiable behavior. In A. Jacobs & L. B. Sachs (Eds.), *The psychology of private events.* New York: Academic Press, 1971, pp. 61-75.

Sachs, L. B., & Anderson, W. L. Modification of hypnotic susceptibility. *International Journal of Clinical and Experimental Hypnosis*, 1967, *15*, 172-180.

Sanders, R. S., & Reyher, J. Sensory deprivation and the enhancement of hypnotic susceptibility. *Journal of Abnormal Psychology*, 1969, *74*, 375-381.

Sarbin, T. R. Contributions to role-taking theory: I. Hypnotic behavior. *Psychological Review*, 1950, *57*, 255–270.

Sarbin, T. R., & Coe, W. *Hypnosis: A social psychological analysis of influence communication*. New York: Holt, Rinehart & Winston, 1972.

Sargent, J. D., Green, E. E., & Walters, E. D. Preliminary report on the use of autogenic feedback training in the treatment of migraine and tension headaches. *Psychosomatic Medicine*, 1973, *35*, 129–135.

Schachtel, E. G. *Metamorphosis*. New York: Basic Books, 1959.

Scheffler, I. *Science and subjectivity*. Indianapolis: Bobbs-Merrill, 1967.

Scheibe, K. E., Gray, A. L., & Keim, C. S. Hypnotically induced deafness and delayed auditory feedback: A comparison of real and simulating subjects. *International Journal of Clinical and Experimental Hypnosis*, 1968, *16*, 158–164.

Schneck, J. M. *Hypnosis in modern medicine* (3rd ed.). Springfield, Ill.: Charles C. Thomas, 1963.

Schulman, R. E., & London, P. Hypnotic susceptibility and MMPI profiles. *Journal of Consulting Psychology*, 1963, *27*, 157–160.

Shapiro, A. K. Placebo effects in medicine, psychotherapy, and psychoanalysis. In A. E. Bergin and S. L. Garfield (Eds.), *Handbook of psychotherapy and behavior change: An empirical analysis*. New York: John Wiley & Sons, 1971.

Shapiro, J. L., & Diamond, M. J. Increases in hypnotizability as a function of encounter group training. *Journal of Abnormal Psychology*, 1972, *79*, 112–115.

Sheehan, P. W. A methodological analysis of the simulating technique. *International Journal of Clinical and Experimental Hypnosis*, 1971, *19*, 83–99.

Sheehan, P. W. Hypnosis and the manifestations of "imagination." In E. Fromm & R. E. Shor (Eds.), *Hypnosis: Research developments and perspectives*. Chicago: Aldine-Atherton, 1972, pp. 293–319.

Sheehan, P. W. Escape from the ambiguous: Artifact and methodologies of hypnosis. *American Psychologist*, 1973, *28*, 983–993.

Shor, R. E. Hypnosis and the concept of the generalized reality-orientation. *American Journal of Psychotherapy*, 1959, *13*, 582–602.

Shor, R. E. The frequency of naturally occurring "hypnotic-like" experiences in the normal college population. *International Journal of Clinical and Experimental Hypnosis*, 1960, *8*, 151–163.

Shor, R. E. Three dimensions of hypnotic depth. *International Journal of Clinical and Experimental Hypnosis*, 1962, *10*, 23–38.

Shor, R. E. Physiological effects of painful stimulation during hypnotic analgesia. In J. E. Gordon (Ed.), *Handbook of clinical and experimental hypnosis*. New York: Macmillan, 1967, pp. 511–549.

Shor, R. E. The three-factor theory of hypnosis as applied to the book-reading fantasy and to the concept of suggestion. *International Journal of Clinical and Experimental Hypnosis*, 1970, *18*, 89–98.

Shor, R. E. The fundamental problem in hypnosis research as viewed from historic perspectives. In E. Fromm & R. E. Shor (Eds.), *Hypnosis: Research developments and perspectives*. Chicago: Aldine-Atherton, 1972, pp. 15–40.

Shor, R. E., & Cobb, J. C. An exploratory study of hypnotic training using the concept of plateau responsiveness as a referent. *American Journal of Clinical Hypnosis*, 1968, *10*, 178–193.

Shor, R. E., & Orne, E. C. *Harvard Group Scale of Hypnotic Susceptibility*. Palo Alto, Calif.: Consulting Psychologists' Press, 1962.

Shor, R. E., & Orne, E. C. Norms on the Harvard Group Scale of Hypnotic Susceptibility, Form A. *International Journal of Clinical and Experimental Hypnosis*, 1963, *11*, 39–47.

Shor, R. E., & Orne, M. T. *The nature of hypnosis: Selected basic readings*. New York: Holt, Rinehart & Winston, 1965.

Shor, R. E., Orne, M. T., & O'Connell, D. N. Validation and cross validation of a scale of self-reported personal experiences which predicts hypnotizability. *Journal of Psychology*, 1962, *53*, 55–75.

Shor, R. E., Orne, M. T., & O'Connell, D. N. Psychological correlates of plateau hypnotizability in a special volunteer sample. *Journal of Personality and Social Psychology*, 1966, *3*, 80–95.

Shutz, J. H., & Luthe, W. *Autogenic therapy*. New York: Grune & Stratton, 1969.

Silverman, J. A. Paradigm for the study of altered states of consciousness. *British Journal of Psychiatry*, 1968, *114*, 1201–1218.

Sinclair-Gieben, A. H. C., & Chalmers, D. Evaluation of treatment of warts by hypnosis. *Lancet*, 1959, October 3, 480–482.

Singer, J. L. Theoretical implications and fantasy techniques. *Contemporary Psychoanalysis*, 1971, *8*, 82–95.

Sjoberg, B. M., & Hollister, L. F. The effects of psychotomimetic drugs on primary suggestibility. *Psychopharmacologia*, 1965, *8*, 251–262.

Smith, M. C., & Groen, M. Evidence for semantic analysis of unattended verbal items. *Journal of Experimental Psychology*, 1974, *102*, 595–603.

Solursh, L. P., & Rae, J. M. LSD, suggestion and hypnosis. *International Journal of Neuropsychiatry*, 1966, *2*, 60–64.

Spanos, N. P. Goal-directed fantasy and the performance of hypnotic test suggestions. *Psychiatry*, 1971, *34*, 86–96.

Spanos, N. P., & Barber, T. X. "Hypnotic" experiences as inferred from auditory and visual hallucinations. *Journal of Experimental Research in Personality*, 1968, *3*, 136–150.

Spanos, N. P., & Barber, T. X. Cognitive activity during "hypnotic" suggestibility: Goal-directed fantasy and the experience of nonvolition. *Journal of Personality*, 1972, *40*, 510–524.

Spanos, N. P., & Barber, T. X. Toward a convergence in hypnosis research. *American Psychologist*, 1974, *29*, 500–511.

Spanos, N. P., & Ham, M. L. Cognitive activity in response to hypnotic suggestion: Goal-directed fantasy and selective amnesia. *American Journal of Clinical Hypnosis*, 1973, *15*, 191–198.

Surman, O. S., Gottlieb, S. K., Hackett, T. P., & Silverberg, E. L. Hypnosis in the treatment of warts. *Archives of General Psychiatry*, 1973, *28*, 439–441.

Sutcliffe, J. P. "Credulous" and "skeptical" views of hypnotic phenomena: A review of certain evidence and methodology. *International Journal of Clinical and Experimental Hypnosis*, 1960, *8*, 73–101.

Sutcliffe, J. P. "Credulous" and "skeptical" views of hypnotic phenomena: Experiments on esthesia, hallucination, and delusion. *Journal of Abnormal and Social Psychology*, 1961, *62*, 189–200.

Sutcliffe, J. P., Perry, C. W., & Sheehan, P. W. Relation of some aspects of imagery and fantasy to hypnotic susceptibility. *Journal of Abnormal Psychology*, 1970, *76*, 279–287.

Szasz, T. S. *The myth of mental illness*. New York: Hoeber-Harper, 1964.

Tart, C. T. *Altered states of consciousness: A book of readings*. New York: John Wiley & Sons, 1969.

Tart, C. T. Increases in hypnotizability resulting from a prolonged program for enhancing personal growth. *Journal of Abnormal Psychology*, 1970, *75*, 260–266.(a)

Tart, C. T. Self report scales of hypnotic depth. *International Journal of Clinical and Experimental Hypnosis*, 1970, *18*, 105–125.(b)

Tart, C. T. States of consciousness and state specific sciences. *Science*, 1972, *176*, 1203–1210.(a)

Tart, C. T. Measuring the depth of an altered state of consciousness with particular reference to self-report scales of hypnotic depth. In E. Fromm & R. E. Shor (Eds.), *Hypnosis: Research developments and perspectives.* Chicago: Aldine-Atherton, 1972, pp. 445–477.(b)

Tellegen, A., & Atkinson, G. Openness to absorbing and self altering experiences ("absorption"), a trait related to hypnotic susceptibility. *Journal of Abnormal Psychology,* 1974, *83,* 268–277.

Travis, T. A., Kondo, C. Y., & Knott, J. R. Alpha conditioning: A controlled study. *Journal of Nervous and Mental Disease,* 1974, *158,* 163–173.

Ullman, M. On the psyche and warts: I. Suggestions and warts: A review and comment. *Psychosomatic Medicine,* 1959, *21,* 473–488.

Van Doren, C. *Benjamin Franklin.* New York: Garden City Publishing, 1938.

Van Nuys, D. Meditation, attention, and hypnotic susceptibility: A correlational study. *International Journal of Clinical and Experimental Hypnosis,* 1973, *21,* 59–69.

Wallach, M. A., & Leggett, M. I. Testing the hypothesis that a person will be consistent: Stylistic consistency versus situational specificity in size of children's drawings. *Journal of Personality,* 1972, *40,* 309–330.

Weitzenhoffer, A. *Hypnotism: An objective study in suggestibility.* New York: John Wiley & Sons, 1953.

Weitzenhoffer, A. M., & Hilgard, E. R. *Stanford Hypnotic Susceptibility Scale Forms A and B.* Palo Alto, Calif.: Consulting Psychologists' Press, 1959.

Weitzenhoffer, A. M., & Hilgard, E. R. *Stanford Hypnotic Susceptibility Scale, Form C.* Palo Alto, Calif.: Consulting Psychologists' Press, 1962.

Wietzenhoffer, A. M., & Hilgard, E. R. *Revised Stanford Profile Scales of Hypnotic Susceptibility, Forms I and II.* Palo Alto, Calif.: Consulting Psychologists' Press, 1967.

Weitzenhoffer, A. M., & Sjoberg, B. M. Suggestibility with and without "induction of hypnosis." *Journal of Nervous and Mental Disease,* 1961, *132,* 205–220.

White, R. W. Two types of hypnotic trance and their personality correlates. *Journal of Psychology,* 1937, *3,* 279–289.

White, R. W. A preface to the theory of hypnotism. *Journal of Abnormal and Social Psychology,* 1941, *36,* 477–505.

Wickramasekera, I. The effects of sensory restriction on susceptibility to hypnosis: A hypothesis, some preliminary data, and theoretical speculation. *International Journal of Clinical and Experimental Hypnosis,* 1969, *17,* 217–224.

Wickramasekera, I. Effects of sensory restriction on susceptibility to hypnosis: A hypothesis and more preliminary data. *Journal of Abnormal Psychology,* 1970, *76,* 69–75.

Wickramasekera, I. Effects of electromyographic feedback on hypnotic susceptibility: More preliminary data. *Journal of Abnormal Psychology,* 1973, *83,* 74–77.

Williamsen, J. A., Johnson, H. J., & Eriksen, C. W. Some characteristics of posthypnotic amnesia. *Journal of Abnormal Psychology,* 1965, *70,* 123–131.

Wolberg, L. R. *Medical hypnosis* (2 vols.). New York: Grune & Stratton, 1948.

Young, P. C. Antisocial uses of hypnosis. In L. M. LeCron (Ed.), *Experimental hypnosis.* New York: Macmillan, 1952, pp. 376–409.

Zuckerman, M. Perceptual isolation as a stress situation: A review. *Archives of General Psychiatry,* 1964, *11,* 255–276.

Name Index

Allen, J. L., 124
Allington, H. V., 141
Anderson, J. A. D., 147
Anderson, W. L., 81, 82
Appignanesi, A., 120
As, A., 79, 80, 98, 99, 116, 117
Atkinson, G., 119, 120

Bakal, D. A., 147
Bakan, P., 126, 127
Banford, S. A., 80
Barber, T. X., 3, 6, 9, 10, 14, 25, 28, 29,
    35, 42, 49, 54, 55, 62, 65, 85, 86,
    87, 88, 89, 95, 96, 97, 105, 108,
    111, 117, 125, 129
Barnett, L. W., 151
Basker, M. A., 147
Beecher, H. K., 23
Bentler, P. M., 66
Bernheim, H., 53, 54, 56, 70, 85
Bexton, W. H., 72
Blanchard, E. B., 152
Boag, T. J., 54
Bowers, K. S., 16, 17, 20, 27, 43, 44,
    45, 48, 56, 72, 87, 94, 97, 112,
    115, 117, 118, 120, 123, 125
Bowers, P. G., 72, 94, 120, 123, 125
Branch, L. G., 151
Brenman, M., 93, 98, 140, 150
Brunn, J. T., 134
Burgess, T. O., 103

Calverley, D. S., 49, 55, 86, 87, 96,
    108, 117
Chalmers, D., 143
Charcot, J., 6
Chaves, J. F., 3
Cheek, D. B., 134, 136
Clawson, T.A., 142, 144, 145, 151
Cobb, J. C., 80, 83, 131
Coe, W. C., 3, 6, 25, 85, 93, 95, 119,
    124, 125
Cooper, G. W., Jr., 111
Cooper, L. M., 41, 67, 68, 77, 80, 81,
    117, 131
Crasilneck, H. B., 151

Dalal, A. S., 96
Dalton, R., 147
Dana, R. H., 111
Darnton, R., 8
Davert, E. C., 70
Day, M. E., 125
Deckert, G. H., 111
Deikman, A. J., 94, 98
Deslon, C., 8, 61
Diamond, M. J., 71, 74, 80, 82
Dixon, N. F., 105, 130
Dubin, L. L., 145
Duke, J., 125

Edmonston, W. E., 78
Ellenberger, H. F., 105

Subject Index